Keep Your Glow On

A Comprehensive Guide to America's Lighthouses

wendy brewer

Schiffer Publishing Ltd®

4880 Lower Valley Road, Atglen, Pennsylvania 19310

Dedication

In memory of my mother, Sylvia Michaels, who loved books and founded
the North Babylon Public Library, and my father, Ackerman Michaels,
who greatly influenced my personality.

This book is dedicated to:
my children, Cassie and Kevin Brewer, who complete my life,
my brother, Alan Michaels who protected me throughout my recovery
and who kissed my head when I lost my hair, and
my sisters, Phyllis Taylor and Jamie Rose, who I love.

Copyright © 2011 by Wendy Brewer

Library of Congress Control Number: 2010943238

Designed by Mark David Bowyer
Type set in GoudyHandtooled BT / Zurich BT

ISBN: 978-0-7643-3704-8
Printed in China

Schiffer Books are available at special discounts for bulk purchases for sales promotions or premiums. Special editions, including personalized covers, corporate imprints, and excerpts can be created in large quantities for special needs. For more information contact the publisher:

Published by Schiffer Publishing Ltd.
4880 Lower Valley Road
Atglen, PA 19310
Phone: (610) 593-1777; Fax: (610) 593-2002
E-mail: Info@schifferbooks.com

For the largest selection of fine reference books on this and related subjects, please visit our web site at **www.schifferbooks.com**
We are always looking for people to write books on new and related subjects.
If you have an idea for a book please contact us at the above address.

This book may be purchased from the publisher.
Include $5.00 for shipping.
Please try your bookstore first.
You may write for a free catalog.

In Europe, Schiffer books are distributed by
Bushwood Books
6 Marksbury Ave.
Kew Gardens
Surrey TW9 4JF England
Phone: 44 (0) 20 8392 8585; Fax: 44 (0) 20 8392 9876
E-mail: info@bushwoodbooks.co.uk
Website: www.bushwoodbooks.co.uk

Contents

Point Judith Lighthouse,
Rhode Island

Introduction

I have a good life, not only because I do what I love but because I've always been able to love what I do. It was winter in Savannah, Georgia, and I had already begun to write *Keep Your Glow On* when I had my first day as a volunteer at the Tybee Island Lighthouse. The weather was wet and foggy and, for me, the mist increased the romance of the day's experience. Many people think the fog increases the spookiness of a lighthouse. In fact many lighthouses are thought to be haunted.

I grew up on Long Island, New York, and lived near the Fire Island Lighthouse. Until 2004, when I visited the lighthouse for the first time, I had taken it for granted; usually ignoring it. At the age of 53, I finally appreciated it and fell in love with its beauty. Majestically it rose 168 feet above the surrounding beach and ocean landscape. Its beacon shined so brightly that it was visible in the daylight and its wide black and white stripes provided a crisp contrast to its surroundings.

In 2005 while in San Diego, California, I visited the old Point Loma Lighthouse. It is located at the top of a high cliff, is short (46 feet), and painted white. The sky was brilliant blue that day and the contrast between the lighthouse and its surroundings is still vivid in my mind.

Until then I thought all lighthouses were tall towers (painted black and white). There at Point Loma was a lighthouse situated on a tall cliff that dropped sharply into the water below. It did not require the height of a tower. In fact, the cliff itself acted as the tower.

That's when I became interested in lighthouses and although I was hooked, I didn't realize it yet. I also didn't realize until I started collecting data that the Point Loma Lighthouse has the highest focal plane (462 feet) of all American lighthouses. A lighthouse with a high focal plane can be viewed from a farther distance in the water. High focal planes also increase the visual drama of the sharp descent into the ocean. I later learned that there was an unpredictable problem with the site chosen for the Point Loma Lighthouse. Because it was built on such a tall cliff, it was often obscured by low-flying clouds and fog. Less than 40 years after the (old) Point Loma Lighthouse was built, a skeletal lighthouse was built nearby at a lower elevation. The New Point Loma Lighthouse replaced the original picturesque lighthouse.

I lived in Washington, D.C., in 2005 and in my spare time I began researching lighthouses and their locations in nearby Virginia and Maryland. I was lucky enough to find www.LighthouseFriends.com, a wonderfully informative web site that contains coordinates and directions, as well as lots of other useful information. On weekends I began taking day-trips to lighthouses in the general area and soon began traveling to multiple lighthouses in Maryland, Virginia, Delaware, and southern New Jersey. In Delaware I saw my second "lightship," the *Overfalls*, and it was then that my interest blossomed beyond my control. Although it was actually quite thrilling, it caused me to panic slightly wondering how obsessive I would become.

After working 34 years for the federal government, I retired on April Fool's Day, 2006. I immediately packed and stored everything I owned and headed out in my car to see the majority of America's lighthouses and figure out what I wanted to be when I grew up.

This may seem rather spontaneous, but I had spent hundreds of hours since I visited the Point Loma Lighthouse, collecting lighthouse coordinates (latitude and longitude — most lighthouses do not have street addresses), locating lighthouses using mapping software, and preparing a national map that provided me with the directions I needed to and from every American lighthouse I planned to visit. I knew, then, that, as soon as possible, I would begin to live in a new way… and this is how I felt when I set out on the road.

Although the cold and hot weather resulted in my changing itineraries twice, I traveled the American east, north (Great Lakes), and west coasts and had the experiences of my life.

Point Loma Lighthouse, California

At some point in my travels between the north and west coasts, I realized that I had health issues. For this reason, I did not travel along the Gulf Coast. Instead, I quickly drove to and settled in Tybee Island, Georgia, where I stayed only three months before being diagnosed with breast cancer.

In 2008, I moved to New York where I had a radical mastectomy followed by chemo and radiation treatments. I moved back to Tybee Island as soon as my health permitted. The Tybee Island Lighthouse and all of the island's surroundings were great motivators for me to get well as quickly as possible. Until that time and throughout my treatments, I recaptured my experiences by writing *Keep Your Glow On.* I looked forward to the future when I could again visit lighthouses that I hadn't seen yet. As I started to recuperate, I returned to some of the lighthouses that I have seen previously, because you never know what will be illuminated.

Throughout America's history, lighthouses helped sailors reach the safety of land. It's pleasantly ironic that throughout one of the stormiest periods of my life (breast cancer and its treatments) lighthouses helped guide me out of the storm and into the safety of the future. Indeed, I have a good life and I've kept my glow on every step of the way.

I didn't become obsessive about lighthouses, but I continue to have a healthy passion for them that will thrive for many years. I want to channel my passion to help ensure their survival.

Tybee Island
Lighthouse,
Georgia

Montauk Point
Lighthouse,
New York (end
of day)

General Information About Lighthouses

Boston Harbor Lighthouse, Massachusetts

As a lighthouse enthusiast with a mission to help save lighthouses, I hope to convey the essence of life saving stations, beacons, and light keepers and their families, so that, today, it matters that they existed, gave their entireties, and persevered under extreme circumstances that we cannot even grasp from our "saw/heard it on the news" experience. I invite you to share the journey.

Lighthouses are towers, buildings, or frameworks designed to transmit light from a system of lamps and lenses. They were built as aids to navigation that marked dangerous coastlines, hazardous shoals (shallow waters), rocks, and safe harbor entries. Some even point to a direction.

Lighthouses and their keepers saved countless lives. Like majestic guardians they stood watch, showed how to reach the shore, and warned of various dangers. Lighthouse keepers sacrificed much to maintain the lighthouse beacons. Many lived secluded lives and worked hard day in and day out. Without their dedication, lighthouses would have long ago fallen into disrepair and night beacons would not have shone. With a few exceptions in today's world, it's hard to imagine such constant dedication and physical labor.

Very sadly (yet reasonably in our technical world), American lighthouses are mostly obsolete. They've been replaced by sonar depth finders and Global Positioning Systems (GPS).

Progress is good most of the time but it's important that you know and remember what came before. It feels right to honor lighthouse keepers who sacrificed themselves to save others. Lighthouses help keep us connected with America's simple past and selfless nature.

All American lighthouses are now automated and on-site lighthouse keepers are no longer needed, although keepers still operate the Boston Harbor Lighthouse in Massachusetts. Boston Harbor was the site of America's first lighthouse and the Boston Harbor Lighthouse continues to shine brightly, reminding us of America's inextinguishable spirit.

In 1716, the first American lighthouse was built on Little Brewster Island at the Boston Harbor entrance. Because the lighthouse and harbor were under Britain's control in 1775, the Massachusetts Minutemen burned the lighthouse. The following year, the British blew up the remains before permanently leaving Boston Harbor. In 1783 a new lighthouse was constructed. In 1859 the Boston Harbor Lighthouse's tower height was raised from 75 feet to its current 89-foot height and a 12-sided second order Fresnel lens was installed. This remains the only American lighthouse that is still manually operated. The oldest standing (original) American lighthouse is the Sandy Hook Lighthouse in New Jersey, which was first lit in 1764.

Sandy Hook Lighthouse,
New Jersey

On August 7, 1789, the original Congress passed America's very first Public Works Act when it created the Lighthouse Service and placed it in control of the Department of Treasury. Two hundred years later, Congress passed a resolution to designate August 7 as "National Lighthouse Day." Quite a few people (myself included) consider every day, as Lighthouse Day.

Many national and local lighthouse societies and associations have emerged. These organizations are dedicated to preserving, restoring, and maintaining America's maritime buildings and history. Without the efforts of these employees and volunteers, we'd lose many more irreplaceable lighthouses. In 2005 Hurricane Katrina destroyed five lighthouses. Many others are in sorry states of disrepair. They are listed on the lighthouse "Doomsday List" and the "Watch List of Threatened Lighthouses" (see Chapter 8). Without intervention, they too will soon perish.

One sad loss occurred in 2007, when a lightship was sold as scrap. For the sake of simplicity, a lightship is a floating lighthouse. A paragraph in Chapter 5 now reads: "Today only 15 life-saving lightships remain." When I began this journey there were 16. This tragic loss could have been prevented. There were gallant efforts, but none of them succeeded in saving the New Bedford Lightship from its unwholesome fate: the scrap pile. Despite the money needed, I had fully expected that someone would see the lightship's historic value and save it from such a shameful ending. Short of that I had naively hoped that efforts to scrap it would be stalled long enough for the profits from *Keep Your Glow On* to make a difference in its ultimate fate.

I was sadly mistaken. But the loss of the New Bedford Lightship gave me a new drive and desire to help save other lighthouses and lightships from a similar fate. Even in these trying financial times, we, as Americans, can join together and preserve our own maritime history.

Tall Lighthouses

Having grown up on Long Island, New York, my own original (and simple) lighthouse perception was of a tall, black and white tower near the ocean. Little did I know that most American lighthouses did not fit this general description. I grew up near the Fire Island Lighthouse. It's tall. It has black and white bands (day marks). It's near the ocean. Hmmmmmm…

When first thinking about lighthouses most of us envision the tall ones unless we live near or visit some of America's other beautifully interesting lighthouses. For this reason alone, I'm addressing tall tower (over 99 feet) lighthouses as a separate chapter. However, to fall in love with the others, simply read on.

Fire Island Lighthouse, New York

I've learned a few interesting facts about lighthouses. The first is that when we conjure up lighthouse locations, many of us think of North Carolina. The most obvious reason is that the Cape Hatteras Lighthouse, on North Carolina's Outer Banks, is America's tallest existing lighthouse (197 feet). Almost 60 percent of North Carolina's 14 lighthouses are taller than 99 feet. Only Florida has more tall lighthouses than North Carolina.

The most surprising fact is that Michigan has far more lighthouses (135) than any other state. Following in a not-so-close second place, is New York with 79 lighthouses (see Chapter 9, List 4 for additional state-by-state information).

The volume of American lighthouses varies because sources define and list them differently. *Keep Your Glow On* estimates that there are almost 800 American lighthouses and about 150 of them are more than 99 feet tall. In addition to lighthouses, these 800 include lightships, replicas, partial "ruins," and a few faux lighthouses.

Volunteers at different lighthouses can tell you from what distance the lighthouse if visible from a boat on the water. There are many (internal and external) factors that impact just how far a lighthouse can be viewed, but it's not more than 18-20 miles away. This limitation is due to the earth's round shape (curvature). Once you travel further than 18-20 miles away, the view of the distant lighthouse beacon and horizon literally curves away from your sight.

Cape Hatteras Lighthouse,
North Carolina

Each "tall" tower lighthouses is unique and different from all the rest. These visual variations are called "day marks" and they helped sailors identify each tall tower by its color and pattern combination during daylight hours. (All lighthouses also have "night marks." Because night marks pertain to the lens they are discussed in Chapter 6.) Most day mark colors are white, black, and red, but they not limited to these colors. The marks can be stripes, wide bands, solid color, diamonds, spirals, squares, etc. The day mark colors also vary on the exterior lantern room trim and the watch room. In other words, two tall towers might look identical, but on closer examination, one top may be black and the other may be white. Similarly, if two towers each consist of six stripes (three black, three white), one tower's top stripe may be white and its bottom stripe black, and the other tower's top stripe may be black with a white stripe at the bottom. Day marks are important so sailors knew exactly where they are headed ashore. Here are some interesting day marks:

Point Lookout Lighthouse,
North Carolina

Barnegat Lighthouse, New Jersey

New Cape Henry Lighthouse, Virginia

Assateague Island Lighthouse, Virginia

A **light station** consists of the lighthouse and all of the outbuildings (e.g. keeper's quarters, boathouse, fog signal building, etc.). There are specific terms for different lighthouse parts.

The **lighthouse** consists of a tower that supports the lantern room at the top.

The **lantern room** is the glassed-in room at the top of a lighthouse tower that contains the lamp and lens.

The round, storm-proof **ventilator** is located above the lantern room. It removes heat and smoke from the lamps that builds up during the day.

A **lightening rod** sits on top of the ventilator. The grounding system is usually connected to the metal cupola roof and provides a safe conduit for direct lightning strikes.

The **watch room**, which is directly below the lantern room, is where the lighthouse keeper stood watch at night and prepared the lights so they would efficiently function each evening.

The **gallery** is an open walkway on the outside of a lighthouse's upper portion (generally located outside the watch room). The gallery was needed to access and clean the external lantern room windows. A bonus of visiting a lighthouse is the view from the gallery. It is great to feel the sun and the rush of the wind from the top of the tower.

From the lighthouse gallery, the contrast of the metal with the water and sky often makes a wonderful sight. Beyond that is the horizon and surrounding landscape of usually isolated shore lines.

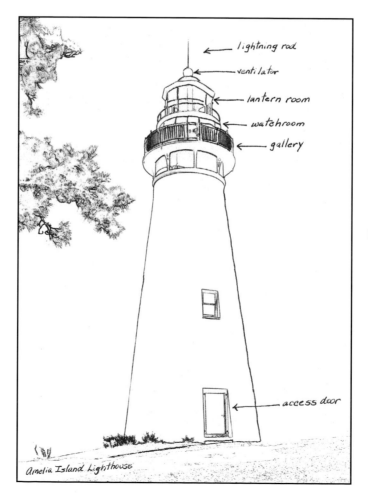

lightning rod

ventilator

lantern room

watchroom

gallery

access door

Amelia Island Lighthouse

Parts of a lighthouse

Most lighthouses have spiral staircases and many of them are very artsy. As you ascend a lighthouse, you'll notice that the stairs grow narrower the closer you get to the top. Although not always visible, the walls also grow narrower nearer the top. Lighthouses are tapered to provide the tower with strength and stability, and to reduce wind resistance. In various places on the walls (on the inside and outside) you can see vents that allow air to circulate within the tower.

Ponce de Leon Inlet Lighthouse, Florida

Barnegat Lighthouse, New Jersey

Many lighthouses show the year they were built somewhere on the building itself. The Old Michigan City Lighthouse in Indiana is a beautiful example.

Now that we know about tall towers, let's find out about other lighthouse types that are generally taller than 100 feet.

Texas towers were named because they resembled off-shore oil platforms in the Gulf of Mexico. Texas tower lighthouses replaced some Atlantic Ocean lightships in the 1960s. The first American Texas tower lighthouse was the Buzzards Bay Lighthouse in Massachusetts. The framework of four steel, concrete-filled piles was driven deep into the ocean floor and supported a square platform. The lighthouse tower was attached to one corner of the platform. Only five other Texas tower lighthouses were constructed: Ambrose, New York; Chesapeake, Maryland; Diamond Shoal, North Carolina; Frying Pan Shoals, North Carolina; and Savannah, Georgia. In 1996 the Ambrose and the Savannah Lights were struck by ships. The Diamond Shoal and Frying Pan Shoals Light were sunk and became artificial reefs. The Buzzards Bay light was demolished and replaced with a smaller light. The Chesapeake Light remains.

Skeletal lighthouses (skeletons) were built between 1861 and 1910. The first three onshore skeletal towers were built in Michigan. Of these, the Whitefish Point Lighthouse was the first American skeleton lighthouse and it remains in pristine condition. The tower had a square design, but the watch room and lantern room are octagonal. The lowest section of the tower was vertical rather than pyramidal, which differs from all the subsequent designs. The design was changed twice to increase the sturdiness. However, the basic idea of the skeletal lighthouse has remained constant; allowing wind and storms to pass harmlessly through them.

Old Michigan City Lighthouse, Indiana

Whitefish Point Lighthouse, Michigan

Reedy Island Range Rear Lighthouse, Delaware

Integral lighthouses incorporate the keepers dwelling and tower into a single structure. They are sometimes referred to as "schoolhouse" lighthouses because, except for the tower surmounted to the top of the building that supports them, they resemble an old one-room schoolhouse. The tower was usually short and buildings were typically constructed of wood or brick.

Morgan Point Lighthouse, Connecticut

Range Lights and Twin Lights were built in sets of two and were typically located on shore. From the water, once range lights are aligned (one in front of the other), they show how to enter the area they mark (e.g. harbor) and then mark the sea entry lane. Twin lights were similar to range lights and were first built to help distinguish different light stations from one another.

Cape Ann
Lighthouses,
Massachusetts

Cape Ann
Lighthouses,
Massachusetts

Lighthouses are also categorized by the years in which they were built.

Pre-Constitution Era lighthouses were built between 1716 and 1789. They include Sandy Hook, New Jersey, and Boston Harbor, Massachusetts, lighthouses.

Early Federal Period lighthouses, which include Old Cape Henry, Virginia, Montauk Point, New York, and Bald Head Island, North Carolina, lighthouses, were built between 1789 and 1820.

Fifth Order of the Treasury lighthouses, which were inferior structures in constant need of repair and replacement, were built between 1820 and 1852. The Matinicus Rock Lighthouse, Maine, was built during this period although relatively few lighthouses from this time exist. The lighting system used was also inferior to that used in European lighthouses.

Portland Head Lighthouse, Maine

Charlotte-Genesee Lighthouse, New York

Lighthouse Board lighthouses include Brandywine Shoal, New Jersey, and Thomas Point Shoals, Maryland, lighthouses. These lighthouses were built between 1852 and 1903. American caissons and screw pile lighthouses were built during this period. The Light House Board improved lighthouses and created charts/maps showing current lighthouse locations, day marks (colors and patterns of towers), and night marks (color and flashing patterns of beacons).

Admiralty Head
Lighthouse, Washington

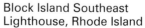

Block Island Southeast
Lighthouse, Rhode Island

Proudly Petite Lighthouses

There are two different height measures that are used for lighthouses; the tower height and the focal plane height. These measurements are not interchangeable and are usually different. Tower height is the measurement from the ground to the top of the tower. The focal plane is the height from the mean water level to the middle of the light source. Lighthouses surrounded by water generally have a lower focal plane than lighthouses built on land. Lighthouses located on cliffs have higher focal planes than ones built near a flat shoreline. Focal planes influence how far from the lighthouse it first can be seen from the water. It was important for lost sailors to see the lighthouse beacon as soon as possible so it could guide ships safely to shore.

Let's consider the 54-foot tower of the Split Rock Lighthouse on Lake Superior in Minnesota, which sits atop an almost 130-foot cliff. This lighthouse's focal plane is 168 feet. If the Split Rock Lighthouse was built on North Carolina's flat shoreline, its focal plane would probably be between 50 and 60 feet.

Split Rock Lighthouse,
Minnesota

You also begin to see that "proudly petite" lighthouses have their own charm, color, and style.

Short, conical lighthouses (cottages) are almost always white (stone or glazed brick) with some black trim. They were built on land near the shoreline. Many were easy-to-build, wood-frame towers that housed little more than the lantern.

Drum Point Lighthouse, Maryland

Castle Hill Lighthouse, Rhode Island

Screw pile lighthouse design was invented in the 1830s by a blind civil engineer from Ireland, Alexander Mitchell. In 1850 America first used the new design to build the Brandywine Shoal Lighthouse, New Jersey, in the Delaware Bay. The screw pile lighthouse construction was a light-weight wooden tower supported by wrought-iron stilts, often resembling a spider. The bottoms of the stilts had corkscrew-like, cast-iron flanges that were "screwed" into the ground under waters with shifting sand or muddy bottoms. This engineering technology permitted lighthouse construction on sites that were previously too soft to support the weight of a heavy lighthouse tower.

Caisson lighthouses were made of cast iron, built to last, and were located in bodies of water. The underwater base was filled with concrete and stone and then leveled. A multi-storied iron or brick tower was built atop. Caissons were more complicated and more expensive than screw pile lighthouses, but they better withstood pressure from ice. In 1976-1977 an ice floe permanently leaned the Sharps Island Lighthouse at a 15 degree angle.

Sharps Island Lighthouse,
Maryland

Crib foundation lighthouse construction, which replaced lightships, was used extensively on the hard rock bottoms of the Great Lakes. Wooden cribs were constructed ashore, towed to the site and filled with stone. Once the crib settled to the bottom, it was capped with concrete and leveled (by adding weight to one side). The construction was such that the monolithic base acted as a massive, single block of stone that has endured the Great Lake's ice floes.

Buffalo Intake Crib
Lighthouse, New York

Lightships

In simple terms, lightships were floating lighthouses. Between 1820 and 1985 lighthouses and lightships were essential components of America's commitment to safely navigate its waters. Lightships could be moored where, at the time, it would be impractical or impossible to place a lighthouse. They were easily stationed in deep water many miles from shore and served as a landfall or a point of departure for long ocean voyages. Because lightships were versatile and provided a variety of functions, they satisfied multiple requirements and were readily repositioned to meet changing needs. Early "light boats" did not have engines and had to be towed to and from their assigned stations.

In 1819 Congress authorized the construction of America's first three lightships. The first light boat was started in 1819 and was completed in 1820. The first five lightships warned of dangers in the Chesapeake Bay. In 1832 the first American "outside" lightship was anchored in the ocean near Sandy Hook, New Jersey.

By the end of the 1800s, lightships were uniformly designed. Most had flat bottoms, were approximately 135 feet long, and had heavy mushroom anchors. In the early 1900s, radios became standard equipment and in the 1920s lightships used radio beacons that helped other ships plot their locations. Although it's hard to imagine now, like lighthouses, lightships existed at a time before satellites and GPS. In all, 179 lightships were built.

Lightship Columbia, Oregon

Identifying lightships is not as simple as one might think. At first, these vessels were designated only with the name of the light station where they were located. The lightship's name was painted on its hull. But as lightships were replaced with newer ones, or transferred from one location to another, keeping track of the older ones became more difficult. In 1867, America started using numbers to identify lightships. The numbering series began with LV (presumably for "light vessel"). In 1950 active lightships were renumbered with a series that began with WAL and renumbered again in 1965 replacing WAL with WLV. Today there are three lightships called "Nantucket" but they all have different numbers.

Other ships depended on the fixed position of the lightship's light and radio beacons, as well as its fog horn, to help them find their way. While other ships headed for refuge, lightships remained anchored as violent waters erupted all around them. At least four lightships and their crews were sunk during violent storms and 150 collisions involved lightships, five of which sank with crew members aboard.

In 1909, the number of lightships maintained at any single time peaked at 56 but by 1927, 68 lightships had been discontinued or replaced by lighthouses or buoys. Typically, lightships were more costly to operate than lighthouses. New lighthouse technologies like screw pile lighthouses in the Chesapeake Bay, crib foundation lighthouses in the Great Lakes, and Texas towers in the Atlantic Ocean, replaced many lightships. In 1939, when the Coast Guard assumed responsibility for navigational aids, the number of lightships was reduced to 30. Although three additional lightships were built between 1954 and 1965, the total number of lightships continued to decline steadily until 1983 when the Nantucket I Lightship was replaced with a large navigational buoy. This marked the end of America's lightship era.

Today only 15 life-saving lightships remain, most of which are open to the public. Their current locations and statuses follow. Additional information (e.g. designation numbers, website information, etc.) is in The Listing of U.S. Lighthouses & Lightships in Chapter 9.

Lightship Huron, Michigan. Nautical flags designate Huron's vessel number: LV103.

Ambrose Lightship was launched in 1907 and, after being replaced, was displayed in the 1964 World's Fair. The Ambrose is currently afloat as a museum in New York Harbor, New York, where it was actively located for over 65 years. It is open to the public.

Barnegat Lightship is currently docked and being repaired on the Delaware River in Camden, New Jersey. The private owner tries to maintain it, but the Lightship Barnegat is included on the Doomsday List and is in peril of being permanently lost.

Chesapeake Lightship was active from 1930 to 1970. During World War II, it was painted battleship gray, armed with guns, and patrolled the bay area. The Chesapeake Lightship is currently a museum on Chesapeake Bay and is afloat in the Baltimore Harbor, Maryland. It is open to the public.

Columbia Lightship was one of four vessels that served at the Columbia River Lightship Station. When the last one was decommissioned in 1979, it was the last Pacific coast lightship. It is currently a floating museum on the Columbia River in Astoria, Oregon, and is open to the public.

Frying Pan Lightship was abandoned for 10 years in the Chesapeake Bay. In the mid-1980s the Lightship Frying Pan capsized and sank. It remained underwater for three years before being salvaged and restored (including a new engine). In 1989 the lightship sailed to its current location where it remains afloat in New York Harbor, New York. It is open to the public.

Lightship Chesapeake, Maryland

Huron Lightship is currently a museum on Lake Huron and is dry-berthed at Port Huron, Michigan. It was launched in 1920 and when the Huron was retired in 1970, it was the last lightship on the Great Lakes. It is open to the public.

Liberty Lightship is also known as the Winter Quarter Lightship and is painted with the name "Liberty Landing Marina." The lightship's interior was gutted and renovated and is now used as a floating office building in Liberty State Park in Jersey City, New Jersey.

Nantucket Lightship (has been owned by the U.S. Lightship Museum since 2009. A year later it was moved from New York's Long Island Sound to the Boston Harbor in Massachusetts where it will be refurbished and become a museum that will be open to the public.

Nantucket I Lightship, in 1985, was the last American lightship to be decommissioned. It is located in Nantucket Harbor and is afloat near Nantucket Island, Massachusetts. Its interior has been refurbished. The Nantucket I Lightship is currently a privately owned yacht that is available for hire.

Nantucket II Lightship, in 1952, was the last American lightship to be built. In 1953, a tripod foremast was installed and topped with a lighthouse-style lantern room and new optics that made it the brightest American lightship. It is afloat on the Agawam River in Wareham, Massachusetts.

Overfalls Lightship is afloat on the Delaware Bay in Lewes, Delaware, restoration having been completed in 2010. In 2009, the Lightship Overfalls was returned from Norfolk, Virginia, where its hull underwent major repair work. It is in very good condition and getting better. The Lightship Overfalls is a museum and is open to the public.

Portsmouth Lightship is a museum near the Chesapeake Bay in Portsmouth, Virginia, and is open to the public.

Relief Lightship replaced the previous Relief, which was struck and sunk by the cargo ship, *SS Green Bay*, in New York in 1960. It is currently afloat on the San Francisco Bay, in Oakland, California, and is open to the public.

Swiftsure Lightship is currently afloat in the Northwest Seaport, in Seattle, Washington, and is open to the public.

Umatilla Lightship displays the name "Marine Bio Researcher." It is currently afloat in the Gulf of Alaska, near Pennock Island, Alaska. Despite its rusty exterior appearance, it is in fairly good "original" condition and is privately owned.

Lightship Portsmouth, Virginia

New Bedford Lightship was docked in New Bedford, Massachusetts, where the lightship suffered neglect for many years. In May, 2006, the New Bedford Lightship capsized. It was later re-floated, but in July, 2006, the lightship was vandalized leaving it further exposed to the elements. The City of New Bedford "excessed" the lightship and in June, 2007, it was auctioned and sold for scrap. The New Bedford Lightship had been included on the Doomsday List and is now permanently and sadly lost.

Lightship New Bedford
(October 2006)

The Lens

The most beautiful and artistic item in a lighthouse is its Fresnel lens (pronounced [frey'nel]). The lens is so intricate that it is hard to capture its beauty in a photo. Though it might look like a single piece of glass, in fact it consists of many small pieces.

The Fresnel lens was invented by French physicist Augustin Fresnel (1788-1827). It required far less materials than a conventional spherical lens. Because the Fresnel lens was much thinner than previous lenses, more light could pass through it, making lighthouses visible from much greater distances. The lens bent the light into a narrow beam. Because of its amazing efficiency, a Fresnel lens could easily transmit its light 20 or more miles to the horizon, and it required less fuel oil to do so. Most Fresnel lenses look like barrels or beehives. Later lenses incorporated a bull's eye design into the center of the lens and are shaped like a magnifying glass. This concentrated beam was even more powerful. Some bull's eye lenses contain from two to twenty four different flash panels. Bull's eye lenses with only two panels are called bivalve or clamshell lenses.

Before the Fresnel lens was developed, lighthouses used mirrors to reflect light. A light-reflector behind a light source loses 83% of its light, while the Fresnel lens loses only 17%. The light-reflector system required as many as thirty lamps to provide adequate light. To keep lamps burning at optimum brightness and minimize the soot output, lighthouse keepers spent a lot of time trimming the wicks. Because of this chore, keepers were sometimes called "wickies." Fresnel-equipped lighthouses needed only a single lamp to produce more light (resulting in far less maintenance).

Third Order Fresnel Lens at West Quoddy Lighthouse, Maine

Bivalve Lens on display Navesink Lighthouse, New Jersey

Modern lenses, like the Directional Code Beacons (DCB) have replaced many Fresnel lenses in American lighthouses. Far from the romance and artistry associated with the Fresnel lens, the mechanical-looking DCB is a simple, utilitarian optic that is more economical to maintain that the Fresnel lens. DCB lenses operate from electrical sources rather than fuel oil, which make them almost maintenance-free.

The modern and compact Vega Rotating Beacon (VRB) uses six or eight acrylic Fresnel lenses to rotate around a stationary lamp. The VRB lens can operate in remote, unattended, solar-powered locations and needs only annual maintenance. Like the DCB, the VRB lens is simple and not at all artistic.

In 1822 the first Fresnel lens was used in the Cardovan Tower Lighthouse on the Gironde River in France. In 1841, the first Fresnel lens was sent from France to America for Navesink Lighthouse, New Jersey.

Fresnel lenses originally fell into six sizes, called orders, based on their focal length. The largest (first order) lens was used for lighthouses built on open seacoasts and headlands that needed to be seen from the greatest distances. There are no first order lenses in any of the Great Lakes lighthouses. Completely assembled, a first order lens is about twelve feet tall and has the ability to transmit light approximately 20 miles.

The smallest, sixth order lens was more suitable for lighthouses built in harbors, bays, and on pier heads, as well as in lighthouses built to mark dangers such as shoals and rocks. An intermediate third-and-one-half order lens and seventh and eighth order lenses were developed later.

All lighthouse beacons have either a fixed light or a unique flash sequence and color combination. These integral combinations identify each lighthouse and are called the "night mark." Fixed or stationary lights display a steady beam. Other lights revolve and display a flashing light with varying flash frequencies. The flashing light pattern of each light is called its characteristic.

Bodie Island Lighthouse, North Carolina (morning)

Characteristics include the following:

• An alternating light changes back and forth between two different colors.

• An eclipsed light is fixed, but at defined intervals is briefly interrupted by darkness.

• A flashing light changes back and forth between light and darkness, the total duration of the darkness being greater than the light periods.

• A group-flashing light regularly repeats with the same number of flashes.

• An occulting light changes back and forth between light and darkness with the total duration of the light being greater than the dark periods and the intervals between the two being equal.

Bodie Island Lighthouse, North Carolina (late afternoon)

The longer you remain at a lighthouse on any given day, the more changes you'll notice. As the sun crosses the sky from east to west, it transforms even the day mark colors of the building. In the middle photo, the white day mark temporarily inherits the pink sunset colors allows the windows to be the windows are visible. Although some lighthouse lamps remain lit throughout the day, the Bodie Island Lighthouse is not one of them.

Bodie Island Lighthouse, North Carolina (night)

Revolving, flashing lights often have a number of bull's eye designs that are spaced around the lens' circumference. The concentrated beam from a bull's eye lens makes the light more powerful; the number of bull's eyes determines the flash frequency. Revolving lenses require a large clockwork mechanism that precisely times the lens rotation around the light, which in turn, displays the flash. A rotating lens either floated in a pool of mercury or was mounted on wheels that were controlled by the clockworks.

The clockworks are located in the watch room, just below the lantern room. In addition to the light variations, either fixed or steady, and in addition to white lights, some lighthouses display a green or red light. Still other lighthouses display a white light with a green or red sector. With so many combinations, you begin to see all of the different night mark possibilities.

There are two main factors that determine the distance a light can be seen: the light's intensity (based on the lens size) and the tower height above the water (the focal plane). Weather conditions also affect the light's visibility.

Sand Point (Escabana) Lighthouse, Michigan. Bottom portion of rotating devise.

Sand Point (Escabana) Lighthouse, Michigan. Top lip of rotating devise.

By far, the most beautiful lens I've ever seen is the red and white lens located at Umpqua River Lighthouse in Oregon. The first surprise is that this magnificent first order lens is housed in such a relatively short (61-foot tower) lighthouse. After entering the lighthouse tower, I climbed a few steps and found myself inside the huge lens (looking up at the top of it). Even though I have seen red glass in lenses before, I was in awe of my surroundings. The red glass looked like it was ground from rubies and it radiantly sparkled from the natural sunlight entering through it. There is no substitute for seeing a Fresnel lens with your own eyes and the following photo does not do justice to the Umpqua River Lighthouse lens. It does give you a rough idea of how beautiful and artistic a Fresnel lens can be.

Umpqua River Lighthouse, Oregon. First Order Fresnel Lens.

7

Lighthouse Keepers

Although the days could be boring, lighthouse keepers had no days off. Light keepers were required to fill the oil lamps at the top of the tower, wind clockworks, polish brass, clean the lens and the windows, trim the wicks, paint the lighthouse, maintain and clean the lighthouse, and more. Now we simply "flip a switch" to light a room, but the task of turning the light on and off at least once a day required hard labor. Before electricity and automatic timers, lighting the beacon involved carrying heavy barrels of fuel up the stairs, lighting and trimming the wicks, and cleaning the inevitable soot from the windows to ensure the lights could be seen. They had to work all the time and when the weather was bad, with blinding rain, relentless waves, or gusting winds, they worked even harder to ensure the lamps remained lit. They also risked their own lives to help save others. Because many lighthouses are in remote areas or located on bodies of water, lighthouse keepers often lived in dangerous and isolated places.

The list of brave and dedicated lighthouse keepers is endless. There are many interesting life stories from which to select. I've chosen to provide information about 14 keepers who have been honored by the U.S. Coast Guard (USCG). In the 1990s, the USCG commissioned a new "keeper-class" of coastal buoy tenders (cutters) that are named to honor lighthouse keepers. These 14 stories represent a collective depiction of many lighthouse keepers. Their stories of heroism, dedication, and tragedy follow.

Idawalley Zorada Lewis Wilson (1842-1911) was born in Newport, Rhode Island, and was known for her heroism. In 1854, Ida's father was transferred to the Lighthouse Service and became the keeper at Lime Rock Lighthouse in Rhode Island. In 1858 after her father became disabled by a stroke, Ida and her mother took over his lighthouse keeper duties. After Mr. Lewis died in 1872, Mrs. Lewis was appointed

keeper and Ida continued to help. In 1879, Mrs. Lewis died and Ida was appointed as the keeper. She is credited with saving 18 lives during the 39 years she spent at the Lime Rock Lighthouse and was awarded the Gold Lifesaving Medal. Ida was married for a short time, but she spent most of her life alone at the lighthouse. In 1911, Ida Lewis died of a stroke. The light station was renamed Ida Lewis Rock Lighthouse in her honor. Ida is the only American lightkeeper to be memorialized this way. The *USCGC Ida Lewis* (WLM-551), whose home port is Newport, Rhode Island, was the first keeper-class coastal buoy tender to honor a lighthouse keeper.

Katherine "Kate" Walker (1846-1930) was the wife of the Sandy Hook's Lighthouse keeper, John Walker. In 1883, John was appointed head keeper, with Kate as assistant keeper, at the Robbin's Reef Lighthouse. John died of pneumonia three years later. Kate applied for the appointment as the lightkeeper but, because of her petite stature (4'10", 100 lbs.), objections were raised. Several men turned down the appointment because of the lighthouse's isolation before Kate's application was reconsidered and she was appointed in 1895. Kate is reported to have saved at least 50 lives. She retired in 1919. The Robbin's Reef Lighthouse is often referred to as "Kate's Light." The *USCGC Katherine Walker* (WLM-552), whose home port is Bayonne, New Jersey, was named in her honor.

Abigail "Abbie" Burgess Grant (1839-1892) was born in Maine, the daughter of Sam Burgess. In 1853, Sam was appointed lighthouse keeper at Matinicus Rock. As a teenager, Abbie was left alone twice to tend to the lighthouse while her father went to the mainland for provisions. Severe storms prevented Mr. Burgess from returning to the island for four weeks the first time and three weeks, the second time. Not only did Abbie take care of the Matinicus Lighthouse in his absence, she cared for her invalid mother and her siblings. Abbie remained on the island for many years and later married Isaac Grant whose father, John, was the Matinicus lightkeeper after her father. Abbie did much of the work while her father and father-in-law were keepers at the Matinicus Lighthouse. In 1873, Isaac was appointed keeper at White Head Lighthouse where he and Abbie tended the lights. Two years later, Abbie was appointed the assistant keeper there, where she remained until she retired in 1890. The *USCGC Abbie Burgess* (WLM-553), whose homeport is Rockland, Massachusetts, was named in her honor.

Marcus A. Hanna (1842-1921), born in Bristol, Maine, was the lighthouse keeper in two Maine lighthouses. His father was the keeper of the Franklin Island Lighthouse. When the Civil War began, Marcus enlisted in the Navy for one year and then fought in volunteer regiments until the war ended. In 1895, Marcus received the Medal of Honor for volunteering (in 1863) to carry water behind enemy lines. In 1869, Marcus was appointed keeper at the Pemaquid Point Lighthouse, and in 1873 he was transferred as head keeper to the Cape Elizabeth Lighthouse. In 1885, Marcus was awarded the Gold Lifesaving Medal for saving two sailors when their schooner wrecked near the Cape Elizabeth Lighthouse. The *USCGC Marcus Hanna* (WLM-554), whose homeport is South Portland, Maine, was named in his honor.

James Rankin (1844-1921) was born in Ireland and immigrated to America in 1867. In 1877, he served for one year as the keeper of East Brother Island Lighthouse in California before transferring to the Fort Point Lighthouse in San Francisco. James remained at Fort Point until he retired in 1919. During his years as lightkeeper, James saved 18 lives. *The USCGC James Rankin* (WLM-555), whose homeport is Baltimore, Maryland, was named in his honor.

Joshua Appleby (1770-1846) was born in Rhode Island and served as lighthouse keeper in the Sand Key Lighthouse in Florida. In 1820, Joshua sailed to the Florida Keys where he made his living by fishing and salvaging shipwrecks. He was accused of conspiring to intentionally run ships aground, then salvage and sell the cargo. In 1823 he was arrested but was later released. In 1837, Joshua was appointed head keeper of the Sand Key Lighthouse. While he was there, hurricanes hit the Keys in 1841, 1842, and 1844. The lighthouse was damaged and repaired after the 1842 and 1844 hurricanes. In 1846, the Great Havana Hurricane hit the area. By the hurricane's end, Sand Key was totally submerged under water. The following day there was no evidence that the lighthouse had been there. Joshua's daughter, grandson, and two friends had been visiting him when the hurricane landed. All of them lost their lives along with over 250 other hurricane victims. *The USCGC Joshua Appleby* (WLM-556), whose homeport is St Petersburg, Florida, was named in his honor. Also see the story of Barbara Mabrity who was impacted by the same hurricane.

Frank Albert Drew (1864-1931) was a hero to mariners who sailed on Lake Michigan. From 1899-1903, Frank served as the assistant lighthouse keeper at the Pilot Island Lighthouse. He began in 1903, as the assistant keeper, and finished his career in 1929, as head keeper of Wisconsin's Green Island Lighthouse. Frank's father, Samuel, was the original keeper of the Green Island Lighthouse (1824-1882). Frank became well known and received many citations for his numerous, heroic rescues. The *USCGC Frank Drew* (WLM-557), whose homeport is Portsmouth, Virginia, was named in his honor.

Anthony Petit (?-1946) was the head lightkeeper of a five-member crew at the Scotch Cap Lighthouse in Alaska. On April 1, 1946 a tsunami struck the light station destroying it and killing everyone at the lighthouse. The *USCGC Anthony Petit* (WLM-558), whose homeport is Ketchikan, Alaska, was named in his honor.

Barbara Mabrity (1782-1867) was the longest-serving lighthouse keeper at the Key West Lighthouse in Florida. In 1826, Barbara was the wife and assistant to Key West Lighthouse's original keeper, Michael. After Michael died in 1832, Barbara was appointed head keeper. In early October 1846, as the weather began to change in Key West, a severe hurricane swept across Cuba. Barbara had experience; she (and the lighthouse) survived hurricanes in 1835, 1841 and 1842. On October 10, a few residents took shelter inside the lighthouse. As the hurricane raged, a huge wave washed away everything. All six of Barbara's children died in the storm. Barbara served as lighthouse keeper the following year when a new lighthouse was built. In 1864, Barbara was accused of making remarks disloyal to the Union and was urged to retire. She refused to leave and she was fired. She died three years later. The *USCGC Barbara Mabrity* (WLM-559), whose homeport is Mobile, Alabama, was named in her honor. Also see the story of Joshua Appleby who was impacted by the same hurricane.

William J. Tate (1869-1953) was a man of action. He was the keeper of the North Landing Lighthouse in North Carolina from 1915-1939. William was frequently cited for saving lives and property and as a result he was one of the best-paid keepers in the U.S. Lighthouse Service. William was also an aviation pioneer who had been involved in helping the Wright brothers with their first powered flight in 1903. Among other things, he helped them assemble their aircraft at Kill Devil Hill on North Carolina's Outer Banks. William combined his aviation interests with his duty as a lighthouse keeper. He was the first U.S. Lighthouse Service member to inspect lighted navigation aids from an airplane (1920). As a result, the Coast Guard Aviation currently plays a large role in monitoring and servicing American navigation aids. The *USCGC William Tate* (WLM-560), whose homeport is Philadelphia, Pennsylvania, was named in his honor.

Harry C. Claiborne (1859-1918) was a New Orleans native who, in 1887, began his career as the second assistant keeper of the Southwest Pass Lighthouse located near New Orleans, Louisiana. Two years later he was appointed as the head keeper of the Pass a l'Outre Lighthouse in Louisiana and in 1895 he was transferred to the Bolivar Point Lighthouse near Galveston, Texas. Harry was on duty when the Galveston Hurricane hit in 1900. Over 100 people took refuge inside the lighthouse where Harry oversaw their care until additional help came. In 1915, he again cared for 50 hurricane refugees who took shelter in the lighthouse. Both times, Galveston had been devastated by the hurricanes. Both times, Harry oversaw the rebuilding of the damaged lighthouse. In 1915 all of the light station buildings (except the tower) were put on stilts for improved hurricane protection in the future. The improvements were successful; the light station has not been destroyed since. Harry passed away while still working at the lighthouse. Up until the end, Harry was a dedicated and compassionate lighthouse keeper. *The USCGC Harry Claiborne* (WLM-561), whose homeport is Galveston, Texas, was named in his honor.

Maria Herrick Bray (1828?-1921) was a naturalist and an author. She was married to Alexander Bray, who was the lighthouse keeper at the twin Thacher Island Lighthouses in Massachusetts. In 1864, Alexander took a sick assistant keeper to the mainland and became stranded there for several days. During that absence Maria took care of both lights. The *USCGC Maria Bray* (WLM-562), whose homeport is Atlantic Beach, FL, was named in her honor.

Henry Blake (1837-1871), who was born in England, arrived in the Washington territory in 1857. A year later he was appointed as the original keeper at the New Dungeness Lighthouse in Washington. Henry was a compassionate man who helped those in need. In 1868, the S'Klallam Indians (who lived near the lighthouse) attacked and killed the Tsimshian Indians (who lived on Vancouver Island and were camping nearby). Henry immediately went to the site but found no survivors. The next morning a 17-year old, pregnant, Tsimshian woman named Nusee-chus, arrived at the lighthouse. Although she survived the attack, she was badly slashed and bleeding. Henry and his wife, Mary Ann, nursed the woman back to health and took her to a temporary safe home on the mainland. The *USCGC Henry Blake* (WLM-563), whose homeport is Everett, Washington, was named in his honor.

George D. Cobb served at the Point Bonita Lighthouse near San Francisco, California. On Christmas day in 1896, George saw three sailors tossed into the bay when their sailboat capsized. In gale-force winds and high waves, George risked his own life when he quickly rowed out and saved the men from drowning. For his heroism and valor, he was awarded the Silver Lifesaving Medal. The *USCGC George Cobb* (WLM-564), whose homeport is San Pedro, CA, was named in his honor.

8

Recycling Lighthouses

Before lighthouses were automated, lighthouse keepers literally turned the lights on and off at least once every day. In addition, they performed daily maintenance work that kept the equipment and property in good working order. After lighthouses were automated, staff was needed only for periodic maintenance visits. Today, most boats and ships have sonar and/or global positioning systems that provide current location information. These technologies eliminated the need for visual lighthouse sightings, rendering them obsolete. Lighthouses have simply outlived their usefulness. It would be wasteful for the government to spend money maintaining these unneeded properties. However, it would be indefensible to abandon them and allow lighthouses and the histories they represent to perish from neglect and decay.

As a result, the U.S. government is in the process of transferring/auctioning many lighthouse properties to organizations dedicated to maritime restorations and others. The U.S. Coast Guard (USCG) must first declare a lighthouse property to be "surplus," although the actual beacons and fog horns generally remain the direct property of the U.S. government.

Most often and as a result of the National Historic Lighthouse Preservation Act (NHLPA), lighthouse ownership is transferred from the federal government to a federal, state, or local government, a non-profit organization, or an educational agency. In 2000, the government realized that a dedicated non-profit organization could raise funds and obtain grants to maintain these historical landmarks. Through this process, the new owners must comply with strict NHLPA guidelines and be financially able to maintain the lighthouse and property. Additionally, the lighthouse must benefit education, park, recreation, or preservation efforts, and be available to the general public at reasonable times and under reasonable conditions. Only light stations that are eligible for listing in the National Register of Historic Places

can be conveyed through the NHLPA. When there is no interest in a lighthouse through the NHLPA transfer process, it can be auctioned to private citizens who then "bid" on the posted properties. Lighthouses purchased through private auction must comply with state and federal requirements for historic preservation.

Restoration is the only way to ensure that America's lighthouses remain in the present and are secured for future generations. Once a lighthouse or lightship is gone, it is lost forever; although there are a handful of groups that have built replicas of "lost lighthouses." There are many different lighthouse associations that volunteer their time and dedicate thousands of hours to preserve lighthouses. I've had the pleasure to meet many selfless and dedicated individuals who tirelessly work for a single mission: to preserve and maintain America's lighthouses and maritime histories. I find that people involved with renovations share a similar, goal-driven dedication. They seem simultaneously committed to the past and the future and are willing to spend the present to merge the two. Just as past lighthouse keepers helped save human lives and properties, today's lighthouse keepers tirelessly work to save the lives of the very lighthouses themselves.

The two biggest challenges that face today's lighthouse keepers are time, which is running out, and money, which is hard to raise. However, if we don't do something now, there may be no lighthouses to save later. Without continued American dedication and commitment, lighthouses will become extinct. The Lighthouse Depot developed the lighthouse "Doomsday List" (DDL), which contains endangered American lighthouses, lightships, and others. A similar compilation, "The Watch List of Threatened Lighthouses" (WLTL), was produced by the University of North Carolina at Chapel Hill. These lists can be viewed by accessing: www.unc.edu/rowlett/lighthouse/watch.html or www.lighthousedepot.com/lite_explorer.asp?action=search_lighthouses&doomsday=Y.

Both lists help identify lighthouses that are in various stages of disrepair or neglect and are at risk of crumbling to an inglorious end. Although neither list is updated on a regular basis, there's no doubt that being on either list helps to save lighthouses by drawing attention to their condition and need. In Chapter 9 you will find an extensive Listing of U.S. Lighthouses and Lightships. Under the column heading "Miscellaneous Information," you'll notice more than 50 lighthouses are notated with either "DDL" or "WLTL." These notations mean that the lighthouse or lightship is at risk. Thankfully, some of them are being restored and given another chance.

Throughout America, employees and volunteers at many lighthouse associations preserve existing lighthouses to ensure future generations can learn about America's maritime past. A handful of on-going lighthouse successes stories follows.

Ruins Minnesota Point
Lighthouse, Minnesota

Avery Point Lighthouse. Since 1997, when this lighthouse was added to the Doomsday List, efforts have been made to restore it. It is located on the Groton campus of the University of Connecticut. As with most lighthouse restoration projects, funding it was the first problem. In 2000, the Avery Point Lighthouse Society was established with simple goals "dedicated to saving, restoring, and relighting the lighthouse." The first major renovation took place in 2001, when the wooden lantern room was removed from the lighthouse and a duplicate room was constructed. In 2002, the Avery Point Lighthouse was placed on the National Register of Historic Places. In 2003, the first and most major portion of the restoration (replacement of the structural blocks) was initiated and completed. In 2005 federal funding was secured, a contract was awarded, and construction of the final structural restoration phase was completed. On October 15, 2006, the Avery Point Lighthouse was relit. Fundraising efforts are ongoing to complete the restoration project, to provide an endowment for the future maintenance, and to create a small museum that will educate people about the important role of the lighthouse and its light keepers.

Avery Point Lighthouse, Connecticut

Sankaty Head Lighthouse. This lighthouse was located on Nantucket Island, Massachusetts only 75 feet from the edge of a swiftly eroding cliff. For it to survive, it had to be moved further away from the cliff. The first step in moving the lighthouse was to raise it with its foundation. One of the two companies in charge of the project had successfully relocated the Block Island Lighthouse in Rhode Island, the Cape Cod Lighthouse in Massachusetts, and the Cape Hatteras Lighthouse in North Carolina. After raising it, the lighthouse was braced and stabilized to prepare it for its move. In 2008, it slowly inched its way along rails and was relocated approximately 280 feet from the cliff. More work is needed to complete the renovation. The 'Sconset Trust will continue to oversee the preservation and restoration efforts.

Esopus Meadows Lighthouse. In 1979, this lighthouse was listed on the National Register of Historic Places. In 1990, the Save the Esopus Lighthouse Commission (SELC) was formed with goals to restore and protect the lighthouse. In 2002, SELC gained stewardship of the lighthouse from the federal government. In 2003, the lighthouse was relit after 38 years of darkness. SELC volunteers continue to work on restoring the lighthouse.

Sankaty Head Lighthouse, Massachusetts

Esopus Meadows Lighthouse, New York

Roanoke River Lighthouse. In 2007 the Roanoke River Lighthouse was relocated to Colonial Park in Edenton, North Carolina, as the first step in its renovation. The renovated screw pile lighthouse will rest on original-looking legs. It will then be opened to the public as a maritime center.

Roanoke River Lighthouse, North Carolina (February 2007)

Morris Island Lighthouse. In 2000, this lighthouse was transferred to the state of South Carolina, which then leased it for 99 years to Save the Light, Inc. The lighthouse, located on a submerged island, is in danger of crumbling into the water. Save the Light, Inc. will coordinate the stabilization, erosion control, and lighthouse restoration, and will raise the funds to reach these goals. In 2007, with the help of the Army Corps of Engineers, Save the Light began restoration efforts. In 2008, a 12-foot cofferdam was completed around the lighthouse's base. The next restoration phase will include injecting concrete into the base, which, before the cofferdam, had been underwater at high tide. Once the foundation work is completed, renovation efforts will focus on the lantern room.

The good news is that many lighthouse organizations are proactive. They obtain and begin restoration efforts on lighthouses and lightships that haven't been officially designated as "doomed" or "threatened," but have been abandoned long ago.

In 2009, I spent five unique, hard-working, and memorable weeks at Alaska's Five Finger Islands Lighthouse, which is located in the Frederick Sound along Stephen's Passage. The lighthouse is located on a very small (less than three acres), unnamed island that can be accessed only by boat, seaplane, or helicopter. The island is located 65 miles south of Juneau and 40 miles north of the small fishing village of Petersburg. In 1997, the USCG awarded a 30-year lease to the Juneau Lighthouse Association (JLA).

Five Finger Islands Lighthouse, Alaska

Morris Island Lighthouse, South Carolina

In 2004, the lighthouse and property were permanently deeded to JLA and the lighthouse was added to the National List of Historic Places. Since 1997, many restorative improvements (requiring hundreds of thousands of dollars and thousands of hours of volunteer labor), have been accomplished to help save this beautiful art deco lighthouse, which was built in 1935; two years after the original wooden lighthouse burned.

The remoteness and size of the island create special challenges when trying to recruit volunteers and raise money. I'll specifically discuss the Five Finger Islands Lighthouse, but keep in mind that similar challenges and opportunities pertain to most lighthouse (and lightship) restoration projects.

Some lighthouses are so remote that receiving provisions and supplies is an incredible challenge that is hard to imagine in our modern lives. At the Five Finger Islands Lighthouse, shipments can be made only at high tide and the words "weather permitting" are realistically included when discussing arrivals and departures of any kind. Loading and unloading supplies are often labor- and time-intensive tasks.

Five Finger Islands
Lighthouse, Alaska

Working on a lighthouse restoration project can include lots of manual labor, dirt, sore muscles, long hours, and diminished contact with the rest of the world. So, why would any sensible person volunteer for that? The most obvious reasons include the personal satisfaction of keeping a lighthouse from fading into oblivion, and seeing immediate results. The camaraderie with other volunteers is infectious and the dedication and commitment of the lighthouse keepers are endless and inspiring. Even when my body said "no," I wanted to accomplish more.

There are other surprising or unexpected benefits that are different on each project. Some of the most memorable moments at the Five Finger Islands Lighthouse began when the lighthouse keeper or a volunteer shouted, "Whales!!" This signaled that at least one whale was very close to the island. The Five Finger Islands are surrounded by southeast Alaska's most densely populated waters of humpback whales in the summer months, which wonderfully coincides with the lighthouse's volunteer season.

The restoration projects at the Five Finger Islands Lighthouse have come a long way to meet its light keepers' end goals. These include the creation of "a marine mammal research site and a public educational facility focusing on the maritime and marine significance of the region. Visitors and guests to the island will experience the workings of a lighthouse on a remote site while enjoying the unparalleled beauty of the area." I'm content to have been a tiny part of this dream.

You can help to keep the glow on at a lighthouse or a lightship. There are many different ways to help with this goal and it's easier than you might think. Here are lots of ways you can help give back to our planet and our communities:

• Visit a lighthouse and join a lighthouse association.
• Contribute money to a national (or regional) lighthouse organization or directly to a local lighthouse.
• Donate products (e.g. baskets of homemade jams, baked goods, etc.) or services (e.g. spa treatments, car detailing, home carpet cleaning, dinner for two, etc.) to local lighthouses that they can use in fund raising auctions and events.
• If you're artistic, create artwork and donate it to local lighthouses that they can use in fund raising auctions and events.

Wind Point Lighthouse, Wisconsin. Renovation in progress - August, 2007

• If you're musical, donate your band's time to give a concert to help in local fund raising efforts.
• Volunteer your time for manual labor (e.g. clean, paint, electrical work, roofing, plumbing, etc.) or become a tour guide at a local lighthouse.
• If you live in a state that has special lighthouse license plates, buy and display them on your car.
• If you have office skills, volunteer your time to create or maintain a local lighthouse website, help write grants requesting funds or assist with mail outs.
• Contact federal and state legislators and inform them that you are interested in lighthouse preservation.
• If one does not currently exist, establish a non-profit organization. Convince local government (or spearhead an effort) to assume lighthouse ownership. There are many groups around who can provide information and direction with this. Contact groups that have succeeded.

Website addresses are included in **The Complete Listing of American Lighthouses** in Chapter 9 for anyone who is interested in more detailed information, wants to help save these lighthouses, or wants to make a direct contribution to the current preservation efforts. If we pull together, we can positively influence the future history of our American lighthouses. It doesn't take much to help save the planet and community. Join the effort to recycle lighthouses.

9

Just the Facts

I researched numerous lighthouse-related databases. Although there is a wealth of information, it is inconsistent, mainly due to lack of controlled documentation and changes in the "keepers" of the documents.

I made every effort to verify all of the data included in *Keep Your Glow On.* Other lighthouse sources may reflect different data. In cases where I used a specific date or tower height, I attempted to define my use of the data. Please be cautious and verify all data you reference. I created a series of simple and complex lists that contain different data sets to view lighthouse information from different perspectives.

List 1

Oldest American Lighthouses

A list of the 20 oldest continuously standing American lighthouses follows. The year listed reflects the "first lit" date of the current lighthouse tower. This is different from the date the lighthouse was commissioned. It also will be different if a current tower was built atop an existing base (e.g. Tybee Island Lighthouse, Georgia) or is built on the same site as a previously existing lighthouse (e.g. Boston Harbor Lighthouse, Massachusetts).

All lighthouses listed in List 1 are included in the National Park Services (NPS) inventory.

Sandy Hook, NJ	1764
Portland Head, ME	1791
Old Cape Henry, VA	1792
Montauk Point, NY	1797
Eatons Neck, NY	1799

New London Harbor, CT	1801
Faulkners Island, CT	1802
Old Point Comfort, VA	1802
New Point Comfort, VA	1806
Sands Point, NY	1809
Scituate, MA	1811
Bald Head Island, NC	1817
Bird Island, MA	1819
Long Island Head, MA	1819
Amelia Island, FL	1820
Sapelo Island, GA	1820
Bakers Island, MA	1821
Burnt Island, ME	1821
Marblehead, OH	1821
Charlotte-Genesee, NY	1822

List 2

Tallest American Lighthouses
in the National Park Services Inventory

The following shows the 21 tallest (over 149 feet) American lighthouses. The tower height begins at ground level (and does not include any underground measurements). Some lighthouse data sources include the antenna height; while other sources do not. Generally, there is no notation about whether or not the antenna height is included or excluded, which may account for 3-6 foot discrepancies. Different sources list the Cape Hatteras Lighthouse's height between

191 and 210 feet. This may be partially due because approximately 10 additional feet of it are underground. These factors contribute to lighthouse height discrepancies (from one lighthouse data source to another).

Cape Hatteras, NC	197-foot tower
Cape Charles, VA	191-foot tower
Ponce de Leon Inlet, FL	175-foot tower
Diamond Shoal, NC	175-foot tower
Barnegat, NJ	172-foot tower
Bodie Island, NC	170-foot tower
Cape Lookout, NC	169-foot tower
Oak Island, NC	169-foot tower
Absecon, NJ	169-foot tower
Fire Island, NY	168-foot tower
St Augustine, FL	165-foot tower
New Cape Henry, VA	163-foot tower
Currituck Beach, NC	162-foot tower
Morris Island, SC	161-foot tower
Sombrero Key, FL	160-foot tower
Dry Tortugas, FL	157-foot tower
Cape May, NJ	157-foot tower
Tybee Island, GA	154-foot tower
Pensacola, FL	150-foot tower
Cape Romain, SC	150-foot tower

All lighthouses listed in List 2 are included in the National Park Services (NPS) inventory. Please note that two lighthouses are excluded from List 2 because they are not included in the NPS lighthouse inventory. They are: the Perry Memorial Lighthouse (OH) at 352 feet, and the Rappahannock Shoal Channel South Range Rear Lighthouse (VA) at 224 feet.

List 3

Focal Plane Heights Over 150 Feet

Seventy-six American lighthouses are 100 feet or taller. The number of lighthouses doubles with a focal plane over 100 feet. The focal plane measures the height from the middle of the lens to the water's mean level. While most of the tall American lighthouses are located on the east coast, the west coast lays claim to more lighthouses with high focal planes.

Lighthouse Name, State		Focal Plane	Tower Height
Old Point Loma, CA	NPS	462 ft focal plane	46 feet
Cape Mendocino, CA	NPS	422 ft focal plane	43 feet
Makapu'u, HI	NPS	420 ft focal plane	46 feet
Farallon Island, HI	NPS	358 ft focal plane	41 feet
Perry Memorial, OH	—	335 ft focal plane	352 feet
Point Reyes, CA	NPS	294 ft focal plane	35 feet
Anacapa Island, CA	NPS	277 ft focal plane	40 feet
Point Sur, CA	NPS	273 ft focal plane	48 feet
Block Island Southeast, RI	NPS	261 ft focal plane	52 feet
Marcus Hook, DE	NPS	250 ft focal plane	100 feet
Navesink, NJ	NPS	246 ft focal plane	73 feet
Cape Blanco, OR	NPS	245 ft focal plane	59 feet
Cape Hinchinbrook, AK	NPS	235 ft focal plane	67 feet
Staten Island Range, NY	NPS	231 ft focal plane	90 feet
Old Plantation Flats, VA	—	220 ft focal plane	224 feet
Boyer Bluff, WI	—	220 ft focal plane	80 feet
Cape Disappointment, WA	NPS	220 ft focal plane	53 feet
Cape Meares, OR	NPS	217 ft focal plane	38 feet
Kilauea, HI	NPS	216 ft focal plane	52 feet
Alcatraz Island, CA	NPS	214 ft focal plane	84 feet
Moloka`i, HI	NPS	213 ft focal plane	138 feet
Skunk Bay, WA	—	210 ft focal plane	30 feet
Heceta Head, OR	NPS	205 ft focal plane	56 feet
Huron Island, MI	NPS	197 ft focal plane	39 feet
Trinidad Head, CA	NPS	196 ft focal plane	25 feet
North Head, WA	NPS	194 ft focal plane	65 feet
Cape Hatteras, NC	NPS	192 ft focal plane	197 feet
Pensacola, FL	NPS	191 ft focal plane	150 feet

New Dorp, NY	NPS	190 ft focal plane	80 feet
Seguin Island, ME	NPS	186 ft focal plane	53 feet
Point Vicente, CA	NPS	185 ft focal plane	67 feet
Cape Charles, VA	NPS	180 ft focal plane	191 feet
Fire Island, NY	NPS	180 ft focal plane	168 feet
Monhegan Island, ME	NPS	178 ft focal plane	47 feet
Cape Sarichef, AK	—	177 ft focal plane	35 feet
Liston Range Rear, DE	NPS	176 ft focal plane	120 feet
Table Bluff, CA	NPS	176 ft focal plane	35 feet
Cape May, NJ	NPS	175 ft focal plane	157 feet
Michigan Island (New), WI	NPS	170 ft focal plane	118 feet
Gay Head, MA	NPS	170 ft focal plane	51 feet
Cape Cod, MA	NPS	170 ft focal plane	66 feet
Montauk Point, NY	NPS	168 ft focal plane	110 feet
Absecon, NJ	NPS	168 ft focal plane	169 feet
Split Rock, MN	NPS	168 ft focal plane	54 feet
Cape Ann, MA	NPS	166 ft focal plane	124 feet
Cape Flattery, WA	NPS	165 ft focal plane	65 feet
Umpqua River, OR	NPS	165 ft focal plane	61 feet
Barnegat, NJ	NPS	165 ft focal plane	172 feet
New Cape Henry, VA	NPS	164 ft focal plane	163 feet
Kevich, WI	—	163 ft focal plane	50 feet
Charleston, SC	NPS	163 ft focal plane	140 feet
Yaquina Head, OR	NPS	162 ft focal plane	93 feet
Cape Romain, SC	NPS	161 ft focal plane	150 feet
Yaquina Bay, OR	NPS	161 ft focal plane	51 feet
St Augustine, FL	NPS	161 ft focal plane	165 feet
Ponce de Leon Inlet, FL	NPS	159 ft focal plane	175 feet
Morris Island, SC	NPS	158 ft focal plane	161 feet
Currituck Beach, NC	NPS	158 ft focal plane	162 feet
Sankaty Head, MA	NPS	158 ft focal plane	70 feet
Cape Lookout, NC	NPS	156 ft focal plane	169 feet
Bodie Island, NC	NPS	156 ft focal plane	170 feet
Cape Kumukahi, HI	NPS	156 ft focal plane	125 feet
Point Arena, CA	NPS	155 ft focal plane	115 feet
North Point, WI	NPS	154 ft focal plane	74 feet
Assateague Island, VA	NPS	154 ft focal plane	142 feet
Dry Tortugas, FL	NPS	151 ft focal plane	157 feet

Only lighthouses indicated as "NPS" in List 3 are included in the National Park Services lighthouse inventory.

List 4

General Information - By State

State	Number of Lighthouses		Tower Height Over 99' Tall		Focal Point Height			Older Than 1820*	
	Qty	%	Qty	%	99 - 249'	250-462'	Total	Qty	%
Alabama	3	<1%	1	1%	1	–	1	–	–
Alaska	15	2%	–	–	3	–	3	–	–
California	48	6%	2	3%	13	6	19	–	–
Connecticut	21	3%	–	–	–	–	–	3	12%
Delaware	16	2%	4	5%	3	1	4	–	–
Florida	35	4%	15	20%	19	–	19	1	4%
Georgia	8	1%	2	3%	2	–	2	1	4%
Hawaii	11	1%	2	3%	5	–	5	1	4%
Illinois	8	1%	1	1%	1	–	1	–	–
Indiana	6	1%	–	–	–	–	–	–	–
Louisiana	13	2%	4	5%	3	–	3	–	–
Maine	66	8%	2	3%	11	–	11	2	8%
Maryland	27	3%	1	1%	2	–	2	–	–
Massachusetts	65	8%	4	5%	9	–	9	5	20%
Michigan	135	17%	8	11%	9	–	9	–	–
Minnesota	8	1%	–	–	1	–	1	–	–
Mississippi	3	<1%	–	–	–	–	–	–	–
New Hampshire	5	1%	–	–	–	–	–	–	–
New Jersey	24	3%	4	5%	6	–	6	1	4%
New York	79	10%	3	4%	6	–	6	4	16%
North Carolina	14	2%	8	11%	5	–	5	2	8%
Ohio	23	3%	1	1%	1	1	2	1	4%
Oregon	13	2%	–		10	–	10	–	–
Pennsylvania	4	<1%	–		1	–	1	–	–
Rhode Island	21	3%	–		–	1	1	1	4%
South Carolina	12	2%	4	5%	5	–	5	–	–
Texas	7	1%	1	1%	–	–	–	–	–
Vermont	6	1%	–	–	–	–	–	–	–
Virginia	17	2%	5	7%	3	–	3	3	12%
Washington	28	3%	1	1%	7	–	7	–	–
Wisconsin	55	7%	3	4%	11	–	11	–	–
Total	**796**	**100%**	**74**	**100%**	**137**	**9**	**146**	**25**	**100%**

*Based on the year the existing completed tower was lit. Rebuilt (and partially rebuilt) towers show the last date the current tower was completed (and lit), not the date of the previous tower(s).

List 4 includes lighthouses not listed in the National Park Services lighthouse inventory.

The Listing of
U.S. Lighthouses & Lightships

In the pages that follow is a compilation of information about individual American lighthouses or lightships. It is sorted by state and then by lighthouse name.
Information includes:

- The body of water it is on
- The nearest town or city
- The latitude and longitude of its location
- If the lighthouse is included in the National Park Service lighthouse inventory
- The year it was first lit
- The height and general category of the lighthouse
- The focal plane
- Current lens information
- Miscellaneous interesting information about each lighthouse or lightship
- Internet addresses where you can learn more about a particular lighthouse.

Please note that the information listed in *Keep Your Glow On* may be different from data located elsewhere. There are numerous discrepancies among published lighthouse data sources. In most cases, I tried to locate more than one source with matching data. In other cases, I selected the data element that seemed most probable.

Wherever possible, I tried to explain a discrepancy by defining the data element. For example, *Keep Your Glow On* uses the "first lit" date of the existing tower to define the age of the lighthouse. If a lighthouse tower was rebuilt, or partially rebuilt, the first lit date reflects that of the new tower, not the original tower.

Lighthouse height discrepancies may be caused because one source includes the measurement of the lightning rod while another source excludes the lightning rod height. Similarly and most notably, the tallest American lighthouse, Cape Hatteras in North Carolina, is listed with varying heights (191-207 feet). Ten feet of the Cape Hatteras tower are underground. The heights listed throughout *Keep Your Glow On* start at ground level. In general you should verify data before referencing it.

Alabama

MOBILE BAY (MIDDLE BAY) LIGHTHOUSE
Body of Water: Mobile Bay
Near: Mobile, AL
Lat & Long: 30.43745, -88.01165
National Park Service Inventory
First Lit: 1885
Height & Type: 54 ft screwpile
Focal Plane: 54 ft fp
Current Lens Information: (inactive) 155 MM
Miscellaneous Information:
 • Refurbished (1985) by Alabama Lighthouse Association
Volunteer & Contribution Information:
 www.alabamalighthouses.com

MOBILE POINT LIGHTHOUSE
Body of Water: Mobile Bay
Near: Mobile, AL
Lat & Long: 30.2278, -88.0239
National Park Service Inventory
First Lit: 1873
Height & Type: 30 ft skeleton
Focal Plane: 110 ft fp
Current Lens Information: none
Miscellaneous Information:
 • Can be viewed on cruise from Daulin Island
Volunteer & Contribution Information:
 www.alabamalighthouses.com

SAND ISLAND LIGHTHOUSE
Body of Water: Mobile Bay & Gulf of Mexico
Near: Dauphin Island, AL
Lat & Long: 30.1966, -88.0534
National Park Service Inventory
First Lit: 1873
Height & Type: 131 ft tower
Focal Plane:
Current Lens Information: none

Miscellaneous Information:
- DDL
- Second order Fresnel lens displayed in Ft. Morgan Museum

Volunteer & Contribution Information:
www.alabamalighthouses.com

Alaska

CAPE DECISION LIGHTHOUSE
Body of Water: Pacific Ocean
Near: Petersburg, AK
Lat & Long: 56.0014, -134.1369
National Park Service Inventory
First Lit: 1932
Height & Type: 76 ft tower
Focal Plane: 96 ft fp
Current Lens Information: VRB-25
Miscellaneous Information:
- Last light station to be established in Alaska

Volunteer & Contribution Information:
www.capedecisionlight.org

CAPE HINCHINBROOK LIGHTHOUSE
Body of Water: Pacific Ocean
Near: Cordova, AK
Lat & Long: 60.2383, -146.6466
National Park Service Inventory
First Lit: 1934
Height & Type: 67 ft tower
Focal Plane: 235 ft fp
Current Lens Information: VRB-25 SP
Miscellaneous Information:
- Accessible only by boat
- Original third-order Fresnel lens displayed in Valdez Museum

CAPE SARICHEF LIGHTHOUSE
Body of Water: Bering Sea
Near: Anchorage, AK
Lat & Long: 54.59861, -164.92667
First Lit: 1950
Height & Type: 35 ft tower
Focal Plane: 177 ft fp
Current Lens Information: 375 MM
Miscellaneous Information:
- Most westerly and isolated US lighthouse
- Located on Unimak Island

CAPE SPENCER LIGHTHOUSE
Body of Water: Gulf of Alaska
Near: Juneau, AK
Lat & Long: 58.1984, -136.64
National Park Service Inventory
First Lit: 1925
Height & Type: 25 ft tower with house
Focal Plane: 105 ft fp
Current Lens Information: VRB-25 SP
Miscellaneous Information:
- Accessible only by boat
- Original third-order Fresnel lens displayed in Juneau's Alaska State Museum

CAPE ST ELIAS LIGHTHOUSE
Body of Water: Pacific Ocean
Near: Cordova, AK
Lat & Long: 59.7983, -144.5983
National Park Service Inventory
First Lit: 1916
Height & Type: 55 ft tower
Focal Plane: 85 ft fp

Current Lens Information: VRB-25 SP
Miscellaneous Information:
- Original third order Fresnel lens displayed at Cordova Museum

Volunteer & Contribution Information:
www.kayakisland.org

ELDRED ROCK LIGHTHOUSE
Body of Water: Pacific Ocean
Near: Haines, AK
Lat & Long: 58.9717, -135.22
National Park Service Inventory
First Lit: 1905
Height & Type: 56 ft octagonal tower
Focal Plane: 91 ft fp
Current Lens Information: 250 MM SP
Miscellaneous Information:
- Accessible only by boat

Volunteer & Contribution Information:
www.sheldonmuseum.org

FIVE FINGER ISLANDS LIGHTHOUSE
Body of Water: Gulf of Alaska
Near: Petersburg, AK
Lat & Long: 57.2698, -133.6322
National Park Service Inventory
First Lit: 1935
Height & Type: 68 ft tower
Focal Plane: 81 ft fp

Current Lens Information: VRB-25 SP
Miscellaneous Information:
- 2006 USPS stamp
- Owned and being renovated by Juneau Lighthouse Association

Volunteer & Contribution Information:
www.5fingerlighthouse.com

GUARD ISLAND LIGHTHOUSE
Body of Water: Gulf of Alaska
Near: Ketchikan, AK
Lat & Long: 55.4466, -131.8817
National Park Service Inventory
First Lit: 1924
Height & Type: 30 ft tower
Focal Plane: 23 ft fp
Current Lens Information: VRB-25 SP

Five Finger Islands Lighthouse, Alaska

Miscellaneous Information:
- Guard Island Heritage Inc. hopes to obtain and restore the lighthouse

Volunteer & Contribution Information:
www.lighthouseexcursion.com

UMATILLA LIGHTSHIP
Body of Water: Gulf of Alaska
Near: Ketchikan, AK
Lat & Long: 55.3325, -131.6594
First Lit: 1946
Height & Type: lightship
Current Lens Information: duplex 550 MM electric
Miscellaneous Information:
- WLV-196
- Privately owned

MARY ISLAND LIGHTHOUSE
Body of Water: Gulf of Alaska
Near: Ketchikan, AK
Lat & Long: 55.0895, -131.1836
National Park Service Inventory
First Lit: 1937
Height & Type: 61 ft tower
Focal Plane: 76 ft fp
Current Lens Information: 250 MM
Miscellaneous Information:
- Accessible only by boat

ODIAK PHAROS LIGHTHOUSE
Body of Water: Gulf of Alaska
Near: Cordova, AK
Lat & Long: 60.53714, -145.76288
Height & Type: short tower
Focal Plane: 26 ft fp
Miscellaneous Information:
- Privately owned
- Cordova Rose Lodge

Volunteer & Contribution Information:
www.cordovarose.com (general info)

POINT RETREAT LIGHTHOUSE
Body of Water: Pacific Ocean
Near: Juneau, AK
Lat & Long: 58.4087, -134.9559

National Park Service Inventory
First Lit: 1924
Height & Type: 25 ft tower with house
Focal Plane: 63 ft fp
Current Lens Information: 300 MM SP
Miscellaneous Information:
- Accessible only by boat
- Currently being renovated

Volunteer & Contribution Information:
www.aklighthouse.org

POINT SHERMAN LIGHTHOUSE
Body of Water: Pacific Ocean
Near: Juneau, AK
Lat & Long: 58.855, -135.1517
First Lit: 1904
Height & Type: ruins
Current Lens Information: none
Miscellaneous Information:
- Accessible only by boat

SENTINEL ISLAND LIGHTHOUSE
Body of Water: Pacific Ocean
Near: Juneau, AK
Lat & Long: 58.5464, -134.9231
National Park Service Inventory
First Lit: 1935
Height & Type: 51 ft tower
Focal Plane: 86 ft fp
Current Lens Information: VRB-25 SP
Miscellaneous Information:
- Owned and being renovated by Gastineau Channel Historical Society

Volunteer & Contribution Information:
www.gastineauchannel.blogspot.com

TREE POINT LIGHTHOUSE
Body of Water: Gulf of Alaska
Near: Ketchikan, AK
Lat & Long: 54.8021, -130.9339
National Park Service Inventory
First Lit: 1935
Height & Type: 66 ft tower
Focal Plane: 86 ft fp
Current Lens Information: 300 MM

Miscellaneous Information:
- Fourth-order Fresnel displayed at Tongass Historical Museum

Sentinel Island Lighthouse, Alaska

California

ALCATRAZ ISLAND LIGHTHOUSE
Body of Water: San Francisco Bay
Near: San Francisco, CA
Lat & Long: 37.8262, -122.4222
National Park Service Inventory
First Lit: 1909
Height & Type: 84 ft tower
Focal Plane: 214 ft fp
Current Lens Information: DCB-24
Miscellaneous Information:
- Site of first Pacific Coast lighthouse (1854)
- Accessible by ferry

Volunteer & Contribution Information:
www.alcatraztickets.com (general info)

ANACAPA ISLAND LIGHTHOUSE
Body of Water: Santa Barbara Channel
Near: Oxnard, CA
Lat & Long: 34.0156, -119.3584
National Park Service Inventory
First Lit: 1932
Height & Type: 40 ft tower
Focal Plane: 277 ft fp
Current Lens Information: DCB-24
Miscellaneous Information:
- Accessible only by boat or ferry
- Located in Channel Island National Park

ANO NUEVO LIGHTHOUSE
Body of Water: Pacific Ocean
Near: Santa Cruz, CA
Lat & Long: 37.1078, -122.336
First Lit: 1890
Height & Type: ruins
Current Lens Information: first order Fresnel
Miscellaneous Information:
- Located in Ano Nuevo California State Reserve

BATTERY POINT (CRESCENT CITY) LIGHTHOUSE
Body of Water: Pacific Ocean
Near: Crescent City, CA
Lat & Long: 41.744, -124.2032

National Park Service Inventory
First Lit: 1856
Height & Type: 45 ft tower with house
Focal Plane: 77 ft fp
Current Lens Information: fifth order Fresnel
Miscellaneous Information:
- Reactivated (1982)
- Museum

Volunteer & Contribution Information:
www.delnortehistory.org

CAPE MENDOCINO LIGHTHOUSE
Body of Water: Pacific Ocean
Near: Shelter Cove, CA
Lat & Long: 40.0225 -124.0694
National Park Service Inventory
First Lit: 1868
Height & Type: 43 ft tower 16-sided pyramid
Focal Plane: 422 ft fp
Current Lens Information:
Miscellaneous Information:
- Located in Mel Coombs Park

Volunteer & Contribution Information:
www.hmdb.org (general info)

CAPE MENDOCINO LIGHTHOUSE (REPLICA)
Body of Water: Pacific Ocean
Near: Ferndale, CA
Lat & Long: 40.02319, -124.06852
Height & Type: 43 ft tower – replica
Current Lens Information: none
Miscellaneous Information:
- Replica contains the original first order Fresnel lens

CARQUINEZ STRAIT LIGHTHOUSE
Body of Water: San Pablo Bay
Near: Vallejo, CA
Lat & Long: 38.0682, -122.2125
National Park Service Inventory
First Lit: 1910
Height & Type: keepers quarters only
Focal Plane: 56 ft fp
Current Lens Information: none

Miscellaneous Information:
- Owned by Western Water Ways, Inc.

EAST BROTHER LIGHTHOUSE
Body of Water: San Francisco Bay
Near: Richmond, CA
Lat & Long: 37.9633, -122.433
National Park Service Inventory
First Lit: 1874
Height & Type: 48 ft square tower with house
Focal Plane: 61 ft fp
Current Lens Information: FA 251
Miscellaneous Information:
- Bed & breakfast

Volunteer & Contribution Information:
www.ebls.org

FARALLON ISLAND LIGHTHOUSE
Body of Water: Pacific Ocean
Near: San Francisco, CA
Lat & Long: 37.6983, -123.0016
National Park Service Inventory
First Lit: 1855
Height & Type: 41 ft tower without lantern
Focal Plane: 358 ft fp
Current Lens Information: none
Miscellaneous Information:
- Accessible only by boat
- Fresnel lens displayed at Maritime National Historic Park Visitor Center

FORT POINT LIGHTHOUSE
Body of Water: Pacific Ocean
Near: San Francisco, CA
Lat & Long: 37.8108, -122.4771
National Park Service Inventory
First Lit: 1864
Height & Type: 27 ft skeleton
Focal Plane: 110 ft fp
Current Lens Information: none
Miscellaneous Information:
- Located under Golden Gate Bridge

HUMBOLDT HARBOR LIGHTHOUSE
Body of Water: Pacific Ocean
Near: Eureka, CA

Lat & Long: 40.7691, -124.221
First Lit: n/a
Height & Type: ruins
Current Lens Information: none
Miscellaneous Information:
- Collapsed in 1933

RELIEF LIGHTSHIP
Body of Water: San Francisco Bay
Near: Oakland, CA
Lat & Long: 37.7956, -122.2804
First Lit: 1907
Height & Type: lightship
Current Lens Information: two 375mm lanterns
Miscellaneous Information:
- WLV-605
- Owned by U.S. Lighthouse Society
Volunteer & Contribution Information:
www.uslhs.org

LIME POINT LIGHTHOUSE
Body of Water: San Francisco Bay
Near: San Francisco, CA
Lat & Long: 37.82557, -122.47856
First Lit: 1900
Height & Type: 20 ft tower – partial ruins
Focal Plane: 33 ft fp
Current Lens Information: 250 MM SP
Miscellaneous Information:
- Located under Golden Gate Bridge

LONG BEACH HARBOR ("ROBOT LIGHT") LIGHTHOUSE
Body of Water: Los Angeles/Long Beach Harbors
Near: Long Beach, CA
Lat & Long: 33.72322, -118.1868
First Lit: 1949
Height & Type: 42 ft tower
Miscellaneous Information:
- Always automated
- **National Park Service Inventory**
"significant unmanned aid"

LIONS LIGHTHOUSE FOR SIGHT LIGHTHOUSE
Body of Water: Los Angeles/Long Beach Harbors

Near: Long Beach, CA
Lat & Long: 33.72322, -118.1868.
First Lit: 2000
Height & Type: 65 ft tower – faux lighthouse
Focal Plane: 105 ft fp
Miscellaneous Information:
- Owned by City of Long Beach

LOS ANGELES HARBOR (ANGEL'S GATE) LIGHTHOUSE
Body of Water: Los Angeles Harbor
Near: Los Angeles, CA
Lat & Long: 33.7088, -118.2512
National Park Service Inventory
First Lit: 1913
Height & Type: 69 ft tower
Focal Plane: 73 ft fp
Current Lens Information: DCB-24 SP
Miscellaneous Information:
- Original fourth order Fresnel lens displayed at LA Maritime Museum

MILE ROCKS LIGHTHOUSE
Body of Water: Pacific Ocean
Near: San Francisco, CA
Lat & Long: 37.7927, -122.5102
First Lit: 1906
Height & Type: tower without lantern room
Focal Plane: 49 ft fp
Miscellaneous Information:
- Converted to pad for helicopter landing

NEW POINT LOMA LIGHTHOUSE
Body of Water: Pacific Ocean
Near: San Diego, CA
Lat & Long: 32.6651, -117.24249
National Park Service Inventory
First Lit: 1891
Height & Type: 70 ft skeleton
Focal Plane: 88 ft fp
Current Lens Information: third order Fresnel
Miscellaneous Information:
- Original third order lens had 12 bulls eyes with alternating red glass

OAKLAND HARBOR LIGHTHOUSE
Body of Water: Pacific Ocean

Near: Oakland, CA
Lat & Long: 37.7809, -122.2434
National Park Service Inventory
First Lit: 1903
Height & Type: tower with house
Current Lens Information: none
Miscellaneous Information:
- Converted into Quinn's Lighthouse Restaurant & Pub
Volunteer & Contribution Information:
www.quinnslighthouse.com (general info)

OLD POINT LOMA LIGHTHOUSE
Body of Water: Pacific Ocean
Near: San Diego, CA
Lat & Long: 32.67171, -117.24086
National Park Service Inventory
First Lit: 1855
Height & Type: 46 ft tower with house
Focal Plane: 462 ft fp
Current Lens Information: (inactive) third order Fresnel
Miscellaneous Information:
- High focal point obscured light with cloud cover and fog

PIEDRAS BLANCAS LIGHTHOUSE
Body of Water: Pacific Ocean
Near: San Simeon, CA
Lat & Long: 35.665, -122.2434
National Park Service Inventory
First Lit: 1875
Height & Type: 74 ft tower without lantern room
Focal Plane: 142 ft fp
Current Lens Information: VRB-25
Miscellaneous Information:
- Maintained by Bureau of Land Management since 2001
Volunteer & Contribution Information:
www.piedrasblancas.gov

PIGEON POINT LIGHTHOUSE
Body of Water: Pacific Ocean
Near: Santa Cruz, CA

Lat & Long: 37.18185, -122.39353
National Park Service Inventory
First Lit: 1872
Height & Type: 115 ft tower
Focal Plane: 148 ft fp
Current Lens Information: DCB-24
Miscellaneous Information:
  • Hostel accommodations available on lighthouse property
Volunteer & Contribution Information:
  www.norcalhostels.org/pigeon/local-sights (general info)

POINT ARENA LIGHTHOUSE
Body of Water: Pacific Ocean
Near: Point Arena , CA
Lat & Long: 38.9546, -123.7406
National Park Service Inventory
First Lit: 1908
Height & Type: 115 ft tower
Focal Plane: 155 ft fp
Current Lens Information: DCB-224
Miscellaneous Information:
  • Lighthouse lodging available
Volunteer & Contribution Information:
  www.pointarenalighthouse.com

Point Arena Lighthouse,
California

POINT ARGUELLO LIGHTHOUSE
Body of Water: Pacific Ocean
Near: Lompoc, CA
Lat & Long: 34.5778, -120.6475
First Lit: 1901
Height & Type: 20 ft post w/ navigation aid
Miscellaneous Information:
- Located on Vandenberg Air Force Base
- Currently two rotating lights atop a steel tower

POINT BLUNT LIGHTHOUSE
Body of Water: Pacific Ocean
Near: San Francisco, CA
Lat & Long: 37.8533, -122.42
National Park Service Inventory
First Lit: 1956
Height & Type: fog signal building with navigation aid
Miscellaneous Information:
- Accessible by (and best seen from) boat or ferry

POINT BONITA LIGHTHOUSE
Body of Water: San Francisco Bay
Near: Sausalito, CA
Lat & Long: 37.8155, -122.5297
National Park Service Inventory
First Lit: 1877
Height & Type: 33 ft tower
Focal Plane: 140 ft fp
Current Lens Information: second order Fresnel
Miscellaneous Information:
- Last CA lighthouse to be automated
- Accessible three days a week
Volunteer & Contribution Information:
www.NationalParkServiceInventory.gov/goga/pobo

POINT CABRILLO LIGHTHOUSE
Body of Water: Pacific Ocean
Near: Mendocino, CA
Lat & Long: 39.3487, -123.8261
National Park Service Inventory
First Lit: 1909
Height & Type: 47 ft tower with house
Focal Plane: 84 ft fp
Current Lens Information: DCB-224
Miscellaneous Information:
 • Bed & breakfast
Volunteer & Contribution Information:
 www.mendocinolighthouse.pointcabrillo.org

Point Cabrillo Lighthouse,
California

POINT CONCEPTION LIGHTHOUSE
Body of Water: Pacific Ocean
Near: Las Cruces, CA
Lat & Long: 34.449, -120.4707
National Park Service Inventory
First Lit: 1882
Height & Type: 52 ft tower
Focal Plane: 133 ft fp
Current Lens Information: none
Miscellaneous Information:
- Best viewed from boat or plane
- Privately owned property

POINT DIABLO LIGHTHOUSE
Body of Water: Pacific Ocean
Near: San Francisco, CA
Lat & Long: 37.82, -122.49965
First Lit: 1923
Height & Type: small beacon on shack
Miscellaneous Information:
- **National Park Service Inventory**
"significant unmanned aid"
- Best viewed from boat

POINT FERMIN LIGHTHOUSE
Body of Water: San Pedro Harbor
Near: San Pedro, CA
Lat & Long: 33.7053, -118.2937
National Park Service Inventory
First Lit: 1874
Height & Type: 30 ft tower with house

Current Lens Information: none
Miscellaneous Information:
- Early "Stick" style Victorian architecture
- Museum
Volunteer & Contribution Information:
www.pointferminlighthouse.org

POINT HUENEME LIGHTHOUSE
Body of Water: Port Hueneme
Near: Point Hueneme , CA
Lat & Long: 34.145, -119.2098
National Park Service Inventory
First Lit: 1941
Height & Type: 48 ft square tower
Focal Plane: 52 ft fp
Current Lens Information: fourth order Fresnel
Miscellaneous Information:
- Accessible third Saturday each month (February - October)
Volunteer & Contribution Information:
www.huenemelight.org

POINT KNOX LIGHTHOUSE
Body of Water: Pacific Ocean
Near: Tiburon, CA
Lat & Long: 37.8561, -122.4423
First Lit: 1900
Height & Type: ruins
Miscellaneous Information:
- Located in Angel Island Park
- Best viewed from boat or plane

POINT MONTARA LIGHTHOUSE
Body of Water: San Francisco Bay
Near: Montara , CA
Lat & Long: 37.5363, -122.519
National Park Service Inventory
First Lit: 1928
Height & Type: 30 ft tower
Focal Plane: 70 ft fp
Current Lens Information: FA 251
Miscellaneous Information:
   • One of California's converted lighthouse hostels
Volunteer & Contribution Information:
   www.norcalhostels.org/montara (general info)

Point Montara Lighthouse, California

POINT PINOS LIGHTHOUSE
Body of Water: Monterey Bay
Near: Pacific Grove, CA
Lat & Long: 36.63357, -121.93348
National Park Service Inventory
First Lit: 1855
Height & Type: 43 ft tower with house
Focal Plane: 89 ft fp
Current Lens Information: third order Fresnel
Miscellaneous Information:
  • Oldest active lighthouse on west coast
Volunteer & Contribution Information:
    www.pacificgroveheritage.org (general info)

POINT REYES LIGHTHOUSE
Body of Water: Gulf of Farallones
Near: San Rafael, CA
Lat & Long: 37.9957, -123.02327
National Park Service Inventory
First Lit: 1870
Height & Type: 35 ft tower
Focal Plane: 294 ft fp
Current Lens Information: first order Fresnel
Miscellaneous Information:
  • Pathway consists of more than 300 steps
    leading to the lighthouse

POINT SUR LIGHTHOUSE
Body of Water: Monterey Bay
Near: Big Sur, CA
Lat & Long: 36.3063, -121.9016
National Park Service Inventory
First Lit: 1889
Height & Type: 48 ft tower with house
Focal Plane: 273 ft fp
Current Lens Information: DCB-224
Miscellaneous Information:
  • Lantern room restoration complete (2001)
Volunteer & Contribution Information:
    www.pointsur.org

POINT VICENTE LIGHTHOUSE
Body of Water: Pacific Ocean
Near: Rancho Palo Verdes, CA
Lat & Long: 33.7419, -118.4106
National Park Service Inventory

First Lit: 1926
Height & Type: 67 ft tower
Focal Plane: 185 ft fp
Current Lens Information: third order Fresnel
Miscellaneous Information:
  • USCG personnel assigned nearby live in
    lighthouse housing

PUNTA GORDA LIGHTHOUSE
Body of Water: Pacific Ocean
Near: Petrolia, CA
Lat & Long: 40.2493, -124.3503
National Park Service Inventory
First Lit: 1912
Height & Type: 27 ft tower
Focal Plane: 75 ft fp
Current Lens Information: none
Miscellaneous Information:
  • Part of the King Range National
    Conservation Area

SAN LUIS OBISPO (PORT HARTFORD) (PORT SAN LUIS) LIGHTHOUSE
Body of Water: San Luis Obispo Bay
Near: San Luis Obispo, CA
Lat & Long: 35.1601, -120.76
National Park Service Inventory
First Lit: 1890
Height & Type: 40 ft tower
Focal Plane: 116 ft fp
Current Lens Information: none
Miscellaneous Information:
  • Ownership transferred to the Port San Luis
    Harbor District (1992)
Volunteer & Contribution Information:
    www.sanluislighthouse.org

SANTA BARBARA LIGHTHOUSE
Body of Water: Pacific Ocean
Near: Santa Barbara , CA
Lat & Long: 34.3958, -119.7232
First Lit: 1856
Height & Type: 24 ft tower without lantern (ruins)
Miscellaneous Information:
  • Earthquake toppled lighthouse and
    shattered Fresnel lens (1925)

SANTA CRUZ (MARK ABBOTT MEMORIAL) LIGHTHOUSE
Body of Water: Santa Cruz Bay
Near: Santa Cruz, CA
Lat & Long: 36.9515, -122.0268
First Lit: 1967
Height & Type: 39 ft tower
Focal Plane: 60 ft fp
Miscellaneous Information:
  • WLTL surfing museum located inside the
    lighthouse
Volunteer & Contribution Information:
    www.santacruzsurfingmuseum.org (general info)

SANTA CRUZ BREAKWATER (WALTON) LIGHTHOUSE
Body of Water: Santa Cruz Harbor
Near: Santa Cruz, CA
Lat & Long: 36.9604, -122.0023
First Lit: 2001
Height & Type: 42 ft tower
Focal Plane: 36 ft fp
Miscellaneous Information:
  • Funded by private donations
  • Signal is green

SOUTHAMPTON SHOALS LIGHTHOUSE
Body of Water: Sacramento River
Near: Stockton , CA
Lat & Long: 38.0359, -121.4942
National Park Service Inventory
First Lit: 1905
Height & Type: tower without lantern room
Focal Plane: 52 ft fp
Current Lens Information: none
Miscellaneous Information:
  • Privately owned
  • St. Francis Yacht Club
  • Top two stories moved to Tinsley Island (1960)

ST GEORGE REEF LIGHTHOUSE
Body of Water: Pacific Ocean
Near: Crescent City, CA
Lat & Long: 41.83662, -124.38652
National Park Service Inventory
First Lit: 1892

Height & Type: 90 ft tower
Focal Plane: 144 ft fp
Miscellaneous Information:
- 2006 USPS stamp
- Accessible by boat or helicopter

Volunteer & Contribution Information:
www.stgeorgereeflighthouse.us

TABLE BLUFF LIGHTHOUSE
Body of Water: Pacific Ocean
Near: Eureka, CA
Lat & Long: 40.8081, -124.1654
National Park Service Inventory
First Lit: 1892
Height & Type: 35 ft tower
Focal Plane: 176 ft fp
Current Lens Information: none
Miscellaneous Information:
- Original Fresnel lens sent to and used in Old Point Loma Lighthouse

TRINIDAD HEAD LIGHTHOUSE
Body of Water: Pacific Ocean
Near: Trinidad, CA
Lat & Long: 41.0518, -124.1514
National Park Service Inventory
First Lit: 1871
Height & Type: 25 ft square tower
Focal Plane: 196 ft fp
Current Lens Information: 375 MM
Miscellaneous Information:
- Automated (1974) but USCG remained there until 2000

TRINIDAD (HEAD) MEMORIAL LIGHTHOUSE
Body of Water: Trinidad Harbor
Near: Trinidad, CA
Lat & Long: 41.058, -124.1431
First Lit: 1949
Height & Type: 25 ft tower – white/red replica
Current Lens Information: fourth order Fresnel
Miscellaneous Information:
- Original Fresnel lens from Trinidad Head is displayed in the replica

YERBA BUENA (GOAT ISLAND) LIGHTHOUSE
Body of Water: Pacific Ocean
Near: San Francisco, CA
Lat & Long: 37.8073, -122.3625
National Park Service Inventory
First Lit: 1875
Height & Type: 25 ft tower
Focal Plane: 95 ft fp
Current Lens Information: fifth order Fresnel
Miscellaneous Information:
- Can be viewed from Alemeda Oakland ferry

Connecticut

AVERY POINT
Body of Water: Atlantic Ocean
Near: Groton, CT
Lat & Long: 41.3196, -72.067
First Lit: 1945
Height & Type: 41 ft tower
Focal Plane: 55 ft fp
Current Lens Information: flashing green light
Miscellaneous Information:
- DDL
- University of Connecticut
- Renovated and relit (2006)

Volunteer & Contribution Information:
www.lighthousefoundation.org

FAULKNERS ISLAND LIGHTHOUSE
Body of Water: Long Island Sound
Near: Guilford, CT
Lat & Long: 41.2117, -72.6533
National Park Service Inventory
First Lit: 1802
Height & Type: 46 ft tower
Focal Plane: 94 ft fp
Current Lens Information: 190 MM SP
Miscellaneous Information:
- Best viewed from boat
- Part of Stewart B. McKinney National Wildlife Refuge

Volunteer & Contribution Information:
www.lighthouse.cc/FLB

FAYERWEATHER ISLAND (BLACK ROCK HARBOR) LIGHTHOUSE
Body of Water: Black Rock Harbor
Near: Bridgeport, CT
Lat & Long: 41.1424, -73.2167
National Park Service Inventory
First Lit: 1823
Height & Type: 41 ft tower
Focal Plane: 44 ft fp
Current Lens Information: none / fifth order Fresnel
Miscellaneous Information:
- Located at Seaside Park

Fayerweather Island (Black Rock Harbor) Lighthouse, Connecticut

FIVE MILE POINT (OLD NEW HAVEN) LIGHTHOUSE
Body of Water: Long Island Sound
Near: New Haven, CT
Lat & Long: 41.2483, -72.9039
National Park Service Inventory
First Lit: 1845
Height & Type: 70 ft tower
Focal Plane: 97 ft fp
Current Lens Information: fourth order Fresnel
Miscellaneous Information:
- Located at Lighthouse Point Park

GREAT CAPTAIN ISLAND LIGHTHOUSE
Body of Water: Long Island Sound
Near: Greenwich, CT
Lat & Long: 40.9825, -73.6235
National Park Service Inventory
First Lit: 1868
Height & Type: 51 ft tower with house
Focal Plane: 74 ft fp
Current Lens Information: none
Miscellaneous Information:
- Owned by Town of Greenwich
- Accessible by boat or ferry

GREENS LEDGE LIGHTHOUSE
Body of Water: Long Island Sound
Near: Norwalk, CT
Lat & Long: 41.0417, -73.4434
National Park Service Inventory
First Lit: 1902
Height & Type: 52 ft caisson
Focal Plane: 62 ft fp
Current Lens Information: VRB-25
Miscellaneous Information:
- Located at end of private street
- Best seen from boat

LYNDE POINT (SAYBROOK INNER) LIGHTHOUSE
Body of Water: Connecticut River
Near: Old Saybrook, CT
Lat & Long: 41.271373, -72.343254
National Park Service Inventory
First Lit: 1839
Height & Type: 65 ft octagonal tower
Focal Plane: 71 ft fp

Current Lens Information: fifth order Fresnel
Miscellaneous Information:
- Best viewed from boat

MORGAN POINT LIGHTHOUSE
Body of Water: Long Island Sound
Near: Noank, CT
Lat & Long: 41.3167, -71.9894
National Park Service Inventory
First Lit: 1868
Height & Type: 52 ft tower with house
Focal Plane: 61 ft fp
Current Lens Information: none
Miscellaneous Information:
- Privately owned
- Best viewed by boat

MYSTIC SEAPORT (REPLICA) LIGHTHOUSE
Body of Water: Mystic River
Near: Mystic, CT
Lat & Long: 41.3614, -71.9664
First Lit: 1966
Height & Type: 25 ft tower
Current Lens Information: fourth order Fresnel
Miscellaneous Information:
- Replica of (1901) Brant Point Lighthouse
Volunteer & Contribution Information:
www.mysticseaport.org (general info)

NEW LONDON HARBOR LIGHTHOUSE
Body of Water: Long Island Sound
Near: New London , CT
Lat & Long: 41.31666, -72.08997
National Park Service Inventory
First Lit: 1801
Height & Type: 89 ft octagonal tower
Focal Plane: 90 ft fp
Current Lens Information: fourth order Fresnel
Miscellaneous Information:
- Transferred to the New London Maritime Society

NEW LONDON LEDGE LIGHTHOUSE
Body of Water: Long Island Sound
Near: New London , CT
Lat & Long: 41.306121, -72.077286

National Park Service Inventory
First Lit: 1909
Height & Type: 58 ft tower with house
Focal Plane: 58 ft fp
Current Lens Information: VRB-25
Miscellaneous Information:
- Original Fresnel lens displayed at Custom House Maritime Museum
Volunteer & Contribution Information:
www.lighthousefoundation.org

PECK (PECK'S) LEDGE LIGHTHOUSE
Body of Water: Long Island Sound
Near: Norwalk, CT
Lat & Long: 41.0783, -73.3683
National Park Service Inventory
First Lit: 1906
Height & Type: 54 ft caisson
Focal Plane: 61 ft fp
Current Lens Information: 250 MM
Miscellaneous Information:
- Best viewed from boat

PENFIELD REEF LIGHTHOUSE
Body of Water: Long Island Sound
Near: Fairfield, CT
Lat & Long: 41.1163, -73.2218
National Park Service Inventory
First Lit: 1874
Height & Type: 35 ft tower with house
Focal Plane: 51 ft fp
Current Lens Information: DCB-24
Miscellaneous Information:
- Transferred to Beacon Preservation, Inc (2008)
Volunteer & Contribution Information:
www.beaconpreservation.org

SAYBROOK BREAKWATER (SAYBROOK OUTER) LIGHTHOUSE
Body of Water: Connecticut River
Near: Old Saybrook, CT
Lat & Long: 41.2632, -72.34276
National Park Service Inventory
First Lit: 1886
Height & Type: 48 ft tower
Focal Plane: 58 ft fp

Just the Facts **67**

Current Lens Information: 300 MM
Miscellaneous Information:
- Lighthouse image displayed on Connecticut's license plate

SHEFFIELD ISLAND (NORWALK) LIGHTHOUSE
Body of Water: Norwalk River
Near: Norwalk, CT
Lat & Long: 41.0526, -73.4144
National Park Service Inventory
First Lit: 1868
Height & Type: 44 ft tower with house
Focal Plane: 51 ft fp
Current Lens Information: fourth order Fresnel
Miscellaneous Information:
- Accessible by ferry
- Museum

Volunteer & Contribution Information:
www.seaport.org

SOUTHWEST LEDGE (NEW HAVEN BREAKWATER) LIGHTHOUSE
Body of Water: Long Island Sound
Near: New Haven, CT
Lat & Long: 41.325, -72.9116
National Park Service Inventory
First Lit: 1877
Height & Type: 45 ft octagon caisson
Focal Plane: 57 ft fp
Current Lens Information: 190 MM
Miscellaneous Information:
- Best viewed from boat

STAMFORD HARBOR LEDGE (CHATHAM ROCKS) LIGHTHOUSE
Body of Water: Long Island Sound
Near: Stamford, CT

Lat & Long: 41.0133, -73.5433
National Park Service Inventory
First Lit: 1882
Height & Type: 60 ft caisson
Current Lens Information: 200 MM
Miscellaneous Information:
- Privately owned
- Was for sale (1998) but taken off market

STONINGTON HARBOR LIGHTHOUSE
Body of Water: Long Island Sound
Near: Stonington, CT
Lat & Long: 41.3276, -71.9056
National Park Service Inventory
First Lit: 1840
Height & Type: 35 ft octagon stone tower
Focal Plane: 62 ft fp
Current Lens Information: none
Miscellaneous Information:
- Museum
- Fourth order Fresnel lens on display

Volunteer & Contribution Information:
www.stoningtonhistory.org

STRATFORD POINT LIGHTHOUSE
Body of Water: Housatonic River
Near: Stratford, CT
Lat & Long: 41.1517, -73.1033
National Park Service Inventory
First Lit: 1881
Height & Type: 35 ft octagon tower – white/red
Focal Plane: 52 ft fp
Current Lens Information: VRB-25
Miscellaneous Information:
- Original lighthouse was third one built on Long Island Sound (1822)

STRATFORD SHOAL (MIDDLE GROUND) LIGHTHOUSE
Body of Water: Long Island Sound
Near: Bridgeport, CT
Lat & Long: 41.06, -73.1016
National Park Service Inventory
First Lit: 1877
Height & Type: 35 ft tower with house
Focal Plane: 60 ft fp
Current Lens Information: VRB-25
Miscellaneous Information:
- Best viewed from boat or ferry

TONGUE POINT (BRIDGEPORT BREAKWATER) LIGHTHOUSE
Body of Water: Long Island Sound
Near: Bridgeport, CT
Lat & Long: 41.1687, -73.1803
First Lit: 1895
Height & Type: 31 ft tower – black
Focal Plane: 31 ft fp
Current Lens Information: 155 MM
Miscellaneous Information:
- National Park Service Inventory "significant unmanned aid"

Delaware

BAKER RANGE REAR LIGHTHOUSE
Body of Water: Delaware River
Near: New Castle, DE
Lat & Long: 39.5416, -75.5701
First Lit: 1924
Height & Type: skeleton
Miscellaneous Information:
- Located in Augustine Wildlife Area

BELLEVUE RANGE REAR LIGHTHOUSE
Body of Water: Christina & Delaware Rivers
Near: Wilmington, DE
Lat & Long: 39.7201, -75.5181
National Park Service Inventory
First Lit: 1909
Height & Type: 105 ft skeleton – black
Focal Plane: 100 ft fp
Current Lens Information: none
Miscellaneous Information:
- Located in Cherry Island Landfill where it can be viewed

CHERRY ISLAND RANGE LIGHTHOUSE
Body of Water: Delaware Bay
Near: Bellefonte, DE
Lat & Long: 39.76207, -75.48973
First Lit: 1880
Height & Type: 35 ft slender square skeleton
Miscellaneous Information:
- Only skeletons supporting lights remain at both front and rear lights

DELAWARE BREAKWATER LIGHTHOUSE
Body of Water: Delaware Bay
Near: Lewes, DE
Lat & Long: 38.7972, -75.1003
National Park Service Inventory
First Lit: 1885
Height & Type: 49 ft caisson – red/black
Focal Plane: 61 ft fp
Current Lens Information: 375 MM

Miscellaneous Information:
- Assumed duties of Cape Henlopen Lighthouse
Volunteer & Contribution Information:
www.delawarebaylights.org

DELAWARE BREAKWATER RANGE REAR (GREEN HILL) LIGHTHOUSE
Body of Water: Delaware Bay
Near: Lewes, DE
Lat & Long: 38.7896, -75.169
First Lit: n/a
Height & Type: ruins
Current Lens Information: none
Miscellaneous Information:
- Activated 1881
- Defined point of entry into Delaware Bay

FENWICK ISLAND LIGHTHOUSE
Body of Water: Atlantic Ocean
Near: Fenwick Island, DE
Lat & Long: 38.4514, -75.0548
National Park Service Inventory
First Lit: 1859
Height & Type: 84 ft tower
Focal Plane: 83 ft fp
Current Lens Information: third order Fresnel
Miscellaneous Information:
- Southernmost Delaware lighthouse
- Privately owned
Volunteer & Contribution Information:
www.fenwickislandlighthouse.org

FOURTEEN FOOT BANK LIGHTHOUSE
Body of Water: Delaware Bay
Near: Bowers, DE
Lat & Long: 39.04816, -75.18356
National Park Service Inventory
First Lit: 1888
Height & Type: 40 ft tower with house
Focal Plane: 59 ft fp
Current Lens Information: SP
Miscellaneous Information:
- Privately owned since 2007

HARBOR OF REFUGE LIGHTHOUSE
Body of Water: Delaware Bay
Near: Lewes, DE
Lat & Long: 38.8147, -75.09361
National Park Service Inventory
First Lit: 1926
Height & Type: 76 ft caisson
Focal Plane: 72 ft fp
Current Lens Information: DCB-36 SP
Miscellaneous Information:
- Previous lighthouse completed (1908)
Volunteer & Contribution Information:
www.delawarebaylights.org

OVERFALLS LIGHTSHIP
Body of Water: Delaware Bay
Near: Lewes, DE
Lat & Long: 38.779, -75.147
First Lit: 1938
Height & Type: lightship
Current Lens Information: dual 375 MM electric lens lanterns
Miscellaneous Information:
- LV-118 WAL-539 museum WLTL
Volunteer & Contribution Information:
www.overfalls.org

LISTON RANGE FRONT LIGHTHOUSE
Body of Water: Delaware Bay
Near: New Castle, DE
Lat & Long: 39.4829, -75.592
National Park Service Inventory
First Lit: 1906
Height & Type: 45 ft tower with house
Miscellaneous Information:
- Privately owned

LISTON RANGE REAR LIGHTHOUSE
Body of Water: Delaware Bay
Near: New Castle, DE
Lat & Long: 38.7896, -75.639

National Park Service Inventory
First Lit: 1877
Height & Type: 120 ft skeleton – black
Focal Plane: 176 ft fp
Current Lens Information: second order Fresnel
Miscellaneous Information:
- Lens emits continuous red light

MARCUS HOOK (RANGE FRONT) LIGHTHOUSE

Body of Water: Delaware Bay
Near: Bellefonte, DE
Lat & Long:
National Park Service Inventory
First Lit: 1925
Height & Type: 75 ft square pyramidal tower
Focal Plane: 81 ft fp
Current Lens Information: DCB-24
Miscellaneous Information:
- View from Fox Point Park
- Lens emits continuous red light
- 1.5 miles NW from rear range

MARCUS HOOK (RANGE REAR) LIGHTHOUSE

Body of Water: Delaware Bay
Near: Bellefonte, DE
Lat & Long: 39.76223, -75.50317
National Park Service Inventory

First Lit: 1920
Height & Type: 100 ft tower
Focal Plane: 250 ft fp
Current Lens Information: RL-24
Miscellaneous Information:
- Original fourth order Fresnel lens displayed at Philadelphia's Independence Seaport Museum

MISPILLION LIGHTHOUSE

Body of Water: Delaware Bay
Near: Lewes, DE
Lat & Long: 38.9472, -75.3149
National Park Service Inventory
First Lit: 1873
Height & Type: ruins
Focal Plane: 65 ft fp
Current Lens Information: none
Miscellaneous Information:
- Modern lantern was placed atop reconstructed lighthouse in Shipcarpenter Square (2005)

NEW CASTLE LIGHTHOUSE

Body of Water: Delaware Bay
Near: New Castle, DE
Lat & Long: 39.6423, -75.5954
First Lit: 1953
Height & Type: skeleton tower
Focal Plane: 56 ft fp
Miscellaneous Information:
- Property privately owned
- Tower owned by USCG

REEDY ISLAND RANGE REAR LIGHTHOUSE

Body of Water: Delaware Bay
Near: Smyrna, DE
Lat & Long: 39.4064, -75.5898
National Park Service Inventory
First Lit: 1910
Height & Type: 110 ft skeleton – black
Focal Plane: 134 ft fp
Current Lens Information: DCB-224
Miscellaneous Information:
- Delaware River dredged (1899) creating need for more lighthouses

Florida

ALLIGATOR REEF LIGHTHOUSE
Body of Water: Atlantic Ocean
Near: Islamorada , FL
Lat & Long: 24.85167, -80.6183
National Park Service Inventory
First Lit: 1873
Height & Type: 136 ft skeleton – white
Focal Plane: 136 ft fp
Current Lens Information: VRB-25 SP
Miscellaneous Information:
  • Best viewed from boat
Volunteer & Contribution Information:
  www.reeflights.org

AMELIA ISLAND LIGHTHOUSE
Body of Water: Atlantic Ocean
Near: Fernandina Beach, FL
Lat & Long: 30.673, -81.442
National Park Service Inventory
First Lit: 1820
Height & Type: 64 ft tower
Focal Plane: 107 ft fp
Current Lens Information: third order Fresnel
Miscellaneous Information:
  • Oldest (operational) FL lighthouse
  • Northernmost FL lighthouse
Volunteer & Contribution Information:
  www.floridalighthouses.org

AMERICAN SHOAL LIGHTHOUSE
Body of Water: Gulf of Mexico
Near: Sugarloaf Key, FL
Lat & Long: 24.525, -81.52
National Park Service Inventory
First Lit: 1880
Height & Type: 109 ft skeleton – brown
Focal Plane: 109 ft fp
Current Lens Information: VRB-25 SP
Miscellaneous Information:
  • Best viewed from boat
  • 1990 USPS stamp
Volunteer & Contribution Information:
  www.reeflights.org

ANCLOTE KEY LIGHTHOUSE
Body of Water: Gulf of Mexico
Near: Tapron Springs, FL
Lat & Long: 28.168, -82.8458
National Park Service Inventory
First Lit: 1887
Height & Type: 102 ft skeleton – brown
Focal Plane: 101 ft fp
Current Lens Information: none
Miscellaneous Information:
  • Best viewed from boat
  • Relit (2003)
Volunteer & Contribution Information:
  www.anclotecso.com

BOCA GRANDE ENTRANCE RANGE REAR LIGHTHOUSE
Body of Water: Gulf of Mexico
Near: Boca Grande, FL
Lat & Long: 26.7419, -82.2635
National Park Service Inventory
First Lit: 1927
Height & Type: 100 ft skeleton – white
Focal Plane: 105 ft fp
Current Lens Information: 300 MM
Miscellaneous Information:
  • Formerly Delaware Breakwater Rear which relocated from Lewes
Volunteer & Contribution Information:
  www.floridalighthouses.org

Boca Grande Entrance Range Rear
Lighthouse, Florida

CAPE CANAVERAL LIGHTHOUSE
Body of Water: Atlantic Ocean
Near: Cape Canaveral , FL
Lat & Long: 28.4602, -80.5435
National Park Service Inventory
First Lit: 1868
Height & Type: 145 ft tower – black/white stripes
Focal Plane: 137 ft fp
Current Lens Information: DCB-224
Miscellaneous Information:
  • Located on Air Force base
  • Prior reservation needed to tour
Volunteer & Contribution Information:
  www.canaverallight.org

CAPE FLORIDA (CAPE BRAGGS) LIGHTHOUSE
Body of Water: Atlantic Ocean
Near: Key Biscayne, FL
Lat & Long: 25.6666, -80.156
National Park Service Inventory
First Lit: 1845
Height & Type: 95 ft tower
Focal Plane: 100 ft fp
Current Lens Information: 300 MM
Miscellaneous Information:
  • Original lighthouse burned by Seminole warriors (1836)
Volunteer & Contribution Information:
  www.capeflorida.org

CAPE SAN BLAS LIGHTHOUSE
Body of Water: Gulf of Mexico
Near: Apalachicola, FL
Lat & Long: 29.671, -85.3564
National Park Service Inventory
First Lit: 1885
Height & Type: 90 ft tower
Focal Plane: 101 ft fp
Current Lens Information: third order bivalve
Miscellaneous Information:
  • Current lighthouse is fourth one at this location
Volunteer & Contribution Information:
  www.capesanblaslighthouse.com

CAPE ST GEORGE LIGHTHOUSE
Body of Water: Gulf of Mexico
Near: Apalachicola, FL
Lat & Long: 29.5878, -85.04685
National Park Service Inventory
First Lit: 1852
Height & Type: 70 ft tower
Focal Plane: 72 ft fp
Current Lens Information: none
Miscellaneous Information:
  • Accessible only by boat
Volunteer & Contribution Information:
  www.floridalighthouses.org

CARYSFORT REEF LIGHTHOUSE
Body of Water: Atlantic Ocean
Near: North Key Largo, FL
Lat & Long: 25.22167, -80.21167
National Park Service Inventory
First Lit: 1852
Height & Type: 120 ft skeleton – red
Focal Plane: 100 ft fp
Current Lens Information: VRB-25
Miscellaneous Information:
  • Best viewed from boat
Volunteer & Contribution Information:
  www.reeflights.org

CEDAR KEYS (SEAHORSE KEY) LIGHTHOUSE
Body of Water: Gulf of Mexico
Near: Cedar Key, FL
Lat & Long: 29.096483, -83.06533
National Park Service Inventory
First Lit: 1854
Height & Type: 23 ft tower with house
Focal Plane: 75 ft fp
Current Lens Information: none
Miscellaneous Information:
  • Best viewed from boat
  • Part of a Marine Lab used by University of Florida
Volunteer & Contribution Information:
  www.floridalighthouses.org

CROOKED RIVER (CARRABELLE) LIGHTHOUSE
Body of Water: Gulf of Mexico
Near: East Point, FL
Lat & Long: 29.8272, -84.7013
National Park Service Inventory
First Lit: 1895
Height & Type: 100 ft skeleton – red
Focal Plane: 115 ft tp
Current Lens Information: none
Miscellaneous Information:
  • Museum
Volunteer & Contribution Information:
  www.crookedriverlighthouse.org

DRY TORTUGAS (LOGGERHEAD KEY) LIGHTHOUSE
Body of Water: Gulf of Mexico
Near: Key West , FL
Lat & Long: 24.6305, -82.9209
National Park Service Inventory
First Lit: 1858
Height & Type: 157 ft tower – black/white
Focal Plane: 151 ft fp
Current Lens Information: VRB-25 SP
Miscellaneous Information:
  • Accessible only by boat

EGMONT KEY LIGHTHOUSE
Body of Water: Gulf of Mexico
Near: St Petersburg, FL
Lat & Long: 27.6003, -82.7607
National Park Service Inventory
First Lit: 1858
Height & Type: 87 ft tower without lantern room
Focal Plane: 85 ft fp
Current Lens Information: DCB-224
Miscellaneous Information:
  • Accessible by ferry
Volunteer & Contribution Information:
  www.egmontkey.info

FARO BLANCO LIGHTHOUSE
Body of Water: Atlantic Ocean
Near: Marathon, FL
Lat & Long: 24.708856, -81.105266
First Lit: 1950
Height & Type: 65 ft octagon tower – faux lighthouse
Miscellaneous Information:
• Privately owned resort located at 1966 Overseas Hwy

FOWEY ROCKS LIGHTHOUSE
Body of Water: Atlantic Ocean
Near: Key Biscayne, FL
Lat & Long: 25.5899, -80.0965
National Park Service Inventory
First Lit: 1878
Height & Type: 110 ft skeleton – brown/white
Focal Plane: 110 ft fp
Current Lens Information: VRB-25 SP
Miscellaneous Information:
• Best viewed from boat or plane
Volunteer & Contribution Information:
www.reeflights.org

GARDEN KEY (TORTUGAS HARBOR) (FORT JEFFERSON) LIGHTHOUSE
Body of Water: Gulf of Mexico
Near: Key West , FL
Lat & Long: 24.6279, -82.8729
National Park Service Inventory
First Lit: 1826
Height & Type: 82 ft tower – black
Focal Plane: 86 ft fp
Current Lens Information: 3 75-watt incandescent bulbs
Miscellaneous Information:
• Accessible only by boat
Volunteer & Contribution Information:
www.floridalighthouses.org

HILLSBORO INLET LIGHTHOUSE
Body of Water: Atlantic Ocean
Near: Pompano Beach, FL
Lat & Long: 26.2591, -80.0808

National Park Service Inventory
First Lit: 1907
Height & Type: 137 ft skeleton – black/white
Focal Plane: 136 ft fp
Current Lens Information: second order Fresnel bivalve
Miscellaneous Information:
• 2002 USPS stamp
• Brightest Florida lighthouse
Volunteer & Contribution Information:
www.hillsborolighthouse.com

JUPITER INLET LIGHTHOUSE
Body of Water: Atlantic Ocean
Near: Jupiter, FL
Lat & Long: 26.9484, -80.0817
National Park Service Inventory
First Lit: 1860
Height & Type: 108 ft tower – red
Focal Plane: 146 ft fp
Current Lens Information: first order revolving Fresnel
Miscellaneous Information:
• Museum
Volunteer & Contribution Information:
www.jupiterlighthouse.org

Jupiter Inlet Lighthouse, Florida

KEY LARGO LIGHTHOUSE
Body of Water: Atlantic Ocean
Near: Key Largo, FL
Lat & Long: 25.087242, -80.434931
First Lit: 1959
Height & Type: 33 ft tower – white/red checkerboard-faux
Miscellaneous Information:
• Privately owned
• Located on Oleander Circle
• Refurbished lantern room from Rebecca Shoal Lighthouse

KEY WEST LIGHTHOUSE
Body of Water: Atlantic Ocean
Near: Key West , FL
Lat & Long: 24.5506, -81.8007
National Park Service Inventory
First Lit: 1895
Height & Type: 86 ft tower
Focal Plane: 91 ft fp
Current Lens Information: 175 Watt HI-TEK M57
Miscellaneous Information:
• Museum
Volunteer & Contribution Information:
www.kwahs.com

MOLASSES REEF LIGHTHOUSE
Body of Water: Atlantic Ocean
Near: Key Largo, FL
Lat & Long: 25.01, -80.38
First Lit: 1921
Height & Type: 45 ft skeleton
Focal Plane: 45 ft fp
Miscellaneous Information:
• Accessible only by boat

PENSACOLA LIGHTHOUSE
Body of Water: Pensacola Bay
Near: Pensacola , FL
Lat & Long: 30.3458, -87.3084
National Park Service Inventory
First Lit: 1858
Height & Type: 150 ft tower – black/white
Focal Plane: 191 ft fp

Current Lens Information: first order revolving
Miscellaneous Information:
• During Civil War, lighthouse received minimal damage
Volunteer & Contribution Information:
www.pensacolalighthouse.org

PONCE DE LEON (MOSQUITO) INLET LIGHTHOUSE
Body of Water: Atlantic Ocean
Near: Ponce Inlet, FL
Lat & Long: 29.0803, -80.9281
National Park Service Inventory
First Lit: 1887
Height & Type: 175 ft tower – red
Focal Plane: 159 ft fp
Current Lens Information: VRB-25 SP
Miscellaneous Information:
• Tallest Florida lighthouse
Volunteer & Contribution Information:
www.ponceinlet.org

PORT BOCA GRANDE (GASPARILLA ISLAND) LIGHTHOUSE
Body of Water: Gulf of Mexico
Near: Boca Grande, FL
Lat & Long: 26.7173, -82.2608
First Lit: 1890
Height & Type: 44 ft tower with house
Focal Plane: 41 ft fp
Current Lens Information: 375 MM
Miscellaneous Information:
• Located in Gasparilla Island State Park
Volunteer & Contribution Information:
www.floridalighthouses.org

REBECCA SHOAL LIGHTHOUSE
Body of Water: Atlantic Ocean & Gulf of Mexico
Near: Key West , FL
Lat & Long: 24.578, -82.585
First Lit: 1985
Height & Type: 66 ft skeleton – white
Focal Plane: 66 ft fp
Current Lens Information: 250 MM

Miscellaneous Information:
• Accessible only by boat
• 43 miles west of Key West

SAND KEY LIGHTHOUSE
Body of Water: Gulf of Mexico
Near: Key West , FL
Lat & Long: 24.4534, -81.8755
National Park Service Inventory
First Lit: 1853
Height & Type: 120 ft skeleton – red
Focal Plane: 109 ft fp
Current Lens Information: VRB-25 SP
Miscellaneous Information:
• Best viewed by boat
Volunteer & Contribution Information:
www.reeflights.org

SANIBEL ISLAND LIGHTHOUSE
Body of Water: Gulf of Mexico
Near: Sanibel, FL
Lat & Long: 26.45271, -82.0141
National Park Service Inventory
First Lit: 1884
Height & Type: 102 ft skeleton – brown
Focal Plane: 98 ft fp
Current Lens Information: 300 MM
Miscellaneous Information:
• Property transferred to City of Sanibel (2008)
Volunteer & Contribution Information:
www.floridalighthouses.org

SOMBRERO KEY (DRY BANKS) LIGHTHOUSE
Body of Water: Atlantic Ocean
Near: Marathon, FL
Lat & Long: 24.6278, -81.111
National Park Service Inventory
First Lit: 1858
Height & Type: 160 ft skeleton – red
Focal Plane: 142 ft fp
Current Lens Information: VRB-25 SP
Miscellaneous Information:
  • Oldest American straightpile tubular skeleton
Volunteer & Contribution Information:
  www.reeflights.org

ST. AUGUSTINE LIGHTHOUSE
Body of Water: Atlantic Ocean
Near: St Augustine , FL
Lat & Long: 29.88548, -81.28877
National Park Service Inventory
First Lit: 1874
Height & Type: 165 ft tower – black/white spiral stripes
Focal Plane: 161 ft fp
Current Lens Information: first order Fresnel
Miscellaneous Information:
  • First US lighthouse transferred to non-profit organization (2001)
Volunteer & Contribution Information:
  www.staugustinelighthouse.com

ST. JOHNS (MAYPORT) LIGHTHOUSE
Body of Water: Atlantic Ocean
Near: Mayport, FL
Lat & Long: 30.38261, -81.398
First Lit: 1954
Height & Type: 64 ft square tower
Focal Plane: 77 ft fp
Current Lens Information: VRB-25
Miscellaneous Information:
  • Located on Mayport Naval Station
Volunteer & Contribution Information:
  www.floridalighthouses.org

ST. JOHNS RIVER LIGHTHOUSE
Body of Water: Atlantic Ocean
Near: Mayport, FL
Lat & Long: 30.39355, -81.42599
National Park Service Inventory
First Lit: 1859
Height & Type: 81 ft tower – red
Miscellaneous Information:
  • Located on Mayport Naval Station
Volunteer & Contribution Information:
  www.floridalighthouses.org

ST. JOSEPH POINT (BEACON HILL) LIGHTHOUSE
Body of Water: Gulf of Mexico
Near: Port St Joe, FL
Lat & Long: 29.7603, -85.303
National Park Service Inventory
First Lit: 1902
Height & Type: 41 ft tower without lantern room
Focal Plane: 63 ft fp
Current Lens Information: none
Miscellaneous Information:
  • Light placed on skeletal tower (1960)
  • Lantern room destroyed during move

ST. MARKS LIGHTHOUSE
Body of Water: St Marks River
Near: Tallahassee, FL
Lat & Long: 30.0739, -84.179
National Park Service Inventory
First Lit: 1842
Height & Type: 73 ft tower
Focal Plane: 82 ft fp
Current Lens Information: fifth order
Miscellaneous Information:
  • Located in St Marks National Wildlife Refuge
Volunteer & Contribution Information:
  www.floridalighthouses.org

TENNESSEE REEF LIGHTHOUSE
Body of Water:
Near: Key West , FL
Lat & Long: 24.735278, -80.769167
First Lit: 1933

Height & Type: 50 ft skeleton
Focal Plane: 49 ft fp
Miscellaneous Information:
  • Best viewed by boat
  • **National Park Service Inventory** "significant unmanned aid"

Georgia

COCKSPUR ISLAND LIGHTHOUSE
Body of Water: Savannah River
Near: Tybee Island, GA
Lat & Long: 32.0266, -80.8684
National Park Service Inventory
First Lit: 1857
Height & Type: 46 ft tower
Current Lens Information: none
Miscellaneous Information:
  • WLTL
  • On Georgia's "Places In Peril" list

LITTLE CUMBERLAND ISLAND LIGHTHOUSE
Body of Water: Atlantic Ocean
Near: Jekyll Island , GA
Lat & Long: 30.974, -81.4168
National Park Service Inventory
First Lit: 1838
Height & Type: 60 ft tower
Focal Plane: 71 ft fp
Current Lens Information: none
Miscellaneous Information:
  • Accessible only by boat
  • Privately owned island

SAPELO ISLAND LIGHTHOUSE
Body of Water: Atlantic Ocean
Near: Darien, GA
Lat & Long: 31.392, -81.2852
National Park Service Inventory
First Lit: 1820
Height & Type: 70 ft tower-red/white stripes
Focal Plane: 79 ft fp
Miscellaneous Information:
- Accessible by ferry
- Second oldest brick lighthouse in US

Volunteer & Contribution Information:
www.gastateparks.org/Sapelo (general info)

Sapelo Island Lighthouse,
Georgia

SAPELO ISLAND RANGE FRONT LIGHTHOUSE
Body of Water: Atlantic Ocean
Near: Darien, GA
Lat & Long: 31.3895, -81.2773
First Lit: 1877
Height & Type: 25 ft square skeleton

Miscellaneous Information:
- Accessible by ferry

Volunteer & Contribution Information:
www.gastateparks.org/Sapelo (general info)

SAPELO ISLAND LIGHTHOUSE (1905 RUINS)
Body of Water: Atlantic Ocean
Near: Darien, GA
Lat & Long: 31.392, -81.2852
First Lit: n/a
Height & Type: 100 ft skeleton (base only)
Miscellaneous Information:
- Accessible by ferry
- Tower moved to South Fox Island, MI

Volunteer & Contribution Information:
www.gastateparks.org/Sapelo (general info)

SAVANNAH HARBOR (OLD HARBOR) LIGHTHOUSE
Body of Water: Savannah River
Near: Savannah, GA
Lat & Long: 32.0788, -81.0831
First Lit: 1964
Height & Type: lamp post (light tower)
Current Lens Information: DCB-24
Miscellaneous Information:
- In Emmet Park
- Originally Fig Island Range Rear

ST. SIMONS LIGHTHOUSE
Body of Water: Atlantic Ocean
Near: St. Simons Island, GA
Lat & Long: 31.1334, -81.3933
National Park Service Inventory
First Lit: 1872
Height & Type: 104 ft tower
Focal Plane: 106 ft fp
Current Lens Information: third order Fresnel
Miscellaneous Information:
- Transferred to Coastal Georgia Historical Society (2004)

Volunteer & Contribution Information:
www.saintsimonslighthouse.org

TYBEE ISLAND LIGHTHOUSE
Body of Water: Savannah River
Near: Tybee Island, GA
Lat & Long: 32.0273, -80.8509
National Park Service Inventory
First Lit: 1867
Height & Type: 154 ft tower – black/white bands
Focal Plane: 144 ft fp
Current Lens Information: first order Fresnel
Miscellaneous Information:
- Lower 60 feet of tower dates back to 1773
- Six different daymarks
- 2002 USPS stamp
- Museum

Volunteer & Contribution Information:
www.tybeelighthouse.org

Tybee Island Lighthouse, Georgia

Hawaii

ALOHA TOWER (HONOLULU HARBOR) LIGHTHOUSE
Body of Water: Pacific Ocean
Near: Honolulu, HI
Lat & Long: 21.30708, -157.866
First Lit: 1969
Height & Type: tower
Miscellaneous Information:
- Served as navigational aid until 1975

Volunteer & Contribution Information:
www.alohatower.com (general info)

BARBERS POINT LIGHTHOUSE
Body of Water: Pacific Ocean
Near: Honolulu, HI
Lat & Long: 21.2995, -158.1082
National Park Service Inventory
First Lit: 1933
Height & Type: 71 ft tower without lantern room
Focal Plane: 85 ft fp
Current Lens Information: DCB-224
Miscellaneous Information:
- Fresnel lens replaced and light automated lighthouse (1964)

CAPE KUMUKAHI LIGHTHOUSE
Body of Water: Pacific Ocean
Near: Hilo, HI
Lat & Long: 19.5195, -154.8135
National Park Service Inventory
First Lit: 1934
Height & Type: 125 ft skeleton – white
Focal Plane: 156 ft fp
Current Lens Information: DCB-24
Miscellaneous Information:
- Most of light station destroyed in lava flow
- Tower remained intact (1960)

DIAMOND HEAD LIGHTHOUSE
Body of Water: Pacific Ocean
Near: Honolulu, HI
Lat & Long: 21.2554, -157.8095
National Park Service Inventory
First Lit: 1918

Height & Type: 57 ft square tower
Focal Plane: 147 ft fp
Current Lens Information: first order Fresnel
Miscellaneous Information:
• 2006 USPS stamp

KA'ENA POINT LIGHTHOUSE
Body of Water: Pacific Ocean
Near: Oahu, HI
Lat & Long: 24.578, -82.585
First Lit: n/a
Height & Type: 65 ft tower (toppled)
Miscellaneous Information:
• DDL
• Fallen/lies across beach
• **National Park Service Inventory**
"significant unmanned aid"

KAUHOLA POINT LIGHTHOUSE
Body of Water: Pacific Ocean
Near: North Kohala, HI
Lat & Long: 20.2453, -155.7716
First Lit: 1933
Height & Type: 86 ft conical tower
Current Lens Information: red/green alternating flash
Miscellaneous Information:
• Due to erosion replaced with a monopole light
• Tower removed (2009)

KILAUEA LIGHTHOUSE
Body of Water: Pacific Ocean
Near: Kilauea, HI
Lat & Long: 22.2313, -159.4034
National Park Service Inventory
First Lit: 1913
Height & Type: 52 ft tower
Focal Plane: 216 ft fp
Current Lens Information: second order Fresnel
Miscellaneous Information:
• Part of Kilauea Point National Wildlife Refuge
Volunteer & Contribution Information:
www.kilauealighthouse.org

LAHAINA LIGHTHOUSE
Body of Water: Pacific Ocean
Near: Lahaina, HI
Lat & Long: 20.875, -156.6813
First Lit: 1939
Height & Type: 39 ft pyramidal tower
Miscellaneous Information:
• Site of Hawaii's oldest light station (1840)
• **National Park Service Inventory**
"significant unmanned aid"
Volunteer & Contribution Information:
www.lahainarestoration.org

MAKAPU'U LIGHTHOUSE
Body of Water: Pacific Ocean
Near: Oahu, HI
Lat & Long: 21.3089, -157.6513
National Park Service Inventory
First Lit: 1909
Height & Type: 46 ft tower
Focal Plane: 420 ft fp
Current Lens Information: hyper-radiant
Miscellaneous Information:
• Dwellings secretly used to house prosecution witnesses (1970s)

MOLOKAI (KALAUPAPA) LIGHTHOUSE
Body of Water: Pacific Ocean
Near: Molokai, HI
Lat & Long: 21.2091, -156.9699
National Park Service Inventory
First Lit: 1909
Height & Type: 138 ft octagonal tower
Focal Plane: 213 ft fp
Current Lens Information: DCB-24
Miscellaneous Information:
• Tallest Pacific lighthouse
• Part of Kalaupapa National Historic Park

NAWILIWILI LIGHTHOUSE
Body of Water: Pacific Ocean
Near: Lihue, HI
Lat & Long: 21.9558, -159.33009
National Park Service Inventory
First Lit: 1933
Height & Type: 86 ft tower
Focal Plane: 118 ft fp

Current Lens Information: DCB-24
Miscellaneous Information:
• Original fourth order Fresnel lens displayed at Hawaii Maritime Center in Honolulu

Illinois

68TH STREET CRIB (DUNNE CRIB) LIGHTHOUSE
Body of Water: Lake Michigan
Near: Chicago, IL
Lat & Long: 41.786, -87.531
First Lit: 1909
Height & Type: 50 ft skeleton crib – blue
Focal Plane: 61 ft fp
Miscellaneous Information:
• Owned by Chicago Department of Water Management

CHICAGO HARBOR LIGHTHOUSE
Body of Water: Lake Michigan
Near: Chicago, IL
Lat & Long: 41.8906, -87.5878
National Park Service Inventory
First Lit: 1893
Height & Type: 48 ft tower with house
Focal Plane: 82 ft fp
Miscellaneous Information:
• Transferred to the City of Chicago (2009)

CHICAGO HARBOR SOUTHEAST GUIDEWALL LIGHTHOUSE
Body of Water: Lake Michigan
Near: Chicago, IL
Lat & Long: 41.8882, -87.6017
First Lit: 1938
Height & Type: 30 ft square tower – white/turquoise
Focal Plane: 48 ft fp
Miscellaneous Information:
• Best viewed from boat

FOUR MILE CRIB LIGHTHOUSE
Body of Water: Lake Michigan
Near: Chicago, IL

Lat & Long: 41.8734, -87.545
Height & Type: 30 ft crib
Focal Plane: 66 ft fp
Miscellaneous Information:
• Best viewed from boat

GROSSE POINT LIGHTHOUSE
Body of Water: Lake Michigan
Near: Evanston, IL
Lat & Long: 42.0639, -87.6758
National Park Service Inventory
First Lit: 1873
Height & Type: 113 ft tower
Focal Plane: 121 ft fp
Current Lens Information: second order Fresnel
Miscellaneous Information:
• First Great Lakes lighthouse to be designated as National Historic Landmark (1999)
Volunteer & Contribution Information: www.grossepointlighthouse.net

WAUKEGAN HARBOR LIGHTHOUSE
Body of Water: Lake Michigan
Near: Waukegan, IL
Lat & Long: 42.36, -87.8133
First Lit: 1889
Height & Type: 35 ft tower – green/white
Focal Plane: 36 ft fp
Miscellaneous Information:
• Lantern room removed after fire (1967)

WILLIAM E. DEVER CRIB LIGHTHOUSE
Body of Water: Lake Michigan
Near: Chicago, IL
Lat & Long: 41.9167, -87.5717
Height & Type: skeleton on round crib
Focal Plane: 72 ft fp
Miscellaneous Information:
• Best viewed from boat

WILSON AVENUE CRIB LIGHTHOUSE
Body of Water: Lake Michigan
Near: , IL
Lat & Long: 41.9667, -87.5917
Height & Type: 47 ft round tower crib
Focal Plane: 68 ft fp
Miscellaneous Information:
• Best viewed from boat

Indiana

BUFFINGTON HARBOR BREAKWATER LIGHTHOUSE
Body of Water: Lake Michigan
Near: Chicago, IL, East Chicago, IN
Lat & Long: 41.64624, -87.40942
Height & Type: 46 ft tower – red
Miscellaneous Information:
• Owned by City of Gary
• Best viewed from boat

CALUMET HARBOR LIGHTHOUSE
Body of Water: Lake Michigan
Near: Hammond, IN
Lat & Long: 41.7267, -87.4933
Height & Type: 45 ft skeleton
Focal Plane: 40 ft fp
Current Lens Information: none
Miscellaneous Information:
• Can be seen from Calumet Park but best viewed from boat

GARY HARBOR (GARY WEST) BREAKWATER LIGHTHOUSE
Body of Water: Lake Michigan
Near: Gary, IN
Lat & Long: 41.63136, -87.32018
First Lit: 1911
Height & Type: 40 ft (steel plate) tower
Current Lens Information: sixth order Fresnel inactive
Miscellaneous Information:
• **National Park Service Inventory** "significant unmanned aid"
• Best viewed from boat

INDIANA HARBOR EAST BREAKWATER LIGHTHOUSE
Body of Water: Lake Michigan
Near: Gary, IN
Lat & Long: 41.6814, -87.4414
First Lit: 1935
Height & Type: 75 ft tower without lantern
Miscellaneous Information:
• Privately owned (US Steel)
• **National Park Service Inventory** "significant unmanned aid"

MICHIGAN CITY EAST PIERHEAD LIGHTHOUSE
Body of Water: Lake Michigan
Near: Michigan City, IN
Lat & Long: 41.7288, -86.9117
National Park Service Inventory
First Lit: 1904
Height & Type: 49 ft tower with house
Focal Plane: 50 ft fp
Current Lens Information: 2130C rotating
Miscellaneous Information:
• **National Park Service Inventory** "significant unmanned aid"
• Previous tower lit (1858)

OLD MICHIGAN CITY (MICHIGAN CITY) LIGHTHOUSE
Body of Water: Lake Michigan
Near: Michigan City, IN
Lat & Long: 41.7233, -86.9059
National Park Service Inventory
First Lit: 1858
Height & Type: 34 ft tower with house
Focal Plane: 52 ft fp
Current Lens Information: none
Miscellaneous Information:
• Museum
• Hoosier Lighthousing Club rebuilt spiral stairway (2003)
Volunteer & Contribution Information: www.michigancity.com

Louisiana

CHANDELEUR ISLAND LIGHTHOUSE
Body of Water: Gulf of Mexico
Near: Chandeleur Island, LA, Biloxi, MS
Lat & Long: 30.0483, -88.8718
National Park Service Inventory
First Lit: 1896
Height & Type: 100 ft skeleton – brown
Focal Plane: 99 ft fp
Current Lens Information: none
Miscellaneous Information:
- WLTL
- Destroyed by Hurricane Katrina (2005)

NEW CANAL LIGHTHOUSE
Body of Water: Lake Pontchartrain
Near: New Orleans, LA
Lat & Long: 30.0268, -90.1133
National Park Service Inventory
First Lit: 1901
Height & Type: 32 ft tower with house
Focal Plane: 52 ft fp
Current Lens Information: none
Miscellaneous Information:
- Destroyed by Hurricane Katrina (2005)
- Plan to rebuild it
Volunteer & Contribution Information:
www.saveourlake.org

PASS A L'OUTRE LIGHTHOUSE
Body of Water: Gulf of Mexico
Near: New Orleans, LA
Lat & Long: 29.19014, -89.03706
National Park Service Inventory
First Lit: 1855
Height & Type: 85 ft metal tower
Miscellaneous Information:
- DDL
- Best viewed from boat or plane
- Part of Delta Wildlife Refuge

PASS MANCHAC LIGHTHOUSE
Body of Water: Lake Pontchartrain
Near: Hammond, LA

Lat & Long: 30.2967, -90.2982
National Park Service Inventory
First Lit: 1857
Height & Type: 40 ft tower – partial ruins
Focal Plane: 45 ft fp
Current Lens Information: none
Miscellaneous Information:
- DDL
- Pilings surrounding it failed to stop continuing lean but saved it during Hurricane Katrina

PORT PONTCHARTRAIN LIGHTHOUSE
Body of Water: Lake Pontchartrain
Near: New Orleans, LA
Lat & Long: 30.0318, -90.0624
National Park Service Inventory
First Lit: 1855
Height & Type: 42 ft hour-glass tower
Focal Plane: 42 ft fp
Current Lens Information: none
Miscellaneous Information:
- Suffered heavy flooding during Hurricane Katrina lighthouse was not seriously damaged

SABINE PASS LIGHTHOUSE
Body of Water: Gulf of Mexico
Near: Port Arthur, TX, LA
Lat & Long: 29.71696, -93.84741
National Park Service Inventory
First Lit: 1856
Height & Type: 75 ft tower
Focal Plane: 85 ft fp
Current Lens Information: none
Miscellaneous Information:
- DDL
- Museum
Volunteer & Contribution Information:
www.sabinepasslighthouse.org

SHIP SHOAL LIGHTHOUSE
Body of Water: Gulf of Mexico
Near: Houma, LA
Lat & Long: 28.9167, -91.0667

National Park Service Inventory
First Lit: 1859
Height & Type: 125 ft screw pile w/platform
Focal Plane: 117 ft fp
Current Lens Information: third order
Miscellaneous Information:
- DDL
- Best viewed from boat or plane

SOUTH PASS LIGHTHOUSE
Body of Water: Gulf of Mexico
Near: New Orleans, LA
Lat & Long: 29.0152, -89.167
National Park Service Inventory
First Lit: 1847
Height & Type: 116 ft skeleton
Focal Plane: 108 ft fp
Current Lens Information: Doublet
Miscellaneous Information:
- Best viewed from boat or plane
Volunteer & Contribution Information:
www.stjohnparish.com/lakemaurepas

SOUTHWEST PASS LIGHTHOUSE (1871)
Body of Water: Gulf of Mexico
Near: New Orleans, LA
Lat & Long: 28.971, -89.389
First Lit: 1873
Height & Type: 130 ft skeleton
Focal Plane: 128 ft fp
Miscellaneous Information:
- Best viewed from boat or plane

SOUTHWEST PASS ENTRANCE LIGHTHOUSE
Body of Water: Gulf of Mexico
Near: New Orleans, LA
Lat & Long: 28.907, -89.435
National Park Service Inventory
First Lit: 1962
Height & Type: 85 ft tower with house
Focal Plane: 95 ft fp
Current Lens Information: DCB-224
Miscellaneous Information:
- DDL
- Best viewed from boat or plane
- Has boat dock and helipad

Maine

SOUTHWEST REEF LIGHTHOUSE
Body of Water: relocated from Atchaflaya Bay
Near: Berwick, LA
Lat & Long: 29.69412, -91.21619
National Park Service Inventory
First Lit: 1858
Height & Type: 40 ft square tower – red
Focal Plane: 49 ft fp
Current Lens Information: none
Miscellaneous Information:
- Owned by Town of Berwick (2002) on-going restoration

TCHEFUNCTE RIVER LIGHTHOUSE
Body of Water: Lake Pontchartrain
Near: Madisonville, LA
Lat & Long: 30.3799, -90.1692
National Park Service Inventory
First Lit: 1868
Height & Type: 43 ft tower
Focal Plane: 49 ft fp
Current Lens Information: 250 MM
Miscellaneous Information:
- Transferred to Town of Madisonville (1999)
- Currently being renovated
Volunteer & Contribution Information:
www.lpbmm.org

WEST RIGOLETS LIGHTHOUSE
Body of Water: Lake Pontchartrain
Near: New Orleans, LA
Lat & Long: 30.1745, -89.7432
National Park Service Inventory
First Lit: 1855
Height & Type: 30 ft tower
Focal Plane: 30 ft fp
Current Lens Information: none
Miscellaneous Information:
- Destroyed by Hurricane Katrina (2005)

BAKER ISLAND LIGHTHOUSE
Body of Water: Atlantic Ocean
Near: Islesford, ME
Lat & Long: 44.2415, -68.199
National Park Service Inventory
First Lit: 1855
Height & Type: 43 ft tower
Focal Plane: 105 ft fp
Current Lens Information: 300 MM SP
Miscellaneous Information:
- Can be viewed on cruise from Bar Harbor

BASS HARBOR HEAD LIGHTHOUSE
Body of Water: Southwest Harbor
Near: Bass Harbor, ME
Lat & Long: 44.2221, -68.3372
National Park Service Inventory
First Lit: 1858
Height & Type: 32 ft tower
Focal Plane: 56 ft fp
Current Lens Information: fourth order Fresnel
Miscellaneous Information:
- Located in Acadia National Park

BEAR ISLAND LIGHTHOUSE
Body of Water: Northeast Harbor
Near: Northeast Harbor, ME
Lat & Long: 44.2836, -68.2699
National Park Service Inventory
First Lit: 1889
Height & Type: 31 ft tower
Focal Plane: 100 ft fp
Current Lens Information: south tower: VRB-25 SP
Miscellaneous Information:
- Can be viewed on cruise from Bar Harbor

BLUE HILL BAY LIGHTHOUSE
Body of Water: Blue Hill Bay
Near: Brooklin, ME
Lat & Long: 44.2488, -68.4985
National Park Service Inventory
First Lit: 1857
Height & Type: 22 ft tower
Focal Plane: 26 ft fp
Current Lens Information: fifth order Fresnel
Miscellaneous Information:
- Privately owned
- Can be viewed on cruise from Bar Harbor

BOON ISLAND LIGHTHOUSE
Body of Water: Atlantic Ocean
Near: York Harbor, ME
Lat & Long: 43.117, -70.48
National Park Service Inventory
First Lit: 1855
Height & Type: 133 ft tower
Focal Plane: 137 ft fp
Current Lens Information: VRB-25 SP
Miscellaneous Information:
- Can be viewed from shore but best seen by boat
Volunteer & Contribution Information:
www.lighthousefoundation.org

BROWNS HEAD LIGHTHOUSE
Body of Water: West Penobscot Bay
Near: Vinalhaven, ME
Lat & Long: 44.1116, -68.9099
National Park Service Inventory
First Lit: 1857
Height & Type: 20 ft tower
Focal Plane: 39 ft fp
Current Lens Information: fourth order Fresnel
Miscellaneous Information:
- Can be viewed on Vinalhaven ferry

BURNT COAT HARBOR (HOCKAMOCK HEAD) LIGHTHOUSE
Body of Water: Atlantic Ocean
Near: Swan's Island, ME
Lat & Long: 44.1343, -68.4472
National Park Service Inventory
First Lit: 1872
Height & Type: 32 ft tower
Focal Plane: 75 ft fp
Current Lens Information: 250 MM
Miscellaneous Information:
- WLTL

• Accessible by Swans Island ferry
Volunteer & Contribution Information:
www.swansisland.org/

BURNT ISLAND LIGHTHOUSE
Body of Water: Boothbay Harbor
Near: Southport, ME
Lat & Long: 43.825, -69.64
National Park Service Inventory
First Lit: 1821
Height & Type: 30 ft tower
Focal Plane: 61 ft fp
Current Lens Information: 300 MM
Miscellaneous Information:
• Can be viewed on sightseeing cruises
Volunteer & Contribution Information:
www.maine.gov/dmr/burntisland/index.htm

CAPE ELIZABETH LIGHTHOUSE
Body of Water: Casco Bay
Near: Cape Elizabeth , ME
Lat & Long: 43.5666, -70.2
National Park Service Inventory
First Lit: 1874
Height & Type: 67 ft twin towers
Focal Plane: 129 ft fp
Current Lens Information: VRB-25
Miscellaneous Information:
• West tower w/o lantern room
Volunteer & Contribution Information:
www.lighthousefoundation.org

CAPE NEDDICK (NUBBLE) LIGHTHOUSE
Body of Water: Atlantic Ocean
Near: York, ME
Lat & Long: 43.165, -70.5913
National Park Service Inventory
First Lit: 1879
Height & Type: 41 ft tower
Focal Plane: 88 ft fp
Current Lens Information: fourth order Fresnel
Miscellaneous Information:
• Excellent view from Sohier Park
Volunteer & Contribution Information:
www.parksandrec.yorkmaine.org

Cape Neddick (Nubble) Lighthouse, Maine

CUCKOLDS LIGHTHOUSE
Body of Water: Sheepscot Bay
Near: Newagen, ME
Lat & Long: 43.7798, -69.65
National Park Service Inventory
First Lit: 1907
Height & Type: 48 ft round tower
Focal Plane: 59 ft fp
Current Lens Information: VRB-25
Miscellaneous Information:
- Can be viewed on cruises leaving Boothbay Harbor
Volunteer & Contribution Information:
www.cuckolds.org

CURTIS ISLAND (NEGRO ISLAND) LIGHTHOUSE
Body of Water: Camden Harbor
Near: Camden, ME
Lat & Long: 44.2016, -69.049
National Park Service Inventory
First Lit: 1896
Height & Type: 25 ft tower
Focal Plane: 52 ft fp
Current Lens Information: 300 MM SP
Miscellaneous Information:
- Owned by Town of Camden (since 1998)

DICE (DYCE) HEAD LIGHTHOUSE
Body of Water: Castine Harbor
Near: Castine, ME
Lat & Long: 44.38313, -68.81848
National Park Service Inventory
First Lit: 1829
Height & Type: 51 ft tower
Focal Plane: 130 ft fp
Current Lens Information: 250 MM
Miscellaneous Information:
- Current lens installed in 2008

DOUBLING POINT LIGHTHOUSE
Body of Water: Kennebec River
Near: Arrowsic, ME
Lat & Long: 43.8825, -69.806944
National Park Service Inventory
First Lit: 1898
Height & Type: 23 ft tower

Focal Plane: 23 ft fp
Current Lens Information: 250 MM
Miscellaneous Information:
- Lighthouse lifted from foundation to reset granite blocks (1999)
Volunteer & Contribution Information:
www.doublingpoint.org

DOUBLING POINT RANGE FRONT (KENNEBEC RIVER) LIGHTHOUSE
Body of Water: Kennebec River
Near: Arrowsic, ME
Lat & Long: 43.8833, -69.7949
National Park Service Inventory
First Lit: 1899
Height & Type: 21 ft tower
Focal Plane: 18 ft fp
Current Lens Information: 300 MM
Miscellaneous Information:
- Maine's only range lights
Volunteer & Contribution Information:
www.rlk.org

DOUBLING POINT RANGE REAR (KENNEBEC RIVER) LIGHTHOUSE
Body of Water: Kennebec River
Near: Arrowsic, ME
Lat & Long: 43.8833, -69.7949
National Park Service Inventory
First Lit: 1898
Height & Type: 13 ft tower
Focal Plane: 33 ft fp
Current Lens Information: 250 MM
Miscellaneous Information:
- Maine's only range lights
Volunteer & Contribution Information:
www.rlk.org

EAGLE ISLAND LIGHTHOUSE
Body of Water: Penobscot Bay
Near: Sunset, ME
Lat & Long: 44.2183, -68.7683
National Park Service Inventory
First Lit: 1858
Height & Type: 30 ft tower
Focal Plane: 106 ft fp

Current Lens Information: 300 MM
Miscellaneous Information:
- Built in 1839
- Many improvements in 1858 including fourth order Fresnel lens

EGG ROCK LIGHTHOUSE
Body of Water: Frenchmans Bay
Near: Winter Harbor, ME
Lat & Long: 44.3541, -68.138
National Park Service Inventory
First Lit: 1875
Height & Type: 40 ft tower with house
Focal Plane: 64 ft fp
Current Lens Information: VRB-25
Miscellaneous Information:
- Part of Maine Coastal Islands National Wildlife Refuge

FORT POINT LIGHTHOUSE
Body of Water: Penobscot River
Near: Stockton Springs, ME
Lat & Long: 44.4675, -68.8118
National Park Service Inventory
First Lit: 1857
Height & Type: 31 ft tower
Focal Plane: 88 ft fp
Current Lens Information: fourth order Fresnel
Miscellaneous Information:
- Located within Fort Point State Historic site

FRANKLIN ISLAND LIGHTHOUSE
Body of Water: Muscongus Bay
Near: New Harbor, ME
Lat & Long: 43.8917, -69.375
National Park Service Inventory
First Lit: 1855
Height & Type: 45 ft tower
Focal Plane: 57 ft fp
Current Lens Information: 250 MM SP
Miscellaneous Information:
- Two previous lighthouses built on site (1807 & 1831)

GOAT ISLAND LIGHTHOUSE
Body of Water: Cape Porpoise Harbor
Near: Cape Porpoise, ME
Lat & Long: 43.3583, -70.4249
National Park Service Inventory
First Lit: 1859
Height & Type: 25 ft tower
Focal Plane: 38 ft fp
Current Lens Information: 300 MM
Miscellaneous Information:
 • Last Maine lighthouse to be automated (1990)
Volunteer & Contribution Information:
 www.kporttrust.org

GOOSE ROCKS LIGHTHOUSE
Body of Water: Penobscot Bay
Near: North Haven, ME
Lat & Long: 44.1353, -68.8316
National Park Service Inventory
First Lit: 1890
Height & Type: 51 ft caisson
Focal Plane: 51 ft fp
Current Lens Information: 250 MM SP
Miscellaneous Information:
 • "Be A Keeper" Program provides overnight accommodations
Volunteer & Contribution Information:
 www.beaconpreservation.org

GREAT DUCK ISLAND LIGHTHOUSE
Body of Water: Atlantic Ocean
Near: New Brunswick, ME
Lat & Long: 44.1423, -68.246
National Park Service Inventory
First Lit: 1890
Height & Type: 42 ft tower
Focal Plane: 67 ft fp
Current Lens Information: VRB-25 SP
Miscellaneous Information:
 • Can be viewed on cruise from Bar Harbor

GRINDLE POINT LIGHTHOUSE
Body of Water: Gilkey Harbor
Near: Islesboro, ME
Lat & Long: 44.2817, -68.9433

National Park Service Inventory
First Lit: 1874
Height & Type: 39 ft tower
Focal Plane: 39 ft fp
Current Lens Information: 250 MM
Miscellaneous Information:
 • Accessible by ferry

HALFWAY ROCK LIGHTHOUSE
Body of Water: Casco Bay
Near: Portland, ME
Lat & Long: 43.6558, -70.0369
National Park Service Inventory
First Lit: 1871
Height & Type: 76 ft tower
Focal Plane: 77 ft fp
Current Lens Information: VRB-25 SP
Miscellaneous Information:
 • One of Maine's most endangered historic properties (2004)
Volunteer & Contribution Information:
 www.lighthousefoundation.org

HENDRICKS HEAD LIGHTHOUSE
Body of Water: Sheepscot Bay
Near: West Southport, ME
Lat & Long: 43.8234, -69.69
National Park Service Inventory
First Lit: 1875
Height & Type: 39 ft square tower
Focal Plane: 43 ft fp
Current Lens Information: 250 MM
Miscellaneous Information:
 • Privately owned

HERON NECK LIGHTHOUSE
Body of Water: Atlantic Ocean
Near: Vinalhaven, ME
Lat & Long: 44.025, -68.8616
National Park Service Inventory
First Lit: 1854
Height & Type: 30 ft tower
Focal Plane: 92 ft fp
Current Lens Information: 300 MM

Miscellaneous Information:
 • Accessible only by boat

INDIAN ISLAND LIGHTHOUSE
Body of Water: Rockport Harbor
Near: Rockport, ME
Lat & Long: 44.1658, -69.0604
National Park Service Inventory
First Lit: 1074
Height & Type: 31 ft square tower with house
Current Lens Information: none
Miscellaneous Information:
 • Privately owned

ISLE AU HAUT (ROBINSON POINT) LIGHTHOUSE
Body of Water: Isle au Haut Bay
Near: Stonington, ME
Lat & Long: 44.065, -68.6517
National Park Service Inventory
First Lit: 1907
Height & Type: 40 ft tower
Focal Plane: 48 ft fp
Current Lens Information: 250 MM SP
Miscellaneous Information:
 • Bed & breakfast, museum island accessible by mail boat
Volunteer & Contribution Information:
 www.keepershouse.com (for b&b info)

LADIES DELIGHT LIGHTHOUSE
Body of Water: Cobbosseecontee Lake
Near: Manchester, ME
Lat & Long: 44.304, -69.8965
Height & Type: 25 ft tower
Miscellaneous Information:
 • Only remaining lighthouse on the lake

LIBBY ISLAND LIGHTHOUSE
Body of Water: Machias Bay
Near: Machiasport, ME
Lat & Long: 44.5684, -67.3666
National Park Service Inventory
First Lit: 1848
Height & Type: 42 ft tower
Focal Plane: 91 ft fp
Current Lens Information: VRB-25 SP

Miscellaneous Information:
- "Lighthouse In My Life" book

LITTLE RIVER LIGHTHOUSE
Body of Water: Atlantic Ocean
Near: Cutler, ME
Lat & Long: 44.6511, -67.1926
National Park Service Inventory
First Lit: 1876
Height & Type: 41 ft tower
Focal Plane: 56 ft fp
Current Lens Information: 300 MM
Miscellaneous Information:
- Overnight stays available
Volunteer & Contribution Information:
www.littleriverlight.org

LUBEC CHANNEL LIGHTHOUSE
Body of Water: Lubec Channel
Near: Lubec, ME
Lat & Long: 44.8414, -66.9768
National Park Service Inventory
First Lit: 1890
Height & Type: 40 ft caisson
Focal Plane: 53 ft fp
Current Lens Information: 155 MM SP
Miscellaneous Information:
- Can be viewed from shore

MACHIAS SEAL ISLAND LIGHTHOUSE
Body of Water:
Near: Grand Manan, Canada, ME
Lat & Long: 44.5017, -67.1017
Height & Type: tower
Miscellaneous Information:
- Canadian built-not technically U.S. lighthouse

MARK ISLAND (DEER ISLAND THOROFARE) LIGHTHOUSE
Body of Water: Penobscot Bay
Near: Stonington, ME
Lat & Long: 44.1397, -68.7032

National Park Service Inventory
First Lit: 1857
Height & Type: 25 ft tower
Focal Plane: 52 ft fp
Current Lens Information: 250 MM SP
Miscellaneous Information:
- Can be viewed on cruise from Stonington

MARSHALL POINT LIGHTHOUSE
Body of Water: Port Clyde Harbor
Near: Port Clyde, ME
Lat & Long: 43.91806, -69.26111
National Park Service Inventory
First Lit: 1832
Height & Type: 31 ft tower
Focal Plane: 30 ft fp
Current Lens Information: 300 MM
Miscellaneous Information:
- Museum
Volunteer & Contribution Information:
www.marshallpoint.org

MATINICUS ROCK (TWIN TOWERS) LIGHTHOUSE
Body of Water: Atlantic Ocean
Near: Rockland, ME
Lat & Long: 43.7841, -68.8549
National Park Service Inventory
First Lit: 1857
Height & Type: 48 ft tower
Focal Plane: 90 ft fp
Current Lens Information: south tower: VRB-25 SP
Miscellaneous Information:
- North light discontinued (1924)
- Famous lighthouse keeper: Abbie Burgess

MONHEGAN ISLAND LIGHTHOUSE
Body of Water: Atlantic Ocean
Near: Port Clyde, ME
Lat & Long: 43.765, -69.315
National Park Service Inventory
First Lit: 1850

Height & Type: 47 ft tower
Focal Plane: 178 ft fp
Current Lens Information: VRB-25 SP
Miscellaneous Information:
- Accessible by ferry
- Museum
Volunteer & Contribution Information:
www.monheganmuseum.org

MOOSE PEAK (MISTAKE ISLAND) LIGHTHOUSE
Body of Water: Atlantic Ocean
Near: Jonesport, ME
Lat & Long: 44.4745, -67.5331
National Park Service Inventory
First Lit: 1851
Height & Type: 57 ft tower
Focal Plane: 72 ft fp
Current Lens Information: VRB-25
Miscellaneous Information:
- Accessible only by boat

MOUNT DESERT ROCK LIGHTHOUSE
Body of Water: Atlantic Ocean
Near: Frenchboro, ME
Lat & Long: 43.96849, -68.12819
National Park Service Inventory
First Lit: 1847
Height & Type: 58 ft tower
Focal Plane: 75 ft fp
Current Lens Information: VRB-25 SP
Miscellaneous Information:
- Accessible only by boat

NARRAGUAGUS (POND) ISLAND LIGHTHOUSE
Body of Water: Atlantic Ocean
Near: Millbridge, ME
Lat & Long: 44.4554, -67.8332
National Park Service Inventory
First Lit: 1853
Height & Type: 31 ft tower
Current Lens Information: none
Miscellaneous Information:
- Privately owned island

NASH ISLAND LIGHTHOUSE
Body of Water: Atlantic Ocean
Near: Addison, ME
Lat & Long: 44.4638, -67.7457
National Park Service Inventory
First Lit: 1874
Height & Type: 36 ft square tower
Focal Plane: 51 ft fp
Current Lens Information: none
Miscellaneous Information:
- Accessible only by boat

OWL'S HEAD LIGHTHOUSE
Body of Water: Rockland Harbor & Penobscot Bay
Near: Owl's Head, ME
Lat & Long: 44.0921, -69.0441
National Park Service Inventory
First Lit: 1852
Height & Type: 30 ft tower
Focal Plane: 100 ft fp
Current Lens Information: fourth order Fresnel
Miscellaneous Information:
- Original lens still in use
Volunteer & Contribution Information:
www.lighthousefoundation.or

PEMAQUID POINT LIGHTHOUSE
Body of Water: Johns Bay & Muscongus Bay
Near: Pemaquid Point, ME
Lat & Long: 43.8366, -69.5066
National Park Service Inventory
First Lit: 1835
Height & Type: 38 ft tower
Focal Plane: 79 ft fp
Current Lens Information: fourth order Fresnel
Miscellaneous Information:
- On back of Maine's state quarter
Volunteer & Contribution Information:
www.lighthousefoundation.org

Pemaquid Point Lighthouse, Maine

PERKINS ISLAND LIGHTHOUSE
Body of Water: Kennebec River
Near: Georgetown, ME
Lat & Long: 43.7867, -69.7852
National Park Service Inventory
First Lit: 1898
Height & Type: 23 ft tower
Focal Plane: 41 ft fp
Current Lens Information: 250 MM
Miscellaneous Information:
  • DDL
Volunteer & Contribution Information:
  www.lighthousefoundation.org

PETIT MANAN LIGHTHOUSE
Body of Water: Atlantic Ocean
Near: Millbridge, ME
Lat & Long: 44.3684, -67.865
National Park Service Inventory
First Lit: 1855
Height & Type: 119 ft tower
Focal Plane: 123 ft fp
Current Lens Information: VRB-25 SP
Miscellaneous Information:
  • 2nd tallest Maine lighthouse

POND ISLAND LIGHTHOUSE
Body of Water: Atlantic Ocean
Near: Popham Beach, ME
Lat & Long: 43.74, -69.77
National Park Service Inventory
First Lit: 1855
Height & Type: 20 ft tower
Focal Plane: 52 ft fp
Current Lens Information: 250 MM
Miscellaneous Information:
  • Accessible only by boat
  • Can be viewed from Popham Beach

PORTLAND BREAKWATER "BUG LIGHT" LIGHTHOUSE
Body of Water: Casco Bay
Near: South Portland, ME
Lat & Long: 43.6537, -70.2373
National Park Service Inventory
First Lit: 1875
Height & Type: 26 ft tower

Focal Plane: 30 ft fp
Current Lens Information: 250 MM
Miscellaneous Information:
  • Modeled after an ancient Athens monument

PORTLAND HEAD LIGHTHOUSE
Body of Water: Casco Bay
Near: Cape Elizabeth, ME
Lat & Long: 43.6233, -70.2078
National Park Service Inventory
First Lit: 1791
Height & Type: 80 ft tower
Focal Plane: 101 ft fp
Current Lens Information: DCB-224
Miscellaneous Information:
  • Oldest Maine lighthouse
  • Museum
Volunteer & Contribution Information:
  www.portlandheadlight.com (general info)

PROSPECT HARBOR LIGHTHOUSE
Body of Water: Prospect Harbor
Near: Gouldsboro, ME
Lat & Long: 44.4034, -68.0131
National Park Service Inventory
First Lit: 1891
Height & Type: 38 ft tower
Focal Plane: 42 ft fp
Current Lens Information: 250 MM
Miscellaneous Information:
  • Privately owned
Volunteer & Contribution Information:
  www.lighthousefoundation.org

PUMPKIN ISLAND LIGHTHOUSE
Body of Water: Penobscot Bay
Near: Little Deer Isle, ME
Lat & Long: 44.3092, -68.7429
National Park Service Inventory
First Lit: 1854
Height & Type: 28 ft tower
Focal Plane: 43 ft fp
Current Lens Information: none

Miscellaneous Information:
  • Can be viewed from the pier at end of Eggemoggin Road

RAM ISLAND LIGHTHOUSE
Body of Water: Atlantic Ocean
Near: Booth Bay Harbor, ME
Lat & Long: 43.8034, -69.6
National Park Service Inventory
First Lit: 1883
Height & Type: 40 ft tower
Focal Plane: 36 ft fp
Current Lens Information: 250 MM
Miscellaneous Information:
  • Can be viewed from the Maine Maritime Museum in Bath

RAM ISLAND LEDGE LIGHTHOUSE
Body of Water: Casco Bay
Near: Casco Bay, ME
Lat & Long: 43.6317, -70.1867
National Park Service Inventory
First Lit: 1905
Height & Type: 90 ft tower
Focal Plane: 77 ft fp
Current Lens Information: 300 MM
Miscellaneous Information:
  • Can be viewed from Portland Head lighthouse
Volunteer & Contribution Information:
  www.lighthousefoundation.org

ROCKLAND BREAKWATER LIGHTHOUSE
Body of Water: Rockland Harbor
Near: Rockland, ME
Lat & Long: 44.1033, -69.0783
National Park Service Inventory
First Lit: 1902
Height & Type: 25 ft tower
Focal Plane: 39 ft fp
Current Lens Information: VRB-25
Miscellaneous Information:
  • Subject of the book *The Lighthouse at Rockland Breakwater*
Volunteer & Contribution Information:
  www.rocklandlighthouse.com

ROCKLAND HARBOR SOUTHWEST LIGHTHOUSE

Body of Water: Rockland Harbor
Near: Owl's Head, ME
Lat & Long: 44.0856, -69.0913
First Lit: 1987
Height & Type: 44 ft tower
Focal Plane: 44 ft fp
Current Lens Information: fifth order Fresnel
Miscellaneous Information:
- Newest Maine lighthouse
- Privately owned

SADDLEBACK LEDGE LIGHTHOUSE

Body of Water: Atlantic Ocean
Near: Vinalhaven, ME
Lat & Long: 44.015, -68.7266
National Park Service Inventory
First Lit: 1839
Height & Type: 42 ft tower
Focal Plane: 52 ft fp
Current Lens Information: 300 MM
Miscellaneous Information:
- In 1960s keeper's house was blown up in Green Beret assault exercise

SEGUIN ISLAND LIGHTHOUSE

Body of Water: Kennebec River
Near: Georgetown, ME
Lat & Long: 43.70753, -69.75811
National Park Service Inventory
First Lit: 1857
Height & Type: 53 ft tower
Focal Plane: 186 ft fp
Current Lens Information: first order Fresnel
Miscellaneous Information:
- Accessible only by boat
- Highest Maine focal point
Volunteer & Contribution Information:
www.seguinisland.org

SPRING POINT LEDGE LIGHTHOUSE

Body of Water: Casco Bay
Near: South Portland, ME
Lat & Long: 43.6519, -70.2241

National Park Service Inventory
First Lit: 1897
Height & Type: 54 ft caisson
Focal Plane: 54 ft fp
Current Lens Information: 300 MM
Miscellaneous Information:
- One of the few caissons that visitors can "walk" around
Volunteer & Contribution Information:
www.springpoint.org

SQUIRREL POINT LIGHTHOUSE

Body of Water: Kennebec River
Near: Arrowsic, ME
Lat & Long: 43.8166, -69.8016
National Park Service Inventory
First Lit: 1898
Height & Type: 25 ft tower
Focal Plane: 33 ft fp
Current Lens Information: 250 MM
Miscellaneous Information:
- Surrounded by conservation lands

TENANTS HARBOR (SOUTHERN ISLAND) LIGHTHOUSE

Body of Water: Tenants Harbor
Near: St George, ME
Lat & Long: 43.9611, -69.1848
National Park Service Inventory
First Lit: 1857
Height & Type: 27 ft tower
Focal Plane: 25 ft fp
Current Lens Information: none
Miscellaneous Information:
- Privately owned by artist, Jamie Wyeth
- Best viewed by boat

TWO BUSH (ISLAND) LIGHTHOUSE

Body of Water: Tenants Harbor
Near: Spruce Head, ME
Lat & Long: 43.9643, -69.0738
National Park Service Inventory
First Lit: 1907
Height & Type: 42 ft tower
Focal Plane: 65 ft fp
Current Lens Information: VRB-25

Miscellaneous Information:
- Accessible only by boat

WEST QUODDY HEAD LIGHTHOUSE

Body of Water: Bay of Fundy
Near: Lubec, ME
Lat & Long: 44.815, -66.9505
National Park Service Inventory
First Lit: 1858
Height & Type: 49 ft tower – red/white stripes
Focal Plane: 83 ft fp
Current Lens Information: third order Fresnel
Miscellaneous Information:
- Easternmost U.S. land
- 1990 USPS stamp
Volunteer & Contribution Information:
www.westquoddy.com

WHALEBACK LEDGE LIGHTHOUSE

Body of Water: Piscataqua River
Near: New Castle, ME
Lat & Long: 43.0583, -70.6967
National Park Service Inventory
First Lit: 1872
Height & Type: 50 ft tower
Focal Plane: 59 ft fp
Current Lens Information: VRB-25
Miscellaneous Information:
- Accessible only by boat
Volunteer & Contribution Information:
www.lighthousefoundation.org

WHITEHEAD ISLAND LIGHTHOUSE

Body of Water: Tenants Harbor
Near: St George, ME
Lat & Long: 43.9784, -69.125
National Park Service Inventory
First Lit: 1852
Height & Type: 41 ft tower
Focal Plane: 75 ft fp
Current Lens Information: 300 MM
Miscellaneous Information:
- Accessible only by boat

WHITLOCKS MILL LIGHTHOUSE
Body of Water: St. Croix River
Near: Calais, ME
Lat & Long: 45.1625, -67.2275
National Park Service Inventory
First Lit: 1910
Height & Type: 25 ft tower
Focal Plane: 32 ft fp
Current Lens Information: 250 MM
Miscellaneous Information:
    • Original fourth order Fresnel lens at Maine Lighthouse Museum in Rockland
Volunteer & Contribution Information:
    www.stcroixhistorical.org

WINTER HARBOR LIGHTHOUSE
Body of Water: Frenchman Bay
Near: Winter Harbor, ME
Lat & Long: 44.3616, -68.0878
National Park Service Inventory
First Lit: 1856
Height & Type: 19 ft tower
Focal Plane: 37 ft fp
Current Lens Information: none
Miscellaneous Information:
    • Privately owned
    • Can be viewed on cruise from Bar Harbor

WOOD ISLAND LIGHTHOUSE
Body of Water: Atlantic Ocean
Near: Biddeford Pool, ME
Lat & Long: 43.4567, -70.3292
National Park Service Inventory
First Lit: 1858
Height & Type: 47 ft tower
Focal Plane: 71 ft fp
Current Lens Information: VRB-25
Miscellaneous Information:
    • Audubon Society manages most of island as a bird sanctuary
Volunteer & Contribution Information:
    www.woodislandlighthouse.org

Maryland

BALTIMORE LIGHTHOUSE
Body of Water: Chesapeake Bay
Near: Bayhead, MD
Lat & Long: 39.0592, -76.399
National Park Service Inventory
First Lit: 1908
Height & Type: 38 ft tower
Focal Plane: 52 ft fp
Current Lens Information: 300 MM SP
Miscellaneous Information:
    • World's first nuclear-powered lighthouse
Volunteer & Contribution Information:
    www.baltimorelight.org

BETHEL BRIDGE LIGHTHOUSE
Body of Water: Chesapeake Bay
Near: Chesapeake City, MD
Lat & Long: 39.5273, -75.80814
First Lit: 1996
Height & Type: 30 ft square tower – replica
Miscellaneous Information:
    • 2nd St & Bethel Rd.

BLOODY POINT BAR "COFFEE POT" LIGHTHOUSE
Body of Water: Chesapeake Bay
Near: Kent Island, MD
Lat & Long: 38.8332, -76.3914
National Park Service Inventory
First Lit: 1882
Height & Type: 40 ft caisson
Focal Plane: 54 ft fp
Current Lens Information: 300 MM SP
Miscellaneous Information:
    • WLTL
    • Interior fire and explosion (1960)
    • Privately owned
Volunteer & Contribution Information:
    www.cheslights.org

CONCORD POINT LIGHTHOUSE
Body of Water: Chesapeake Bay
Near: Havre de Grace, MD
Lat & Long: 39.5408, -76.0847

National Park Service Inventory
First Lit: 1827
Height & Type: 32 ft tower
Focal Plane: 26 ft fp
Current Lens Information: fifth order Fresnel
Miscellaneous Information:
    • Museum
Volunteer & Contribution Information:
    www.havredegracemd.com

COVE POINT LIGHTHOUSE
Body of Water: Chesapeake Bay
Near: Lusby, MD
Lat & Long: 38.3861, -76.3818
National Park Service Inventory
First Lit: 1828
Height & Type: 51 ft tower
Focal Plane: 45 ft fp
Current Lens Information: fourth order Fresnel
Miscellaneous Information:
    • Acquired by Calvert Marine Museum (2000)
Volunteer & Contribution Information:
    www.calvertmarinemuseum.com

CRAIGHILL CHANNEL LOWER FRONT LIGHTHOUSE
Body of Water: Chesapeake Bay
Near: Fort Howard, MD
Lat & Long: 39.2163, -76.4628
National Park Service Inventory
First Lit: 1875
Height & Type: 25 ft caisson
Focal Plane: 22 ft fp
Current Lens Information: 250 MM SP
Miscellaneous Information:
    • Considered a greater engineering feat than Duxbury Lighthouse
Volunteer & Contribution Information:
    www.craighillrange.org

CRAIGHILL CHANNEL LOWER REAR (MILLERS ISLAND) LIGHTHOUSE
Body of Water: Chesapeake Bay
Near: Ramona Beach, MD
Lat & Long: 39.2291, -76.3942

National Park Service Inventory
First Lit: 1875
Height & Type: 105 ft skeleton
Focal Plane: 105 ft fp
Current Lens Information: fourth order Fresnel
Miscellaneous Information:
• Decayed wooden braces replaced by iron ones (1884)
Volunteer & Contribution Information:
www.craighillrange.org

CRAIGHILL CHANNEL UPPER FRONT (CUT OFF RANGE) LIGHTHOUSE
Body of Water: Patapsco River
Near: Fort Howard, MD
Lat & Long: 39.1972, -76.4482
First Lit: 1903
Height & Type: 22 ft square tower – red/white
Current Lens Information: DCB-24
Miscellaneous Information:
• Original beacon was a "locomotive" type light
Volunteer & Contribution Information:
www.craighillrange.org

CRAIGHILL CHANNEL UPPER REAR (CUT OFF RANGE) LIGHTHOUSE
Body of Water: Chesapeake Bay
Near: Edgemere, MD
Lat & Long: 39.2163, -76.4628
First Lit: 1886
Height & Type: 90 ft square tower
Miscellaneous Information:
• Detailed restoration plan in development
Volunteer & Contribution Information:
www.craighillrange.org

DRUM POINT LIGHTHOUSE
Body of Water: Chesapeake Bay
Near: Solomons, MD
Lat & Long: 38.331, -76.4634
National Park Service Inventory
First Lit: 1883
Height & Type: 47 ft screwpile
Focal Plane: 52 ft fp
Current Lens Information: fourth order Fresnel

Miscellaneous Information:
• Museum
Volunteer & Contribution Information:
www.calvertmarinemuseum.com

FISHING BATTERY LIGHTHOUSE
Body of Water: Susquehanna River
Near: Havre de Grace, MD
Lat & Long: 39.4945, -76.003
National Park Service Inventory
First Lit: 1853
Height & Type: tower with house
Miscellaneous Information:
• DDL
• Accessible only by boat
Volunteer & Contribution Information:
www.cheslights.org

FORT CARROLL LIGHTHOUSE
Body of Water: Chesapeake Bay
Near: Baltimore, MD
Lat & Long: 39.2147, -76.5195
First Lit: 1854
Height & Type: square tower – partial ruins
Miscellaneous Information:
• DDL
• Best viewed by boat
• Privately owned

FORT WASHINGTON LIGHTHOUSE
Body of Water: Potomac River
Near: Fort Washington, MD
Lat & Long: 38.7123, -76.0368
First Lit: 1882
Height & Type: short tower
Miscellaneous Information:
• Located in Fort Washington National Park
Volunteer & Contribution Information:
www.cheslights.org

HOOPER ISLAND LIGHTHOUSE
Body of Water: Chesapeake Bay
Near: Hoopersville, MD
Lat & Long: 38.2564, -76.2499
National Park Service Inventory
First Lit: 1902
Height & Type: 35 ft caisson

Focal Plane: 63 ft fp
Current Lens Information: 300 MM SP
Miscellaneous Information:
• Ownership transferred to US Lighthouse Society (2009)
Volunteer & Contribution Information:
www.cheslights.org

HOOPER STRAIT LIGHTHOUSE
Body of Water: Chesapeake Bay
Near: St Michaels, MD
Lat & Long: 38.788, -76.2186
National Park Service Inventory
First Lit: 1879
Height & Type: 41 ft screwpile
Focal Plane: 41 ft fp
Current Lens Information: fourth order Fresnel
Miscellaneous Information:
• Museum
Volunteer & Contribution Information:
www.cbmm.org

LAZARETTO POINT LIGHTHOUSE
Body of Water: Chesapeake Bay
Near: Baltimore, MD
Lat & Long: 39.262, -76.5715
First Lit: 1954
Height & Type: 31 ft replica of 1831 tower
Miscellaneous Information:
• Privately owned

Lightship name: Chesapeake LIGHTHOUSE
Body of Water: Chesapeake Bay
Near: Baltimore, MD
Lat & Long: 39.2857, -76.6086
First Lit: 1930
Height & Type: lightship
Current Lens Information: 375 MM
Miscellaneous Information:
• LV-116 WAL-538 museum
Volunteer & Contribution Information:
www.baltomaritimemuseum.org

PINEY POINT LIGHTHOUSE
Body of Water: Potomac River
Near: Leonardtown, MD

Lat & Long: 38.1354, -76.5296
National Park Service Inventory
First Lit: 1836
Height & Type: 30 ft tower
Focal Plane: 34 ft fp
Current Lens Information: none
Miscellaneous Information:
  • Piney Point Lighthouse Museum gives lighthouse tours
Volunteer & Contribution Information:
  www.co.saint-marys.md.us/recreate/museums/ppl.asp

POINT LOOKOUT LIGHTHOUSE
Body of Water: Potomac River
Near: Scotland, MD
Lat & Long: 38.0381, -76.3224
National Park Service Inventory
First Lit: 1830
Height & Type: 36 ft tower with house
Focal Plane: 41 ft fp
Current Lens Information: none
Miscellaneous Information:
  • During "Paranormal Night" visitors can visit the lighthouse at night
Volunteer & Contribution Information:
  www.pllps.org

POINT NO POINT LIGHTHOUSE
Body of Water: Chesapeake Bay
Near: Dameron, MD
Lat & Long: 38.1283, -76.29
National Park Service Inventory
First Lit: 1905
Height & Type: 35 ft caisson
Focal Plane: 52 ft fp
Current Lens Information: 375 MM SP
Miscellaneous Information:
  • Best viewed by boat

POOLES ISLAND LIGHTHOUSE
Body of Water: Chesapeake Bay
Near: Edgewood, MD
Lat & Long: 39.2792, -76.2699
National Park Service Inventory
First Lit: 1825

Height & Type: 40 ft tower
Current Lens Information: fourth order Acetylene
Miscellaneous Information:
  • WLTL
  • Best viewed by boat
  • Tower restored (1997)

SANDY POINT SHOAL
Body of Water: Chesapeake Bay
Near: Bayhead, MD
Lat & Long: 39.0167, -76.385
National Park Service Inventory
First Lit: 1883
Height & Type: 37 ft caisson
Focal Plane: 51 ft fp
Current Lens Information: 300 MM SP
Miscellaneous Information:
  • Lighthouse was vandalized; original Fresnel lens smashed (1989)

SEVEN FOOT KNOLL LIGHTHOUSE
Body of Water: Chesapeake Bay
Near: Baltimore, MD
Lat & Long: 39.2836, -76.6054
National Park Service Inventory
First Lit: 1855
Height & Type: 40 ft screwpile
Focal Plane: 40 ft fp
Current Lens Information: none
Miscellaneous Information:
  • Museum
Volunteer & Contribution Information:
  www.baltomaritimemuseum.org

SHARPS ISLAND LIGHTHOUSE
Body of Water: Chesapeake Bay
Near: Tilghman Island, MD
Lat & Long: 38.6382, -76.3749
National Park Service Inventory
First Lit: 1882
Height & Type: 35 ft caisson
Focal Plane: 54 ft fp
Current Lens Information: 250 MM

Miscellaneous Information:
  • DDL
  • Leans from 1977 ice damage

SOLOMONS LUMP LIGHTHOUSE
Body of Water: Chesapeake Bay
Near: Smith Island, MD
Lat & Long: 38.0484, -76.0151
National Park Service Inventory
First Lit: 1895
Height & Type: 35 ft caisson
Focal Plane: 47 ft fp
Current Lens Information: 200 MM
Miscellaneous Information:
  • Best viewed by boat

THOMAS POINT (SHOAL) LIGHTHOUSE
Body of Water: Chesapeake Bay
Near: Annapolis, MD
Lat & Long: 38.8991, -76.436
National Park Service Inventory
First Lit: 1875
Height & Type: 25 ft screwpile
Focal Plane: 43 ft fp
Current Lens Information: 250 MM SP
Miscellaneous Information:
  • Only Chesapeake screwpile still in the Bay
  • Best viewed by boat
Volunteer & Contribution Information:
  www.thomaspointlighthouse.org

TURKEY POINT LIGHTHOUSE
Body of Water: Chesapeake Bay
Near: North East, MD
Lat & Long: 39.4498, -76.0085
National Park Service Inventory
First Lit: 1833
Height & Type: 38 ft tower
Focal Plane: 129 ft fp
Miscellaneous Information:
  • Owned by state of Maryland
Volunteer & Contribution Information:
  www.tpls.org

Massachusetts

Turkey Point Lighthouse, Maryland

ANNISQUAM LIGHTHOUSE
Body of Water: Annisquam Harbor
Near: Gloucester, MA
Lat & Long: 42.6616, -70.6817
National Park Service Inventory
First Lit: 1807
Height & Type: 41 ft tower
Focal Plane: 45 ft fp
Current Lens Information: VRB-25
Miscellaneous Information:
 • Can be viewed from cruise boats

BAKERS ISLAND LIGHTHOUSE
Body of Water: Salem Harbor
Near: Salem, MA
Lat & Long: 42.5364, -70.7861
National Park Service Inventory
First Lit: 1821
Height & Type: 59 ft tower
Focal Plane: 111 ft fp
Current Lens Information: VRB-25
Miscellaneous Information:
 • Can be viewed from Marblehead
 Lighthouse

BASS RIVER (WEST DENNIS) LIGHTHOUSE
Body of Water: Atlantic Ocean
Near: West Dennis, MA
Lat & Long: 41.652, -70.169
National Park Service Inventory
First Lit: 1855
Height & Type: 44 ft tower with house
Focal Plane: 44 ft fp
Current Lens Information: 300 MM
Miscellaneous Information:
 • Inn and restaurant
Volunteer & Contribution Information:
 www.lighthouseinn.com (general info)

BIRD ISLAND LIGHTHOUSE
Body of Water: Buzzards Bay
Near: Marion, MA
Lat & Long: 41.6694, -70.7172

National Park Service Inventory
First Lit: 1819
Height & Type: 31 ft tower
Focal Plane: 31 ft fp
Current Lens Information: 300 MM
Miscellaneous Information:
 • Accessible only by boat

BISHOP AND CLERKS LIGHTHOUSE
Body of Water: Atlantic Ocean
Near: Yarmouth, MA
Lat & Long: 41.6003, -70.218
First Lit: 1851
Height & Type: 45 ft tower
Current Lens Information: none
Miscellaneous Information:
 • Lighthouse demolished 1952

BORDEN FLATS LIGHTHOUSE
Body of Water: Taunton River
Near: Fall River, MA
Lat & Long: 41.705, -71.175
National Park Service Inventory
First Lit: 1881
Height & Type: 50 ft caisson
Focal Plane: 47 ft fp
Current Lens Information: 250 MM
Miscellaneous Information:
 • Privately owned since 2008

BOSTON HARBOR LIGHTHOUSE
Body of Water: Boston Harbor
Near: Boston, MA
Lat & Long: 42.3281, -70.89
National Park Service Inventory
First Lit: 1859
Height & Type: 89 ft tower
Focal Plane: 102 ft fp
Current Lens Information: second order Fresnel
Miscellaneous Information:
 • Site of first U.S. lighthouse (1716); rebuilt
 in 1703
Volunteer & Contribution Information:
 www.fbhi.org

BRANT POINT LIGHTHOUSE
Body of Water: Nantucket Harbor
Near: Nantucket, MA
Lat & Long: 41.28971, -70.09028
National Park Service Inventory
First Lit: 1901
Height & Type: 26 ft tower
Focal Plane: 26 ft fp
Current Lens Information: 250 MM (red)
Miscellaneous Information:
 • Original lighthouse built in 1746

BUTLER FLATS (BUTLER) LIGHTHOUSE
Body of Water: New Bedford Harbor
Near: New Bedford, MA
Lat & Long: 41.6033, -70.895
National Park Service Inventory
First Lit: 1898
Height & Type: 53 ft caisson
Focal Plane: 53 ft fp
Current Lens Information: 300 MM
Miscellaneous Information:
 • Can be viewed from ferries

BUZZARDS BAY (ENTRANCE) LIGHTHOUSE
Body of Water: Buzzards Bay
Near: Cuttyhunk Island, MA
Lat & Long: 41.3962, -71.0336
First Lit: 1961
Height & Type: 66 ft skeleton – red
Focal Plane: 101 ft fp
Current Lens Information: DCB-224
Miscellaneous Information:
 • Replaced by a smaller structure with a solar-powered light (1996)

CAPE ANN (THACHER ISLAND) LIGHTHOUSE
Body of Water: Boston Harbor
Near: Cape Ann, MA
Lat & Long: 42.6372, -70.5752
National Park Service Inventory
First Lit: 1861
Height & Type: 124 ft twin towers
Focal Plane: 166 ft fp

Current Lens Information: So - VRB-25 SP No - 200 MM
Miscellaneous Information:
 • When lined up show true north
 • Accessible only by boat
Volunteer & Contribution Information: www.thacherisland.org

CAPE COD (HIGHLAND) LIGHTHOUSE
Body of Water: Atlantic Ocean
Near: North Truro, MA
Lat & Long: 42.0394, -70.0605
National Park Service Inventory
First Lit: 1857
Height & Type: 66 ft tower
Focal Plane: 170 ft fp
Current Lens Information: VRB-25
Miscellaneous Information:
 • Jacked up and moved back from the eroding cliff (1996)
Volunteer & Contribution Information: www.trurohistorical.org

CAPE POGE (POGUE) LIGHTHOUSE
Body of Water: Atlantic Ocean
Near: Edgartown, MA
Lat & Long: 41.4202, -70.4523
National Park Service Inventory
First Lit: 1893
Height & Type: 35 ft tower
Focal Plane: 65 ft fp
Current Lens Information: 300 MM SP
Miscellaneous Information:
 • Accessible by ferry
 • 7-mile round-trip hike from Dike Bridge
Volunteer & Contribution Information: www.thetrustees.org

CHATHAM LIGHTHOUSE
Body of Water: Chatham Harbor
Near: Chatham, MA
Lat & Long: 41.6717, -69.95
National Park Service Inventory
First Lit: 1877

Height & Type: 48 ft tower
Focal Plane: 80 ft fp
Current Lens Information: DCB-224
Miscellaneous Information:
 • Active USCG station – special arrangements needed to enter

CLARKS POINT LIGHTHOUSE
Body of Water: New Bedford Harbor
Near: New Bedford, MA
Lat & Long: 41.5928, -70.90071
First Lit: 1869
Height & Type: short tower atop fort
Focal Plane: 68 ft fp
Miscellaneous Information:
 • Owned by City of New Bedford

CLEVELAND (EAST) LEDGE LIGHTHOUSE
Body of Water: Buzzards Bay
Near: West Falmouth, MA
Lat & Long: 41.6317, -70.695
National Park Service Inventory
First Lit: 1943
Height & Type: 70 ft caisson
Focal Plane: 74 ft fp
Current Lens Information: 190 MM
Miscellaneous Information:
 • Best viewed by boat

CUTTYHUNK LIGHTHOUSE
Body of Water: Buzzards Bay
Near: Cuttyhunk Island, MA
Lat & Long: 41.4133, -70.95
First Lit: 1891
Height & Type: 60 ft skeleton ruins
Miscellaneous Information:
 • Accessible only by boat
 • Four-mile round-trip hike

DEER ISLAND LIGHTHOUSE
Body of Water: Boston Harbor
Near: Winthrop, MA
Lat & Long: 42.3397, -70.9544
First Lit: 1982

Height & Type: 33 ft tower
Focal Plane: 53 ft fp
Current Lens Information: VRB-25
Miscellaneous Information:
- Can be viewed from ferry
- First U.S. fiberglass lighthouse

DERBY WHARF LIGHTHOUSE
Body of Water: Massachusetts Bay
Near: Salem, MA
Lat & Long: 42.5168, -70.8836
First Lit: 1871
Height & Type: 14 ft tower
Focal Plane: 25 ft fp
Current Lens Information: 155 MM SP
Miscellaneous Information:
- **National Park Service Inventory**
"significant unmanned aid"

DOG BAR (GLOUCESTER) BREAKWATER LIGHTHOUSE
Body of Water: Gloucester Harbor
Near: Gloucester, MA
Lat & Long: 42.583, -70.6723
Height & Type: 37 ft tower
Miscellaneous Information:
- Unique-looking

DUXBURY PIER "BUG LIGHT" LIGHTHOUSE
Body of Water: Duxbury & Plymouth Harbors
Near: Plymouth, MA
Lat & Long: 41.9878, -70.6486
National Park Service Inventory
First Lit: 1871
Height & Type: 47 ft caisson
Focal Plane: 35 ft fp
Current Lens Information: 250 MM SP
Miscellaneous Information:
- First US caisson (1871)
- Pronounced: "ducks-bury"
Volunteer & Contribution Information:
www.buglight.org

EAST CHOP (TELEGRAPH HILL) LIGHTHOUSE
Body of Water: Atlantic Ocean
Near: Oak Bluffs, MA

Lat & Long: 41.4702, -70.5675
National Park Service Inventory
First Lit: 1877
Height & Type: 40 ft tower
Focal Plane: 79 ft fp
Current Lens Information: 300 MM (green)
Miscellaneous Information:
- Stewardship given to Martha's Vineyard Museum (1995)
Volunteer & Contribution Information:
www.mvmuseum.org

EASTERN POINT LIGHTHOUSE
Body of Water: Gloucester Harbor
Near: Gloucester, MA
Lat & Long: 42.5805, -70.6642
National Park Service Inventory
First Lit: 1890

Height & Type: 36 ft tower
Focal Plane: 57 ft fp
Current Lens Information: DCB-24
Miscellaneous Information:
- Shown in movie, "The Perfect Storm"

EDGARTOWN HARBOR LIGHTHOUSE
Body of Water: Edgartown Harbor
Near: Edgartown, MA
Lat & Long: 41.3904, -70.5032
National Park Service Inventory
First Lit: 1875
Height & Type: 45 ft tower
Focal Plane: Current
Current Lens Information: 250 MM SP
Miscellaneous Information:
- Renovation completed by Martha's Vineyard Museum (2007)
Volunteer & Contribution Information:
www.mvmuseum.org

Edgartown Harbor Lighthouse, Massachusetts

FORT PICKERING (WINTER ISLAND) LIGHTHOUSE
Body of Water: Salem Harbor
Near: Salem, MA
Lat & Long: 42.5267, -70.8666
National Park Service Inventory
First Lit: 1871
Height & Type: 32 ft tower
Focal Plane: 28 ft fp
Current Lens Information: 300 MM SP
Miscellaneous Information:
- Located in Winter Island Park

GAY HEAD (AQUINNAH) LIGHTHOUSE
Body of Water: Atlantic Ocean
Near: West Chop, MA
Lat & Long: 41.3483, -70.835
National Park Service Inventory
First Lit: 1856
Height & Type: 51 ft tower
Focal Plane: 170 ft fp
Current Lens Information: DCB-224
Miscellaneous Information:
- Original Fresnel lens on display at Martha's Vineyard Museum
Volunteer & Contribution Information:
www.mvmuseum.org

(THE) GRAVES LIGHTHOUSE
Body of Water: Boston Harbor
Near: Winthrop, MA
Lat & Long: 42.3646, -70.8695
National Park Service Inventory
First Lit: 1905
Height & Type: 113 ft tower
Focal Plane: 98 ft fp
Current Lens Information: VRB-25 SP
Miscellaneous Information:
- Original first order Fresnel displayed at Smithsonian

GREAT POINT (NANTUCKET) LIGHTHOUSE
Body of Water: Atlantic Ocean
Near: Nantucket, MA
Lat & Long: 41.3903, -70.0481
First Lit: 1986

Height & Type: 60 ft tower
Focal Plane: 71 ft fp
Current Lens Information: VRB-25
Miscellaneous Information:
- Can be viewed from ferry
- **National Park Service Inventory** "significant unmanned aid"

HOSPITAL POINT RANGE FRONT LIGHTHOUSE
Body of Water: Beverly Harbor
Near: Beverly, MA
Lat & Long: 42.5463, -70.8564
National Park Service Inventory
First Lit: 1872
Height & Type: 45 ft tower
Focal Plane: 70 ft fp
Current Lens Information: third 1/2 order fresnel
Miscellaneous Information:
- Can be viewed from Bayview Avenue

HOSPITAL POINT RANGE REAR LIGHTHOUSE
Body of Water: none
Near: Beverly, MA
Lat & Long: 42.5487, -70.8782
Height & Type: church steeple
Miscellaneous Information:
- Old lightship equipment adapted/ installed in First Baptist Church steeple

HYANNIS LIGHTHOUSE
Body of Water: Hyannis Harbor
Near: Hyannis, MA
Lat & Long: 41.63607, -70.28833
National Park Service Inventory
First Lit: 1849
Height & Type: 19 ft tower
Current Lens Information: none
Miscellaneous Information:
- Privately owned
- Current tower consists of untraditional lantern

LONG ISLAND HEAD LIGHTHOUSE
Body of Water: Boston Harbor
Near: Boston, MA
Lat & Long: 42.33, -70.9575
National Park Service Inventory
First Lit: 1819
Height & Type: 52 ft tower
Focal Plane: 120 ft fp
Current Lens Information: 250 MM SP
Miscellaneous Information:
- Can be viewed from cruise ship

LONG POINT LIGHTHOUSE
Body of Water: Cape Cod Bay
Near: Provincetown, MA
Lat & Long: 42.033, -70.16873
National Park Service Inventory
First Lit: 1875
Height & Type: 38 ft tower
Focal Plane: 36 ft fp
Current Lens Information: 300 MM SP
Miscellaneous Information:
- Original lighthouse built (1826)
Volunteer & Contribution Information:
www.lighthousefoundation.org

MARBLEHEAD LIGHTHOUSE
Body of Water: Massachusetts Bay
Near: Marblehead, MA
Lat & Long: 42.5052, -70.8335
National Park Service Inventory
First Lit: 1896
Height & Type: 105 ft skeleton – black
Focal Plane: 130 ft fp
Current Lens Information: 300 MM (green)
Miscellaneous Information:
- Owned by Town of Marblehead
- Tower open only by special arrangement

MAYO BEACH LIGHTHOUSE
Body of Water: Atlantic Ocean
Near: Wellfleet, MA

Lat & Long: 41.9305, -70.0323
First Lit: 1881
Height & Type: ruins (35 ft tower)
Current Lens Information: none
Miscellaneous Information:
• Keeper's house is privately owned
• Lighthouse demolished 1939

MINOTS LEDGE LIGHTHOUSE
Body of Water: Massachusetts Bay
Near: Minot, MA
Lat & Long: 42.27, -70.7583
National Park Service Inventory
First Lit: 1860
Height & Type: 114 ft tower
Focal Plane: 85 ft fp
Current Lens Information: 300 MM SP
Miscellaneous Information:
• First US iron lighthouse (1850)
• First US stone lighthouse (1860)

MONOMOY POINT LIGHTHOUSE
Body of Water: Nantucket Harbor
Near: Chatham, MA
Lat & Long: 41.5592, -69.993
National Park Service Inventory
First Lit: 1849
Height & Type: 40 ft tower
Focal Plane: 47 ft fp
Current Lens Information: none
Miscellaneous Information:
• Located in Monomoy Wildlife Refuge
• Accessible by Monomoy ferry

NANTUCKET CLIFF RANGE LIGHTHOUSE
Body of Water: Atlantic Ocean
Near: Nantucket, MA
Lat & Long: 41.2937, -70.1063
Height & Type: 40 ft tower
Miscellaneous Information:
• Purchased (1912) by Gilbreth family who are chronicled in Cheaper By The Dozen

NAUSET LIGHTHOUSE
Body of Water: Atlantic Ocean
Near: North Eastham, MA

Lat & Long: 41.8602, -69.953
National Park Service Inventory
First Lit: 1877
Height & Type: 48 ft tower – red/white
Focal Plane: 102 ft fp
Current Lens Information: DCB-224
Miscellaneous Information:
• Moved from edge of eroding cliff (1996) and restored
Volunteer & Contribution Information:
www.nausetlight.org

NANTUCKET LIGHTSHIP
Body of Water: Boston Harbor
Near: Boston, MA
Lat & Long: 42.372, -71.056
First Lit: 1936
Height & Type: lightship
Current Lens Information: 500 MM electric lens lanterns
Miscellaneous Information:
• Moved from Long Island Sound, NY (2010)
• LV-112 WAL-534
• Owned by US Lightship Museum (2009)
Volunteer & Contribution Information:
www.nantucketlightshiplv-112.org

NANTUCKET I LIGHTSHIP
Body of Water: Nantucket Harbor
Near: various, MA
Lat & Long: 41.63574, -70.91929
First Lit: 1950
Height & Type: lightship
Current Lens Information: duplex 550 MM electric
Miscellaneous Information:
• WLV-612 last decommissioned US lightship (1985)
• Privately owned
Volunteer & Contribution Information:
www.nantucketlightship.com (for rental info)

NANTUCKET II LIGHTSHIP
Body of Water: Agawam River
Near: Wareham, MA
Lat & Long: 41.7562, -70.7124

First Lit: 1952
Height & Type: lightship
Current Lens Information: duplex 375 MM electric
Miscellaneous Information:
• WLV-613
• Last US lightship built

NED'S POINT LIGHTHOUSE
Body of Water: Mattapoisett Harbor
Near: Mattapoisett, MA
Lat & Long: 41.65109, -70.79535
National Park Service Inventory
First Lit: 1838
Height & Type: 39 ft tower
Focal Plane: 41 ft fp
Current Lens Information: 200 MM
Miscellaneous Information:
• Original birdcage-style lantern was replaced with octagonal lantern

NEW BEDFORD (POLLOCK RIP) LIGHTSHIP
Body of Water: Acushnet River
Lat & Long: 41.6352, -70.9184
First Lit: 1930
Height & Type: lightship
Current Lens Information: 375 MM
Miscellaneous Information:
• DDL
• Auctioned as scrap (2007)
• LV-114 WAL-536

NEWBURYPORT HARBOR (PLUM ISLAND) LIGHTHOUSE
Body of Water: Merrimack River
Near: Newburyport, MA
Lat & Long: 42.015, -70.0103
National Park Service Inventory
First Lit: 1898
Height & Type: 45 ft tower
Focal Plane: 50 ft fp
Current Lens Information: fourth order Fresnel
Miscellaneous Information:
• Occasionally open to public

NEWBURYPORT HARBOR RANGE FRONT LIGHTHOUSE
Body of Water: Merrimack River
Near: Newburyport, MA
Lat & Long: 42.8105, -70.86299
National Park Service Inventory
First Lit: 1873
Height & Type: 15 ft tower
Current Lens Information: none
Miscellaneous Information:
  • Listed in National Register

NEWBURYPORT HARBOR RANGE REAR LIGHTHOUSE
Body of Water: none
Near: Newburyport, MA
Lat & Long: 42.811, -70.8657
National Park Service Inventory
First Lit: 1873
Height & Type: 53 ft tower
Focal Plane: 58 ft fp
Current Lens Information: none
Miscellaneous Information:
  • Privately owned
  • Easily viewed from Water Street

NOBSKA POINT LIGHTHOUSE
Body of Water: Atlantic Ocean
Near: Woods Hole, MA
Lat & Long: 41.516, -70.655
National Park Service Inventory
First Lit: 1876
Height & Type: 40 ft tower
Focal Plane: 87 ft fp
Current Lens Information: fourth order Fresnel
Miscellaneous Information:
  • Tours given by USCG Auxiliary Flotilla 11-2

OLD BRANT POINT (BRANT POINT) LIGHTHOUSE
Body of Water: Nantucket Harbor
Near: Nantucket, MA
Lat & Long: 41.2896, -70.0922
Height & Type: 47 ft tower
Current Lens Information: none
Miscellaneous Information:
  • Accessible by ferry

PALMER ISLAND LIGHTHOUSE
Body of Water: New Bedford Harbor
Near: New Bedford, MA
Lat & Long: 41.62637, -70.90948
National Park Service Inventory
First Lit: 1849
Height & Type: 24 ft conical tower
Focal Plane: 34 ft fp
Current Lens Information: 250 MM SP
Miscellaneous Information:
  • Can be viewed from ferry (Cuttyhunk/New Bedford)

PLYMOUTH (GURNET) LIGHTHOUSE
Body of Water: Plymouth Bay
Near: Duxbury, MA
Lat & Long: 42.0036, -70.59978
National Park Service Inventory
First Lit: 1843
Height & Type: 34 ft tower
Focal Plane: 104 ft fp
Current Lens Information: 190 MM
Miscellaneous Information:
  • Moved from edge of eroding cliff (1997)
Volunteer & Contribution Information:
  www.buglight.org

POINT GAMMON LIGHTHOUSE
Body of Water: Atlantic Ocean
Near: West Yarmouth, MA
Lat & Long: 41.61021, -70.26529
Height & Type: 20 ft tower
Focal Plane: 70 ft fp
Miscellaneous Information:
  • Privately owned

RACE POINT LIGHTHOUSE
Body of Water: Cape Cod Bay
Near: Provincetown, MA
Lat & Long: 42.0623, -70.2433
National Park Service Inventory
First Lit: 1876
Height & Type: 45 ft tower

Race Point Lighthouse, Massachusetts

Focal Plane: 41 ft fp
Current Lens Information: VRB-25 SP
Miscellaneous Information:
- Located near Cape Cod's northernmost point

Volunteer & Contribution Information:
www.lighthousefoundation.org

SANDY NECK LIGHTHOUSE
Body of Water: Cape Cod Bay
Near: Barnstable, MA
Lat & Long: 41.7246, -70.2748
National Park Service Inventory
First Lit: 1857
Height & Type: 40 ft tower without lantern room
Focal Plane: 47 ft fp
Current Lens Information: none
Miscellaneous Information:
- Privately owned
- Twelve-mile round-trip hike

Volunteer & Contribution Information:
www.lighthousefoundation.org

SANKATY HEAD LIGHTHOUSE
Body of Water: Atlantic Ocean
Near: Siasconset, MA
Lat & Long: 41.2832, -69.9651
National Park Service Inventory
First Lit: 1850
Height & Type: 70 ft tower – red/white
Focal Plane: 158 ft fp
Current Lens Information: DCB-224
Miscellaneous Information:
- DDL

Volunteer & Contribution Information:
www.sconsettrust.org

SCITUATE LIGHTHOUSE
Body of Water: Scituate Harbor
Near: Scituate, MA
Lat & Long: 42.2049, -70.7155
National Park Service Inventory
First Lit: 1811
Height & Type: 50 ft octagonal tower
Focal Plane: 70 ft fp
Current Lens Information: 250 MM

Miscellaneous Information:
- Tower occasionally open during summer

Volunteer & Contribution Information:
www.scituatehistoricalsociety.org

STAGE HARBOR LIGHTHOUSE
Body of Water: Atlantic Ocean
Near: Chatham, MA
Lat & Long: 41.6584, -69.985
National Park Service Inventory
First Lit: 1880
Height & Type: 36 ft tower without lantern room
Focal Plane: 40 ft fp
Current Lens Information: none
Miscellaneous Information:
- Enoch Eldredge earned $560 per year as first lightkeeper (1880)

STRAITSMOUTH ISLAND (ROCKPORT) LIGHTHOUSE
Body of Water: Atlantic Ocean
Near: Rockport, MA
Lat & Long: 42.662, -70.5881
National Park Service Inventory
First Lit: 1896
Height & Type: 37 ft tower
Focal Plane: 46 ft fp
Current Lens Information: 250 MM SP
Miscellaneous Information:
- DDL
- First lighthouse was deemed a "specimen of contract work of the worst kind" (1842)

TARPAULIN COVE
Body of Water: Vineyard Sound
Near: Gosnold, MA
Lat & Long: 41.4691, -70.7594
National Park Service Inventory
First Lit: 1891
Height & Type: 28 ft tower
Focal Plane: 78 ft fp
Current Lens Information: 300 MM
Miscellaneous Information:
- Best viewed from boat

Volunteer & Contribution Information:
www.cuttyhunkhistoricalsociety.org

TEN POUND ISLAND LIGHTHOUSE
Body of Water: Gloucester Harbor
Near: Gloucester, MA
Lat & Long: 42.6018, -70.6653
National Park Service Inventory
First Lit: 1881
Height & Type: 30 ft tower
Focal Plane: 57 ft fp
Current Lens Information: 250 MM
Miscellaneous Information:
• Winslow Homer painted on this island

THREE SISTERS LIGHTHOUSE
Body of Water: Atlantic Ocean
Near: Eastham, MA
Lat & Long: 41.859, -69.95775
National Park Service Inventory
First Lit: 1892
Height & Type: 29 ft tower
Focal Plane: 95 ft fp
Current Lens Information: none
Miscellaneous Information:
• Three lighthouses
• All had sixth-order Fresnel lenses (1856)

WEST CHOP LIGHTHOUSE
Body of Water: Vineyard Sound
Near: Tisbury, MA
Lat & Long: 41.4808, -70.6
National Park Service Inventory
First Lit: 1891
Height & Type: 52 ft tower
Focal Plane: 84 ft fp
Current Lens Information: fourth order Fresnel
Miscellaneous Information:
• Last Martha's Vineyard lighthouse to be automated (1976)

WINGS NECK LIGHTHOUSE
Body of Water: Buzzards Bay
Near: Pocasset, MA
Lat & Long: 41.6829, -70.6593
National Park Service Inventory
First Lit: 1889
Height & Type: 32 ft tower

Focal Plane: 50 ft fp
Current Lens Information: none
Miscellaneous Information:
• Weekly vacation rental available
Volunteer & Contribution Information:
www.wingsnecklighthouse.com (rent info)

WOOD END LIGHTHOUSE
Body of Water: Cape Cod Bay
Near: Provincetown, MA
Lat & Long: 42.0217, -70.1933
National Park Service Inventory
First Lit: 1873
Height & Type: 39 ft tower
Focal Plane: 45 ft fp
Current Lens Information: VRB-25 SP
Miscellaneous Information:
• 2-mile round-trip hike
Volunteer & Contribution Information:
www.lighthousefoundation.org

Michigan

ALPENA HARBOR LIGHTHOUSE
Body of Water: Lake Huron
Near: Alpena, MI
Lat & Long: 45.0601, -83.4232
First Lit: 1914
Height & Type: 38 ft skeleton – red
Focal Plane: 44 ft fp
Current Lens Information: 250 MM
Miscellaneous Information:
• To differentiate from the increased city lights, lighthouse characteristic changed to occulting white (1918)

AU SABLE POINT LIGHTHOUSE
Body of Water: Lake Superior
Near: Grand Marais, MI
Lat & Long: 46.66314, -86.1391
National Park Service Inventory
First Lit: 1874

Height & Type: 87 ft tower
Focal Plane: 107 ft fp
Current Lens Information: 300 MM SP
Miscellaneous Information:
• 4-mile round trip hike

BEAVER HEAD (BEAVER ISLAND) ST JAMES LIGHTHOUSE
Body of Water: Lake Michigan
Near: Charlevoix, MI
Lat & Long: 45.5773, -85.5763
National Park Service Inventory
First Lit: 1858
Height & Type: 46 ft tower
Focal Plane: 103 ft fp
Current Lens Information: none
Miscellaneous Information:
• Ownership transferred to Charlevoix Public School System (1975)
• Accessible by ferry

BEAVER ISLAND HARBOR (ST JAMES) LIGHTHOUSE
Body of Water: Lake Michigan
Near: Charlevoix, MI
Lat & Long: 45.7425, -85.5088
National Park Service Inventory
First Lit: 1870
Height & Type: 41 ft tower
Focal Plane: 38 ft fp
Current Lens Information: fourth order Fresnel
Miscellaneous Information:
• Ownership transferred to James Township (2004)
• Accessible by ferry
Volunteer & Contribution Information:
www.gllka.com

BETE GRISE (MENDOTA) LIGHTHOUSE
Body of Water: Lake Superior
Near: Mendota, MI
Lat & Long: 47.3742, -87.9669
National Park Service Inventory
First Lit: 1895
Height & Type: 44 ft square tower with house
Focal Plane: 44 ft fp
Current Lens Information: fourth order Fresnel
Miscellaneous Information:
  • Privately owned

BIG BAY POINT LIGHTHOUSE
Body of Water: Lake Superior
Near: Big Bay, MI
Lat & Long: 46.8417, -87.67
National Park Service Inventory
First Lit: 1896
Height & Type: 65 ft tower with house
Focal Plane: 60 ft fp
Current Lens Information: third order Fresnel
Miscellaneous Information:
  • Bed & breakfast
Volunteer & Contribution Information:
  www.bigbaylighthouse.com (for
  reservations)

Big Bay Point Lighthouse, Michigan

BIG SABLE POINT (GRAND POINT AU SABLE) LIGHTHOUSE

Body of Water: Lake Michigan
Near: Ludington, MI
Lat & Long: 44.0572, -86.5144
National Park Service Inventory
First Lit: 1867
Height & Type: 112 ft tower – black/white
Focal Plane: 106 ft fp
Current Lens Information: 300 MM
Miscellaneous Information:
- Deteriorating brick tower encased in steel (1902)

Volunteer & Contribution Information:
www.splka.org

BOIS BLANC ISLAND LIGHTHOUSE

Body of Water: Lake Huron
Near: Mackinaw City, MI
Lat & Long: 45.8111, -84.4208
National Park Service Inventory
First Lit: 1867
Height & Type: 38 ft tower
Focal Plane: 53 ft fp
Current Lens Information: none
Miscellaneous Information:
- Privately owned
- Best viewed from boat

CEDAR RIVER RANGE LIGHTHOUSE

Body of Water: Lake Michigan
Near: Escanaba, MI
Lat & Long: 45.4086, -87.3538
Height & Type: keeper's dwelling only (38 ft tower)
Focal Plane: 66 ft fp
Miscellaneous Information:
- First lit (1889)

CHARITY ISLAND LIGHTHOUSE

Body of Water: Lake Huron
Near: Au Gres, MI
Lat & Long: 44.03745, -83.44109
National Park Service Inventory
First Lit: 1857
Height & Type: 39 ft tower
Focal Plane: 45 ft fp

Miscellaneous Information:
- DDL
- Accessible by ferry

CHARLEVOIX SOUTH PIERHEAD LIGHTHOUSE

Body of Water: Lake Michigan
Near: Charlevoix, MI
Lat & Long: 45.3211, -85.2649
National Park Service Inventory
First Lit: 1948
Height & Type: 36 ft square tower
Current Lens Information: 300 MM
Miscellaneous Information:
- Accessible by Beaver Island ferry
- **National Park Service Inventory** "significant unmanned aid"

CHEBOYGAN CRIB LIGHTHOUSE

Body of Water: Lake Huron
Near: Cheboygan, MI
Lat & Long: 45.6568, -84.465
National Park Service Inventory
First Lit: 1910
Height & Type: 25 ft tower crib – white/red
Focal Plane: 42 ft fp
Miscellaneous Information:
- Moved from its crib to its current location (1984)

Volunteer & Contribution Information:
www.gllka.com

CHEBOYGAN MAIN LIGHTHOUSE

Body of Water: Lake Huron
Near: Cheboygan, MI
Lat & Long: 45.6684, -84.4151
Height & Type: ruins
Focal Plane: 54 ft fp
Miscellaneous Information:
- Original lighthouse built too close to shore and replaced within 8 years

CHEBOYGAN RIVER RANGE FRONT LIGHTHOUSE

Body of Water: Lake Huron
Near: Cheboygan, MI
Lat & Long: 45.6473, -84.4728

NATIONAL PARK SERVICE INVENTORY

National Park Service Inventory
First Lit: 1880
Height & Type: 45 ft square tower
Focal Plane: 75 ft fp
Miscellaneous Information:
- Original lens replaced by locomotive type lights

Volunteer & Contribution Information:
www.gllka.com

CHRISTMAS RANGE (END OF ROAD) (GRAND HARBOR REAR) LIGHTHOUSE

Body of Water: Lake Superior
Near: Christmas, MI
Lat & Long: 46.4367, -86.6913
Height & Type: 62 ft tower – black/white
Current Lens Information: none
Miscellaneous Information:
- Managed by Hiawatha National Forest

CHRISTMAS RANGE (GRAND HARBOR FRONT) LIGHTHOUSE

Body of Water: Lake Superior
Near: Christmas, MI
Lat & Long: 46.4367, -86.6913
Height & Type: tower
Miscellaneous Information:
- Managed by Hiawatha National Forest

COPPER HARBOR

Body of Water: Lake Superior
Near: Copper Harbor, MI
Lat & Long: 47.4744, -87.8602
National Park Service Inventory
First Lit: 1866
Height & Type: 62 ft tower
Focal Plane: 65 ft fp
Current Lens Information: 300 MM
Miscellaneous Information:
- Museum
- Renovated by Michigan Department of Natural Resources

Volunteer & Contribution Information:
www.hal.state.mi.us/mhc/museum/musewil/chlight.html (general info)

COPPER HARBOR RANGE LIGHTS
Body of Water: Lake Superior
Near: Copper Harbor, MI
Lat & Long: 47.4678, -87.8667
First Lit: 1869
Height & Type: 32 ft square skeleton (rear)
Focal Plane: 39 ft fp
Miscellaneous Information:
 • Built to guide ships safely into harbor channel
Volunteer & Contribution Information:
 www.hal.state.mi.us/mhc/museum/musewil/chlight.html (general info)

CRISP POINT LIGHTHOUSE
Body of Water: Lake Superior
Near: Vermilion, MI
Lat & Long: 46.7528, -85.2572
National Park Service Inventory
First Lit: 1904
Height & Type: 58 ft tower with house
Focal Plane: 58 ft fp
Current Lens Information: none
Miscellaneous Information:
 • Original light was fourth order Fresnel lens
Volunteer & Contribution Information:
 www.crisppointlighthouse.org

DETOUR REEF LIGHTHOUSE
Body of Water: Lake Huron
Near: DeTour Village, MI
Lat & Long: 45.9483, -83.9033
National Park Service Inventory
First Lit: 1931
Height & Type: 63 ft square tower
Focal Plane: 74 ft fp
Current Lens Information: VRB-25
Miscellaneous Information:
 • Best viewed from boat but can be viewed from Lighthouse Road
Volunteer & Contribution Information:
 www.drlps.com

DETROIT RIVER (BAR POINT SHOAL) LIGHTHOUSE
Body of Water: Lake Erie
Near: South Rockwood, MI
Lat & Long: 42, -83.1416
National Park Service Inventory
First Lit: 1885
Height & Type: 49 ft tower
Focal Plane: 55 ft fp
Current Lens Information: fourth order Fresnel
Miscellaneous Information:
 • Best viewed from boat

EAGLE HARBOR LIGHTHOUSE
Body of Water: Lake Superior
Near: Eagle Harbor, MI
Lat & Long: 47.4597, -88.1596
National Park Service Inventory
First Lit: 1871
Height & Type: 44 ft tower with house
Focal Plane: 60 ft fp
Current Lens Information: DCB-224
Miscellaneous Information:
 • Museum
 • Original light fourth order Fresnel
Volunteer & Contribution Information:
 www.keweenawhistory.org

EAGLE HARBOR RANGE LIGHTHOUSE
Body of Water: Lake Superior
Near: Eagle Harbor, MI
Lat & Long: 47.4555, -88.1543
First Lit: 1877
Height & Type: tower with house
Miscellaneous Information:
 • Privately owned

EAGLE RIVER LIGHTHOUSE
Body of Water: Lake Superior
Near: Eagle Harbor, MI
Lat & Long: 47.4138, -88.2994
National Park Service Inventory
First Lit: 1874
Height & Type: 24 ft tower with house
Focal Plane: 61 ft fp
Current Lens Information: none
Miscellaneous Information:
 • Privately owned

ESCANABA LIGHTHOUSE
Body of Water: Lake Michigan
Near: Escanaba, MI
Lat & Long: 45.74667, -87.03694
First Lit: 1938
Height & Type: 41 ft square tower
Miscellaneous Information:
 • National Park Service Inventory "significant unmanned aid"

FORT GRATIOT (LAKE HURON) LIGHTHOUSE
Body of Water: Lake Huron
Near: Port Huron, MI
Lat & Long: 43.0062, -82.4226
National Park Service Inventory
First Lit: 1829
Height & Type: 82 ft tower with house
Focal Plane: 86 ft fp
Current Lens Information: DCB-24
Miscellaneous Information:
 • Oldest lighthouse on Lake Huron
Volunteer & Contribution Information:
 www.phmuseum.org

FORTY MILE POINT LIGHTHOUSE
Body of Water: Lake Huron
Near: Rogers City, MI
Lat & Long: 45.4863, -83.9163
National Park Service Inventory
First Lit: 1897
Height & Type: 52 ft square tower
Focal Plane: 66 ft fp
Current Lens Information: fourth order Fresnel
Miscellaneous Information:
 • Museum
 • Located in Lighthouse Park
Volunteer & Contribution Information:
 www.40milepointlighthouse.org

FOURTEEN FOOT SHOAL LIGHTHOUSE
Body of Water: Lake Huron
Near: Cheboygan, MI
Lat & Long: 45.6798, -84.4347
National Park Service Inventory
First Lit: 1930

Height & Type: 55 ft tower with house
Focal Plane: 55 ft fp
Current Lens Information: 250 MM
Miscellaneous Information:
- Can be viewed from Cheboygan Ruins

FOURTEEN MILE POINT LIGHTHOUSE

Body of Water: Lake Superior
Near: Ontonagon, MI
Lat & Long: 46.9919, -89.1202
First Lit: 1894
Height & Type: 55 ft tower with house – ruins
Focal Plane: 60 ft fp
Miscellaneous Information:
- DDL
- Privately owned
- Best viewed from boat or plane

FRANKFORT NORTH BREAKWATER LIGHTHOUSE

Body of Water: Lake Michigan
Near: Frankfort, MI
Lat & Long: 44.6306, -86.2522
National Park Service Inventory
First Lit: 1932
Height & Type: 67 ft tower
Focal Plane: 72 ft fp
Current Lens Information: fourth order Fresnel
Miscellaneous Information:
- Original lighthouse built in 1873

FRANKFORT SOUTH BREAKWATER LIGHTHOUSE

Body of Water: Lake Michigan
Near: Frankfort, MI
Lat & Long: 44.6306, -86.2522
Height & Type: 46 ft tower
Focal Plane: 46 ft fp
Miscellaneous Information:
- Built (1873)
- Replaced by Frankfort North Breakwater light (1912)

FRYING PAN ISLAND LIGHTHOUSE

Body of Water: Lake Huron
Near: Sault Ste. Marie, MI

Lat & Long: 46.5001, -84.3411
First Lit: 1882
Height & Type: 18 ft tower
Focal Plane: 17 ft fp
Miscellaneous Information:
- Transported to current location at USCG Station and restored

GRAND HAVEN SOUTH PIERHEAD - INNER LIGHTHOUSE

Body of Water: Lake Michigan
Near: Grand Haven, MI
Lat & Long: 43.0567, -86.2561
National Park Service Inventory
First Lit: 1905
Height & Type: 51 ft conical tower – red
Focal Plane: 52 ft fp
Current Lens Information: 250 MM
Miscellaneous Information:
- Original Fresnel lens display at Tri-Cities Historical Museum

GRAND HAVEN SOUTH PIERHEAD - OUTER LIGHTHOUSE

Body of Water: Lake Michigan
Near: Grand Haven, MI
Lat & Long: 43.0567, -86.2561
National Park Service Inventory
First Lit: 1905
Height & Type: 36 ft square tower – red
Focal Plane: 42 ft fp
Current Lens Information: 190 MM
Miscellaneous Information:
- Two towers with elevated catwalk

GRAND ISLAND EAST CHANNEL LIGHTHOUSE

Body of Water: Lake Superior
Near: Munising, MI
Lat & Long: 46.4577, -86.6207
National Park Service Inventory
First Lit: 1870
Height & Type: 49 ft square tower
Current Lens Information: none
Miscellaneous Information:
- Privately owned island
- Best viewed from boat

GRAND ISLAND NORTH (OLD NORTH) LIGHTHOUSE

Body of Water: Lake Superior
Near: Munising, MI
Lat & Long: 46.5604, -86.68
National Park Service Inventory
First Lit: 1867
Height & Type: 40 ft square tower
Current Lens Information: none
Miscellaneous Information:
- Privately owned
- Best viewed from plane

GRAND MARAIS HARBOR (OF REFUGE) RANGE FRONT (OUTER) LIGHTHOUSE

Body of Water: Lake Superior
Near: Grand Marais, MI
Lat & Long: 46.6767, -85.9715
National Park Service Inventory
First Lit: 1895
Height & Type: 34 ft skeleton
Focal Plane: 40 ft fp
Miscellaneous Information:
- Light was moved 550 feet on extended pier

GRAND MARAIS HARBOR (OF REFUGE) RNG REAR (INNER) LIGHTHOUSE

Body of Water: Lake Superior
Near: Grand Marais, MI
Lat & Long: 46.6767, -85.9715
National Park Service Inventory
First Lit: 1898
Height & Type: 55 ft skeleton
Focal Plane: 53 ft fp
Current Lens Information: fifth order
Miscellaneous Information:
- Painted white to match front light

GRAND TRAVERSE (CAT'S HEAD) (NORTHPORT) LIGHTHOUSE

Body of Water: Lake Michigan
Near: Northport, MI
Lat & Long: 45.2097, -85.5504
National Park Service Inventory
First Lit: 1858
Height & Type: 47 ft tower with house
Focal Plane: 50 ft fp

Current Lens Information: none
Miscellaneous Information:
- Volunteers can spend one or two weeks working in the lighthouse

Volunteer & Contribution Information:
www.grandtraverselighthouse.com

GRANITE ISLAND LIGHTHOUSE
Body of Water: Lake Superior
Near: Marquette, MI
Lat & Long: 46.7208, -87.4114
First Lit: 1869
Height & Type: 40 ft square tower
Focal Plane: 96 ft fp
Current Lens Information: none
Miscellaneous Information:
- Privately owned
- Website tracks restoration progress

Volunteer & Contribution Information:
www.graniteisland.com

GRAVELLY SHOAL LIGHTHOUSE
Body of Water: Lake Huron
Near: Au Gres, MI
Lat & Long: 44.0184, -83.537
First Lit: 1939
Height & Type: 65 ft square tower
Focal Plane: 75 ft fp
Current Lens Information: 375 MM
Miscellaneous Information:
- View from Charity Island ferry
- **National Park Service Inventory**
"significant unmanned aid"

GRAYS REEF LIGHTHOUSE
Body of Water: Lake Michigan
Near: Mackinaw City, MI
Lat & Long: 45.7656, -85.1542
National Park Service Inventory
First Lit: 1936
Height & Type: 65 ft tower
Focal Plane: 82 ft fp
Current Lens Information: 190 MM
Miscellaneous Information:
- Best viewed from boat

GROSSE ILE (NORTH CHANNEL RANGE FRONT) LIGHTHOUSE
Body of Water: Lake Erie
Near: Grosse Ile, MI
Lat & Long: 42.1683, -83.1419
National Park Service Inventory
First Lit: 1906
Height & Type: 50 ft octagonal tower
Current Lens Information: none
Miscellaneous Information:
- Grosse Ile Lighthouse Renovation Project completed (2009)

GULL ROCK LIGHTHOUSE
Body of Water: Lake Superior
Near: Bete Grise, MI
Lat & Long: 47.4169, -87.6639
National Park Service Inventory
First Lit: 1867
Height & Type: 46 ft tower
Focal Plane: 50 ft fp
Current Lens Information: 250 MM

Miscellaneous Information:
- DDL
- Most of second floor collapsed onto first floor

Volunteer & Contribution Information:
www.gullrocklightkeepers.org

HARBOR BEACH (SAND BEACH) LIGHTHOUSE
Body of Water: Lake Huron
Near: Harbor Beach, MI
Lat & Long: 43.8458, -82.6323
National Park Service Inventory
First Lit: 1885
Height & Type: 45 ft tower
Focal Plane: 54 ft fp
Current Lens Information: 190 MM
Miscellaneous Information:
- Best viewed from boat

Volunteer & Contribution Information:
www.harborbeachchamber.com (general info)

HARSENS ISLAND RANGE REAR AND FRONT LIGHTHOUSE
Body of Water: Lake St Clair
Near: Harsens Island, MI
Lat & Long: 42.5504, -82.6518
Height & Type: 30 ft skeleton
Miscellaneous Information:
- Privately owned
- Best viewed from boat

HOLLAND HARBOR (SOUTH PIERHEAD) "BIG RED" LIGHTHOUSE

Body of Water: Lake Michigan
Near: Holland, MI
Lat & Long: 42.7725, -86.2125
National Park Service Inventory
First Lit: 1936
Height & Type: 32 ft tower with house – red
Focal Plane: 52 ft fp
Current Lens Information: 250 MM
Miscellaneous Information:
    • Vandalized (2009)
    • Owned by Holland Harbor Lighthouse
    Historical Commission
Volunteer & Contribution Information:
    www.holland.org (general info)

Holland Harbor (South Pierhead)
"Big Red" Lighthouse, Michigan

HURON ISLAND LIGHTHOUSE
Body of Water: Lake Superior
Near: L'Anse, MI
Lat & Long: 46.9936, -87.9983
National Park Service Inventory
First Lit: 1877
Height & Type: 39 ft tower
Focal Plane: 197 ft fp
Current Lens Information: electric oscillator
Miscellaneous Information:
  • Best viewed from boat

ISLE ROYALE (MENAGERIE ISLAND) LIGHTHOUSE
Body of Water: Lake Superior
Near: Thunder Bay, MI
Lat & Long: 47.94846, -88.76198
National Park Service Inventory
First Lit: 1875
Height & Type: 61 ft tower
Focal Plane: 72 ft fp
Miscellaneous Information:
  • Accessible only by boat
  • Located in Isle Royale National Park

JACOBSVILLE (PORTAGE RIVER) LIGHTHOUSE
Body of Water: Lake Superior
Near: Jacobsville, MI
Lat & Long: 46.97844, -88.4129
National Park Service Inventory
First Lit: 1870
Height & Type: 45 ft tower
Focal Plane: 65 ft fp
Miscellaneous Information:
  • Bed & breakfast "Jacobsville Lighthouse Inn"
Volunteer & Contribution Information:
  www.jacobsvillelighthouse.com (general info)

KEWEENAW WATERWAY LOWER ENTRANCE (PORTAGE LAKE) LIGHTHOUSE
Body of Water: Lake Superior
Near: Harrisville, MI
Lat & Long: 46.968611, 88.430833
National Park Service Inventory
First Lit: 1920
Height & Type: 31 ft tower
Focal Plane: 68 ft fp
Current Lens Information: fourth order
Miscellaneous Information:
  • Lighthouse has always been automated

KEWEENAW WATERWAY UPPER ENTRANCE LIGHTHOUSE
Body of Water: Lake Superior
Near: Hancock, MI
Lat & Long: 47.2343, -88.6305
Height & Type: tower
Miscellaneous Information:
  • Located in McLain State Park

LAKE ST CLAIR LIGHTHOUSE
Body of Water: Lake St Clair
Near: St Clair Shores, MI
Lat & Long: 42.465, -82.755
Height & Type: 40 ft tower – green/white
Miscellaneous Information:
  • Best viewed from boat

LANSING SHOAL LIGHTHOUSE
Body of Water: Lake Michigan
Near: Gulliver, MI
Lat & Long: 45.9034, -85.5616
National Park Service Inventory
First Lit: 1928
Height & Type: 59 ft square tower
Focal Plane: 69 ft fp
Current Lens Information: VRB-25 SP
Miscellaneous Information:
  • Original third order fresnel lens displayed at Lansing's Michigan Historical Museum

HURON LIGHTSHIP
Body of Water: Lake Huron
Near: Port Huron, MI
Lat & Long: 42.9888, -82.4264
First Lit: 1920
Height & Type: lightship
Current Lens Information: 300 MM
Miscellaneous Information:
  • LV-103 WAL-526 museum
Volunteer & Contribution Information:
  www.phmuseum.org

LITTLE SABLE POINT LIGHTHOUSE
Body of Water: Lake Michigan
Near: Ludington, MI
Lat & Long: 43.6505, -86.5391
National Park Service Inventory
First Lit: 1874
Height & Type: 107 ft tower – brick
Focal Plane: 108 ft fp
Current Lens Information: third order Fresnel
Miscellaneous Information:
  • Maintained by Big Sable Point Light Keepers Association
Volunteer & Contribution Information:
  www.splka.org

LITTLE TRAVERSE (HARBOR POINT) LIGHTHOUSE
Body of Water: Lake Michigan
Near: Harbor Springs, MI
Lat & Long: 45.4188, -84.9782
National Park Service Inventory
First Lit: 1884
Height & Type: 40 ft square tower – brick
Focal Plane: 72 ft fp
Current Lens Information: fourth order Fresnel
Miscellaneous Information:
  • Privately owned

LUDINGTON NORTH PIERHEAD LIGHTHOUSE
Body of Water: Lake Michigan
Near: Ludington, MI
Lat & Long: 43.9533, -86.4622
National Park Service Inventory
First Lit: 1924
Height & Type: 57 ft tower
Focal Plane: 55 ft fp
Current Lens Information: 300 MM
Miscellaneous Information:
  • Original light was fourth order Fresnel lens
Volunteer & Contribution Information:
  www.splka.org

MACKINAC POINT LIGHTHOUSE
Body of Water: Lake Huron
Near: Mackinaw City, MI
Lat & Long: 45.7878, -84.7304

National Park Service Inventory
First Lit: 1892
Height & Type: 40 ft tower
Focal Plane: 62 ft fp
Current Lens Information: none
Miscellaneous Information:
- Museum
Volunteer & Contribution Information:
www.mackinacparks.com/old-mackinac-point-lighthouse

MANISTEE NORTH PIERHEAD LIGHTHOUSE
Body of Water: Lake Michigan
Near: Manistee, MI
Lat & Long: 44.252, -86.3451
National Park Service Inventory
First Lit: 1927
Height & Type: 39 ft tower
Focal Plane: 55 ft fp
Current Lens Information: 300 MM
Miscellaneous Information:
- Previous light was fifth order Fresnel

MANISTIQUE EAST BREAKWATER LIGHTHOUSE
Body of Water: Lake Michigan
Near: Manistique, MI
Lat & Long: 45.945, -86.2466
National Park Service Inventory
First Lit: 1916
Height & Type: 34 ft square tower – red
Focal Plane: 50 ft fp
Current Lens Information: 300 MM
Miscellaneous Information:
- Fourth-order Fresnel lens displayed at Wisconsin Maritime Museum

MANITOU ISLAND LIGHTHOUSE
Body of Water: Lake Superior
Near: Leeland, MI
Lat & Long: 47.4194, -87.5878
National Park Service Inventory
First Lit: 1861
Height & Type: 80 ft skeleton
Focal Plane: 81 ft fp

Current Lens Information: 190 MM
Miscellaneous Information:
- DDL
- Unknown disposition of previous third order Fresnel lens

MARQUETTE BREAKWATER LIGHTHOUSE
Body of Water: Lake Superior
Near: Marquette, MI
Lat & Long: 46.5348, -87.3743
Height & Type: tower-no lantern room red/white
Focal Plane: 40 ft fp
Miscellaneous Information:
- Demolished (1986)
- **National Park Service Inventory** "significant unmanned aid"

MARQUETTE HARBOR LIGHTHOUSE
Body of Water: Lake Superior
Near: Marquette, MI
Lat & Long: 46.5467, -87.3762
National Park Service Inventory
First Lit: 1866
Height & Type: 40 ft square tower with house – red
Focal Plane: 77 ft fp
Current Lens Information: DCB-24
Miscellaneous Information:
- Museum
Volunteer & Contribution Information:
www.mqtmaritimemuseum.com/HLighthouse.html

MARTIN REEF LIGHTHOUSE
Body of Water: Lake Huron
Near: Cedarville, MI
Lat & Long: 45.9132, -84.1484
National Park Service Inventory
First Lit: 1927
Height & Type: 52 ft square tower
Focal Plane: 65 ft fp
Current Lens Information: 200 MM SP
Miscellaneous Information:
- Best viewed from boat or plane

McGULPIN POINT LIGHTHOUSE
Body of Water: Lake Michigan
Near: Mackinaw City, MI
Lat & Long: 45.78672, -84.77302
National Park Service Inventory
First Lit: 1869
Height & Type: 40 ft tower without lantern room
Focal Plane: 102 ft fp
Current Lens Information: 300-MLED
Miscellaneous Information:
- Emmet County bought lighthouse from private owners (2008)
Volunteer & Contribution Information:
www.gllka.com

MENOMINEE NORTH PIERHEAD (MARINETTE) LIGHTHOUSE
Body of Water: Lake Michigan
Near: Menominee, MI
Lat & Long: 45.0969, -87.5856
National Park Service Inventory
First Lit: 1927
Height & Type: 34 ft tower – red
Focal Plane: 46 ft fp
Current Lens Information: 300 MM
Miscellaneous Information:
- Iron catwalk was removed (1972)

MIDDLE ISLAND LIGHTHOUSE
Body of Water: Lake Huron
Near: Alpena, MI
Lat & Long: 45.1933, -83.32151
National Park Service Inventory
First Lit: 1905
Height & Type: 71 ft tower – white/red
Focal Plane: 78 ft fp
Miscellaneous Information:
- Accessible only by boat
- Bed & breakfast

MIDDLE NEEBISH (LOWER NICOLET) RANGE LIGHTHOUSE
Body of Water: Lake Huron / St Marys River
Near: Sault St Marie, MI
Lat & Long: 46.32497, -84.17665
Height & Type: 55 ft tower – red

Miscellaneous Information:
- Can be viewed on Neebish Island ferry

MINNEAPOLIS SHOAL LIGHTHOUSE
Body of Water: Lake Michigan
Near: Escanaba, MI
Lat & Long: 45.5349, -87.0097
National Park Service Inventory
First Lit: 1935
Height & Type: 70 ft tower
Focal Plane: 82 ft fp
Miscellaneous Information:
- Best viewed from boat or plane

MUNISING RANGE FRONT LIGHTHOUSE
Body of Water: Lake Superior
Near: Munising, MI
Lat & Long: 46.415, -86.6616
National Park Service Inventory
First Lit: 1908
Height & Type: 58 ft tower – white
Focal Plane: 79 ft fp
Miscellaneous Information:
- Managed by Pictured Rocks National Lakeshore

MUNISING RANGE REAR LIGHTHOUSE
Body of Water: Lake Superior
Near: Munising, MI
Lat & Long: 46.415, -86.6616
National Park Service Inventory
First Lit: 1908
Height & Type: 33 ft tower
Focal Plane: 104 ft fp
Miscellaneous Information:
- Managed by Pictured Rocks National Lakeshore

MUSKEGON SOUTH BREAKWATER LIGHTHOUSE
Body of Water: Lake Michigan
Near: Muskegon, MI
Lat & Long: 43.225, -86.3422
National Park Service Inventory
First Lit: 1903
Height & Type: 53 ft tower – red
Focal Plane: 70 ft fp
Current Lens Information: 300 MM
Miscellaneous Information:
- In 2008 offered through the National Historic Lighthouse Preservation Act

MUSKEGON SOUTH PIERHEAD LIGHTHOUSE
Body of Water: Lake Michigan
Near: Muskegon, MI
Lat & Long: 43.22412, -86.34711
Height & Type: 50 ft cast iron tower – red
Focal Plane: 50 ft fp
Current Lens Information: 300 MM
Miscellaneous Information:
- In 2008 offered through the National Historic Lighthouse Preservation Act

NORTH MANITOU SHOAL LIGHTHOUSE
Body of Water: Lake Michigan
Near: Leland, MI

Lat & Long: 45.0199, -85.9563
National Park Service Inventory
First Lit: 1935
Height & Type: 63 ft tower
Focal Plane: 79 ft fp
Current Lens Information: VRB-25
Miscellaneous Information:
- Best viewed from boat or ferry

OLD MISSION POINT (MISSION POINT) LIGHTHOUSE
Body of Water: Lake Michigan
Near: Traverse City, MI
Lat & Long: 44.9911, -85.47963
National Park Service Inventory
First Lit: 1870
Height & Type: 30 ft square tower with house
Focal Plane: 36 ft fp
Current Lens Information: none
Miscellaneous Information:
- On private land it can only be visited on tours by Ontonagon County Historical Society
Volunteer & Contribution Information: www.peninsulatownship.com

ONTONAGON LIGHTHOUSE
Body of Water: Lake Superior
Near: Ontonagon, MI
Lat & Long: 46.876, -89.3281
National Park Service Inventory
First Lit: 1866
Height & Type: 34 ft square tower
Focal Plane: 47 ft fp
Current Lens Information: none
Miscellaneous Information:
- WLTL
- Museum
- **National Park Service Inventory**
"significant unmanned aid"

Volunteer & Contribution Information:
www.ontonagonmuseum.org

Ontonagon Lighthouse, Michigan

ONTONAGON WEST PIERHEAD (BREAKWATER) LIGHTHOUSE

Body of Water: Lake Superior
Near: Ontonagon, MI
Lat & Long: 46.8789, -89.3295
Height & Type: 31 ft skeleton
Focal Plane: 31 ft fp
Current Lens Information: 300 MM
Miscellaneous Information:
  • Original tower and red fifth order Fresnel lens lost in storm (1899)

PASSAGE ISLAND LIGHTHOUSE

Body of Water: Lake Superior
Near: Thunder Bay, MI
Lat & Long: 48.2234, -88.3666
National Park Service Inventory
First Lit: 1882
Height & Type: 44 ft tower with house
Focal Plane: 78 ft fp
Current Lens Information: 190 MM
Miscellaneous Information:
  • Accessible by boat

PECHE (PEACH) ISLAND (REAR RANGE) LIGHTHOUSE

Body of Water: Lake St Clair
Near: Marine City, MI
Lat & Long: 42.716348, -82.49177
Height & Type: 66 ft tower
Current Lens Information: sixth order Fresnel
Miscellaneous Information:
  • Originally in Canadian waters
Volunteer & Contribution Information:
  www.visitmarinecity.com (general info)

PENINSULA POINT LIGHTHOUSE

Body of Water: Lake Michigan
Near: Escanaba, MI
Lat & Long: 45.6683, -86.9666
National Park Service Inventory
First Lit: 1866
Height & Type: 40 ft square tower
Focal Plane: 40 ft fp
Miscellaneous Information:
  • Keepers house destroyed by fire (1959)
  • Located in Hiawatha National Forest

PENTWATER PIER LIGHTHOUSE

Body of Water: Lake Michigan
Near: Pentwater, MI
Lat & Long: 43.7816, -86.4434
Height & Type: 34 ft skeleton – red
Focal Plane: 25 ft fp
Miscellaneous Information:
  • Located in Charles Mears State Park

PETOSKEY PIERHEAD LIGHTHOUSE

Body of Water: Lake Michigan
Near: Petoskey, MI
Lat & Long: 45.38, -84.9616
Height & Type: 33 ft tower
Focal Plane: 34 ft fp
Miscellaneous Information:
  • U.S. Army Corps of Engineers repaired damaged pier (2007)

PIPE ISLAND LIGHTHOUSE

Body of Water: Lake Huron
Near: De Tour Village, MI
Lat & Long: 46.0167, -83.9
First Lit: 1888
Height & Type: 44 ft tower
Focal Plane: 37 ft fp
Miscellaneous Information:
  • Private island
  • Best viewed from boat

POE REEF LIGHTHOUSE

Body of Water: Lake Huron
Near: Cheboygan, MI
Lat & Long: 45.6949, -84.362
National Park Service Inventory
First Lit: 1929
Height & Type: 60 ft tower
Focal Plane: 71 ft fp
Current Lens Information: ML 300 series E
Miscellaneous Information:
  • Best viewed from boat but can be viewed from Cheboygan Main

POINT BETSIE LIGHTHOUSE
Body of Water: Lake Michigan
Near: Frankfort, MI
Lat & Long: 44.6917, -86.255
National Park Service Inventory
First Lit: 1858
Height & Type: 37 ft tower with house
Focal Plane: 52 ft fp
Miscellaneous Information:
  • Oldest standing structure in Benzie County
Volunteer & Contribution Information:
  www.pointbetsie.org

POINT IROQUOIS LIGHTHOUSE
Body of Water: Lake Superior
Near: Brimley, MI
Lat & Long: 46.4838, -84.64
National Park Service Inventory
First Lit: 1871
Height & Type: 65 ft tower with house
Focal Plane: 68 ft fp
Current Lens Information: none
Miscellaneous Information:
  • Museum
Volunteer & Contribution Information:
  www.baymillsbrimleyhistory.org

POINTE AUX BARQUES LIGHTHOUSE
Body of Water: Lake Huron
Near: Port Hope, MI
Lat & Long: 44.02299, -82.79358
National Park Service Inventory
First Lit: 1857
Height & Type: 89 ft tower with house
Focal Plane: 93 ft fp
Current Lens Information: DCB-224
Miscellaneous Information:
  • Museum
Volunteer & Contribution Information:
  www.pointeauxbarqueslighthouse.org

PORT AUSTIN REEF LIGHTHOUSE
Body of Water: Lake Huron
Near: Port Austin, MI
Lat & Long: 44.0822, -82.9823
National Park Service Inventory
First Lit: 1878
Height & Type: 60 ft square tower – brick
Focal Plane: 76 ft fp
Current Lens Information: 200 MM
Miscellaneous Information:
  • Best viewed from boat
  • Managed by Port Austin Reef Light Association

PORT SANILAC LIGHTHOUSE
Body of Water: Lake Huron
Near: Port Sanilac, MI
Lat & Long: 43.42876, -82.53992
National Park Service Inventory
First Lit: 1886
Height & Type: 59 ft tower
Focal Plane: 69 ft fp
Current Lens Information: fourth order Fresnel
Miscellaneous Information:
  • Privately owned

PORTAGE RIVER ENTRY LIGHTHOUSE
Body of Water: Lake Superior
Near: Jacobsville, MI
Lat & Long: 46.967, -88.4306
Height & Type: 45 ft tower
Focal Plane: 37 ft fp
Current Lens Information: none
Miscellaneous Information:
  • Privately owned since 1958

POVERTY ISLAND LIGHTHOUSE
Body of Water: Lake Huron
Near: Fairport, MI
Lat & Long: 45.5212, -86.663
National Park Service Inventory
First Lit: 1875
Height & Type: 70 ft tower
Focal Plane: 80 ft fp
Current Lens Information: none

Miscellaneous Information:
  • DDL
  • Best viewed from boat

PRESQUE ISLE (NEW) LIGHTHOUSE
Body of Water: Lake Huron
Near: Presque Isle, MI
Lat & Long: 45.3566, -83.4921
National Park Service Inventory
First Lit: 1871
Height & Type: 109 ft tower
Focal Plane: 113 ft fp
Current Lens Information: third order Fresnel
Miscellaneous Information:
  • Original lens still in use
Volunteer & Contribution Information:
  www.keepershouse.org

PRESQUE ISLE (OLD) LIGHTHOUSE
Body of Water: Lake Huron
Near: Presque Isle, MI
Lat & Long: 45.342, -83.4779
National Park Service Inventory
First Lit: 1840
Height & Type: ruins – partial tower (50 ft tower)
Current Lens Information: none
Miscellaneous Information:
  • Museum
Volunteer & Contribution Information:
  www.keepershouse.org

PRESQUE ISLE HARBOR BREAKWATER LIGHTHOUSE
Body of Water: Lake Superior
Near: Marquette, MI
Lat & Long: 46.575, -87.375
Height & Type: tower – white & red
Miscellaneous Information:
  • **National Park Service Inventory** "significant unmanned aid"

PRESQUE ISLE RANGE FRONT LIGHTHOUSE
Body of Water: Lake Huron
Near: Marquette, MI
Lat & Long: 45.3435, -83.4843
First Lit: 1871
Height & Type: 17 ft tower

Focal Plane: 18 ft fp
Miscellaneous Information:
- **National Park Service Inventory** "significant unmanned aid"

PRESQUE ISLE RANGE REAR LIGHTHOUSE
Body of Water: Lake Huron
Near: Marquette, MI
Lat & Long: 45.3435, -83.4843
First Lit: 1840
Height & Type: 38 ft tower
Focal Plane: 36 ft fp
Miscellaneous Information:
- **National Park Service Inventory** "significant unmanned aid"

ROBERT H MANNING MEMORIAL LIGHTHOUSE
Body of Water: Lake Michigan
Near: Empire, MI
Lat & Long: 44.81332, -86.06748
Height & Type: 35 ft tower
Miscellaneous Information:
- Located in Village Park
- Built in 1991

ROCK HARBOR LIGHTHOUSE
Body of Water: Lake Superior
Near: Grand Portage, MI
Lat & Long: 48.0897, -88.58059
National Park Service Inventory
First Lit: 1855
Height & Type: 50 ft tower
Focal Plane: 70 ft fp
Current Lens Information: none
Miscellaneous Information:
- Located in Isle Royale National Park
- Accessible only by boat

ROCK OF AGES LIGHTHOUSE
Body of Water: Lake Superior
Near: Grand Portage, MI
Lat & Long: 47.8667, -89.3133
National Park Service Inventory
First Lit: 1908
Height & Type: 117 ft caisson
Focal Plane: 130 ft fp

Current Lens Information: 190 MM
Miscellaneous Information:
- Located in Isle Royale National Park
- Best viewed from boat

ROUND ISLAND (ST MARYS RIVER) LIGHTHOUSE
Body of Water: Lake Huron
Near: Jocelyn, ON Canada, MI
Lat & Long: 46.1088, -84.0196
National Park Service Inventory
First Lit: 1892
Height & Type: 35 ft square tower with house
Focal Plane: 40 ft fp
Current Lens Information: none
Miscellaneous Information:
- Privately owned
- Best viewed from boat
- Near Canadian border

ROUND ISLAND OLD (ROUND ISLAND POINT) LIGHTHOUSE
Body of Water: Lake Michigan
Near: St. Ignace, MI
Lat & Long: 45.8295, -84.6002
National Park Service Inventory
First Lit: 1895
Height & Type: 53 ft square tower – brick
Current Lens Information: 300MM SP
Miscellaneous Information:
- Best viewed from boat or ferry

ROUND ISLAND PASSAGE LIGHTHOUSE
Body of Water: Lake Huron
Near: St Ignace, MI
Lat & Long: 45.84337, -84.61498
National Park Service Inventory
First Lit: 1948
Height & Type: 60 ft tower – white/red
Current Lens Information: 190 MM
Miscellaneous Information:
- Best viewed from boat or ferry

SAGINAW RIVER RANGE REAR LIGHTHOUSE
Body of Water: Lake Huron
Near: Bay City, MI
Lat & Long: 43.6366, -83.8534

National Park Service Inventory
First Lit: 1876
Height & Type: 55 ft square tower
Focal Plane: 77 ft fp
Current Lens Information: none
Miscellaneous Information:
- Privately owned commercial property with no entry
- WLTL

SAND HILLS LIGHTHOUSE
Body of Water: Lake Superior
Near: Ameek, MI
Lat & Long: 47.3919, -88.3703
National Park Service Inventory
First Lit: 1919
Height & Type: 91 ft tower with house
Focal Plane: 91 ft fp
Current Lens Information: none
Miscellaneous Information:
- Bed & breakfast
- Sand Hills Lighthouse Inn
Volunteer & Contribution Information:
www.sandhillslighthouseinn.com (reservations)

SAND POINT (BARAGA) LIGHTHOUSE
Body of Water: Keeweenaw Bay
Near: Baraga, MI
Lat & Long: 46.7836, -88.4672
National Park Service Inventory
First Lit: 1878
Height & Type: square tower – brick
Miscellaneous Information:
- Jacked up on greased timbers and moved 200 feet inland onto new foundation (1898)

SAND POINT (ESCANABA) LIGHTHOUSE
Body of Water: Lake Michigan
Near: Escanaba, MI
Lat & Long: 45.7448, -87.0447
National Park Service Inventory
First Lit: 1867
Height & Type: 41 ft square tower
Focal Plane: 44 ft fp
Current Lens Information: fourth order Fresnel
Miscellaneous Information:
- Museum

Volunteer & Contribution Information:
www.deltahistorical.org/lighthouse.htm

SEUL CHOIX POINT LIGHTHOUSE
Body of Water: Lake Michigan
Near: Gulliver, MI
Lat & Long: 45.9216, -85.9116
National Park Service Inventory
First Lit: 1895
Height & Type: 78 ft tower
Focal Plane: 80 ft fp
Current Lens Information: DCB-24
Miscellaneous Information:
• Operated by the Gulliver Historical Society
Volunteer & Contribution Information:
www.greatlakelighthouse.com

SKILLAGALEE ISLAND (ILE AUX GALETS) LIGHTHOUSE
Body of Water: Lake Michigan
Near: Cross Village, MI
Lat & Long: 45.6772, -85.1716
National Park Service Inventory
First Lit: 1888
Height & Type: 58 ft tower
Focal Plane: 58 ft fp
Current Lens Information: 300 MM
Miscellaneous Information:
• Best viewed from boat or plane

SOUTH FOX ISLAND LIGHTHOUSE
Body of Water: Lake Michigan
Near: Charlevoix, MI
Lat & Long: 45.3798, -85.8361
National Park Service Inventory
First Lit: 1868
Height & Type: 30 ft tower

Miscellaneous Information:
• Best viewed from boat or plane – renovated (2008)
• WLTL
Volunteer & Contribution Information:
www.southfox.org

SOUTH FOX ISLAND LIGHTHOUSE
Body of Water: Lake Michigan
Near: Charlevoix, MI
Lat & Long: 45.3798, -85.8361
National Park Service Inventory
First Lit: 1868
Height & Type: 60 ft skeleton – black
Miscellaneous Information:
• Tower relocated from Sapelo Island, GA
• Best viewed from boat or plane
Volunteer & Contribution Information:
www.southfox.org

SOUTH HAVEN SOUTH PIER (HEAD) LIGHTHOUSE
Body of Water: Lake Michigan
Near: South Haven, MI
Lat & Long: 42.4014, -86.288
National Park Service Inventory
First Lit: 1903
Height & Type: 35 ft caisson – red
Focal Plane: 37 ft fp
Current Lens Information: fifth order Fresnel
Miscellaneous Information:
• Fifth order Fresnel lens installed (1902)
Volunteer & Contribution Information:
www.southhaven.com (general info)

SOUTH MANITOU ISLAND LIGHTHOUSE
Body of Water: Lake Michigan
Near: South Manitou Island, MI
Lat & Long: 45.008, -86.0943
National Park Service Inventory
First Lit: 1872
Height & Type: 104 ft tower
Focal Plane: 100 ft fp

Current Lens Information: 155 MM
Miscellaneous Information:
• Accessible by boat or ferry
• Light relit after renovation (2009)
Volunteer & Contribution Information:
www.leelanau.com/lighthouse

SPECTACLE REEF LIGHTHOUSE
Body of Water: Lake Huron
Near: Cheboygan, MI
Lat & Long: 45.7732, -84.1367
National Park Service Inventory
First Lit: 1874
Height & Type: 93 ft tower
Focal Plane: 86 ft fp
Miscellaneous Information:
• Accessible only by boat
• 1994 USPS stamp

SQUAW ISLAND LIGHTHOUSE
Body of Water: Lake Michigan
Near: Manistique, MI
Lat & Long: 45.8393, -85.588
National Park Service Inventory
First Lit: 1892
Height & Type: 50 ft tower
Focal Plane: 57 ft fp
Miscellaneous Information:
• Privately owned island
• Best viewed from plane

ST CLAIR FLATS OLD CHANNEL RANGE REAR LIGHTHOUSE
Body of Water: Lake St Clair
Near: Harsens Island, MI
Lat & Long: 42.53759, -82.68985
National Park Service Inventory
First Lit: 1859
Height & Type: 40 ft tower

Focal Plane: 30 ft fp
Current Lens Information: none
Miscellaneous Information:
• Accessible only by boat
Volunteer & Contribution Information:
www.soschannellights.org

ST CLAIR FLATS OLD CHANNEL RANGE FRONT LIGHTHOUSE
Body of Water: Lake St Clair
Near: Harsens Island, MI
Lat & Long: 42.53759, -82.68985
National Park Service Inventory
First Lit: 1859
Height & Type: 17 ft tower – red brick
Focal Plane: 20 ft fp
Current Lens Information: sixth order
Miscellaneous Information:
• Accessible only by boat
Volunteer & Contribution Information:
www.soschannellights.org

ST HELENA ISLAND LIGHTHOUSE
Body of Water: Lake Michigan
Near: St Ignace, MI
Lat & Long: 45.855, -84.8645
National Park Service Inventory
First Lit: 1873
Height & Type: 71 ft tower
Focal Plane: 71 ft fp
Current Lens Information: 250 MM
Miscellaneous Information:
• Accessible only by boat

Volunteer & Contribution Information:
www.gllka.com

ST JOSEPH NORTH PIERHEAD INNER LIGHTHOUSE
Body of Water: Lake Michigan
Near: St Joseph, MI
Lat & Long: 42.1163, -86.4937
National Park Service Inventory
First Lit: 1907
Height & Type: 57 ft square tower with house
Focal Plane: 53 ft fp
Current Lens Information: fifth order Fresnel
Miscellaneous Information:
• 1994 USPS stamp

ST JOSEPH NORTH PIERHEAD OUTER LIGHTHOUSE
Body of Water: Lake Michigan
Near: St Joseph, MI
Lat & Long: 42.1163, -86.4937
National Park Service Inventory
First Lit: 1906
Height & Type: 35 ft tower
Focal Plane: 31 ft fp
Current Lens Information: fourth order Fresnel
Miscellaneous Information:
• 1994 USPS stamp

ST MARTIN ISLAND LIGHTHOUSE
Body of Water: Lake Michigan
Near: Escanaba, MI
Lat & Long: 45.5049, -86.7586
National Park Service Inventory
First Lit: 1905
Height & Type: 75 ft tower
Focal Plane: 84 ft fp
Current Lens Information: 190 MM
Miscellaneous Information:
• Accessible only by boat

STANNARD ROCK LIGHTHOUSE
Body of Water: Lake Superior
Near: Marquette, MI
Lat & Long: 47.1834, -87.225
National Park Service Inventory
First Lit: 1882
Height & Type: 110 ft tower with house
Focal Plane: 112 ft fp
Current Lens Information: 300MM
Miscellaneous Information:
• Accessible only by boat
• Lens displayed at Marquette Maritime Museum

STURGEON POINT LIGHTHOUSE

Body of Water: Lake Huron
Near: Harrisville, MI
Lat & Long: 44.7122, -83.2726
National Park Service Inventory
First Lit: 1869
Height & Type: 71 ft tower
Focal Plane: 69 ft fp
Current Lens Information: third & half order Fresnel
Miscellaneous Information:
• Museum
• Restored and maintained by Alcona Historical Society
Volunteer & Contribution Information:
www.theenchantedforest.com/ AlconaHistoricalSociety

Sturgeon Point Lighthouse, Michigan

TAWAS (OTTOWA) POINT LIGHTHOUSE
Body of Water: Lake Huron
Near: East Tawas, MI
Lat & Long: 44.2536, -83.4493
National Park Service Inventory
First Lit: 1876
Height & Type: 67 ft tower
Focal Plane: 70 ft fp
Current Lens Information: fourth order Fresnel
Miscellaneous Information:
  • Owned and renovated by Michigan Department of Natural Resources
Volunteer & Contribution Information:
  www.michigan.gov/tawaslighthouse

THUNDER BAY LIGHTHOUSE
Body of Water: Lake Huron
Near: Alpena, MI
Lat & Long: 45.0369, -83.1943
National Park Service Inventory
First Lit: 1857
Height & Type: 50 ft tower
Focal Plane: 69 ft fp
Current Lens Information: 190 MM
Miscellaneous Information:
  • Accessible only by boat
  • Original (1832) tower raised 10 feet

WAUGOSHANCE LIGHTHOUSE
Body of Water: Lake Michigan
Near: Mackinaw City, MI
Lat & Long: 45.8101, -85.1324
National Park Service Inventory
First Lit: 1870
Height & Type: 76 ft tower
Focal Plane: 74 ft fp
Current Lens Information: none
Miscellaneous Information:
  • DDL
  • Can be viewed from boat
  • Dangerous waters
  • Bird-cage lantern room
Volunteer & Contribution Information:
  www.waugoshance.org

WAWATAM (ST IGNACE) LIGHTHOUSE
Body of Water: Lake Michigan
Near: St Ignace, MI
Lat & Long: 45.861361, -84.713877
Height & Type: 52 ft – white & red (faux)
Miscellaneous Information:
  • So State St

WHITE RIVER LIGHTHOUSE
Body of Water: Lake Michigan
Near: Whitehall, MI
Lat & Long: 43.3743, -86.4248
National Park Service Inventory
First Lit: 1875
Height & Type: 38 ft tower
Focal Plane: 57 ft fp
Current Lens Information: none
Miscellaneous Information:
  • Museum
Volunteer & Contribution Information:
  www.whiteriverlightstation.org

WHITE ROCK LIGHTHOUSE
Body of Water: Lake Huron
Near: White Rock, MI
Lat & Long: 43.710476, -82.60940
Height & Type: faux tower
Miscellaneous Information:
  • Privately owned
  • Located at M-25 at White Rock Road

WHITE SHOAL LIGHTHOUSE
Body of Water: Lake Michigan
Near: Mackinaw City, MI
Lat & Long: 45.8417, -85.1349
National Park Service Inventory
First Lit: 1910
Height & Type: 121 ft tower red/white spiral stripes
Focal Plane: 125 ft fp
Current Lens Information: 190 MM
Miscellaneous Information:
  • Lighthouse image displayed on Michigan's license plate

WHITEFISH POINT LIGHTHOUSE
Body of Water: Lake Superior
Near: Paradise, MI
Lat & Long: 46.7716, -84.9567
National Park Service Inventory
First Lit: 1861
Height & Type: 76 ft skeleton – white
Focal Plane: 80 ft fp
Current Lens Information: DCB-24
Miscellaneous Information:
- First lighthouse built on Lake Superior
- Ship Wreck Museum

Volunteer & Contribution Information:
www.shipwreckmuseum.com (for overnight stays)

WILLIAM LIVINGSTONE MEMORIAL LIGHTHOUSE
Body of Water: Lake St Clair
Near: Detroit, MI
Lat & Long: 42.347, -82.9542
Height & Type: 50 ft tower
Miscellaneous Information:
- Only marble Lighthouse in America

WINDJAMMER MARINA LIGHTHOUSE
Body of Water: Lake Huron
Near: Oden, MI
Lat & Long: 45.423917, -84.839514
Height & Type: faux – pale blue
Miscellaneous Information:
- Privately owned
- Located at 3654 US-31

WINDMILL POINT LIGHTHOUSE
Body of Water: Lake St Clair
Near: Detroit, MI
Lat & Long: 42.35812, -82.92983
Height & Type: 40 ft tower
Focal Plane: 47 ft fp
Miscellaneous Information:
- Art Deco architecture

Minnesota

DULUTH HARBOR NORTH BREAKWATER LIGHTHOUSE
Body of Water: Lake Superior
Near: Duluth, MN
Lat & Long: 46.7806, -92.088
National Park Service Inventory
First Lit: 1910
Height & Type: 37 ft tower – black/white
Focal Plane: 46 ft fp
Current Lens Information: fifth order Fresnel
Miscellaneous Information:
- Original fifth order Fresnel lens still in use

DULUTH HARBOR SOUTH BREAKWATER INNER LIGHTHOUSE
Body of Water: Lake Superior
Near: Duluth, MN
Lat & Long: 46.7782, -92.0919
National Park Service Inventory
First Lit: 1901
Height & Type: 67 ft partial skeleton tower
Focal Plane: 68 ft fp
Miscellaneous Information:
- Original 4th order Fresnel lens displayed at Lake Superior Marine Museum

DULUTH HARBOR SOUTH BREAKWATER OUTER LIGHTHOUSE
Body of Water: Lake Superior
Near: Duluth, MN
Lat & Long: 46.7795, -92.0869
National Park Service Inventory
First Lit: 1901
Height & Type: 35 ft tower with house
Focal Plane: 44 ft fp
Current Lens Information: fourth order Fresnel
Miscellaneous Information:
- Original fifth order Fresnel lens transmits continuous green light

GRAND MARAIS LIGHTHOUSE
Body of Water: Lake Superior
Near: Grand Marais, MN
Lat & Long: 47.745, -90.3383
National Park Service Inventory

First Lit: 1922
Height & Type: 34 ft tower
Focal Plane: 48 ft fp
Current Lens Information: fifth order Fresnel
Miscellaneous Information:
- Original fifth order Fresnel lens transmits continuous white light

MINNESOTA POINT LIGHTHOUSE
Body of Water: Lake Superior
Near: Duluth, MN
Lat & Long: 46.7094, -92.0227
Height & Type: ruins – partial tower (50 ft tower)
Focal Plane: 50 ft fp
Miscellaneous Information:
- DDL
- Tower now truncated at about 30 ft

SPLIT ROCK LIGHTHOUSE
Body of Water: Lake Superior
Near: Two Harbors, MN
Lat & Long: 47.1921, -91.38102
National Park Service Inventory
First Lit: 1910
Height & Type: 54 ft octagonal tower
Focal Plane: 168 ft fp
Current Lens Information: third order Fresnel (bivalve)
Miscellaneous Information:
- Museum
- 1994 USPS stamp
- Most photogenic American lighthouse

Volunteer & Contribution Information:
www.mnhs.org (general info)

TWO HARBORS LIGHTHOUSE
Body of Water: Lake Superior
Near: Two Harbors, MN
Lat & Long: 47.0318, -91.6637
National Park Service Inventory
First Lit: 1892
Height & Type: 49 ft tower
Focal Plane: 78 ft fp
Current Lens Information: DCB-224
Miscellaneous Information:
- Bed & breakfast

Volunteer & Contribution Information:
www.lighthousebb.org (general info)

TWO HARBORS (EAST) BREAKWATER LIGHTHOUSE

Body of Water: Lake Superior
Near: Two Harbors, MN
Lat & Long: 47.01038, -91.6695
Height & Type: 37 ft tower
Focal Plane: 33 ft fp
Current Lens Information: fifth order Fresnel
Miscellaneous Information:
- Transmits red flashing light
- **National Park Service Inventory**
"significant unmanned aid"

Two Harbors Lighthouse, Minnesota

Mississippi

BILOXI LIGHTHOUSE
Body of Water: Gulf of Mexico
Near: Biloxi, MS
Lat & Long: 30.3946, -88.9015
National Park Service Inventory
First Lit: 1848
Height & Type: 61 ft tower
Focal Plane: 48 ft fp
Current Lens Information: fifth order Fresnel
Miscellaneous Information:
  • Owned by City of Biloxi
Volunteer & Contribution Information:
  www.biloxi.ms.us/museums/biloxilighthouse

ROUND ISLAND LIGHTHOUSE
Body of Water: Gulf of Mexico
Near: Pascagoula, MS
Lat & Long: 30.2919, -88.5867
First Lit: 1859
Height & Type: ruins
Current Lens Information: fifth order Fresnel
Miscellaneous Information:
  • Destroyed by Hurricane Katrina (2005)
  • Plan to rebuild it
Volunteer & Contribution Information:
  www.roundislandlighthouse.org

SHIP ISLAND LIGHTHOUSE
Body of Water: Gulf of Mexico
Near: Gulfport, MS
Lat & Long: 30.2116, -88.9667
First Lit: 2000
Height & Type: replica (of 1853 lighthouse) – destroyed
Focal Plane: 76 ft fp
Miscellaneous Information:
  • Replica built in 2000 was destroyed by Hurricane Katrina (2005)

New Hampshire

BURKEHAVEN LIGHTHOUSE
Body of Water: Lake Sunapee
Near: Burkehaven, NH
Lat & Long: 43.3913, -72.0598
First Lit: 1983
Height & Type: 20 ft tower (replica)
Current Lens Information: none
Miscellaneous Information:
  • Original (1898) destroyed by ice (1935)
  • Replica built (1980s)
Volunteer & Contribution Information:
  www.lakesunapee.org (general info)

HERRICK COVE LIGHTHOUSE
Body of Water: Lake Sunapee
Near: Georges Cove, NH
Lat & Long: 43.411, -72.0421
Height & Type: 27 ft hexagon tower
Current Lens Information: none
Miscellaneous Information:
  • Accessible only by boat
Volunteer & Contribution Information:
  www.lakesunapee.org (general info)

ISLES OF SHOALS (WHITE ISLAND) LIGHTHOUSE
Body of Water: Atlantic Ocean
Near: Portsmouth, NH
Lat & Long: 42.9676, -70.6237
National Park Service Inventory
First Lit: 1865
Height & Type: 58 ft tower
Focal Plane: 82 ft fp
Current Lens Information: VRB-25 SP
Miscellaneous Information:
  • DDL
  • Owned by NH Division of Parks and Recreation

LOON ISLAND LIGHTHOUSE
Body of Water: Lake Sunapee
Near: Fernwood, NH
Lat & Long: 43.3913, -72.0598
First Lit: 1960
Height & Type: 25 ft tower

Miscellaneous Information:
  • Two previous lighthouses burned (1898 & 1960)
Volunteer & Contribution Information:
  www.lakesunapee.org (general info)

PORTSMOUTH HARBOR (NEW CASTLE) LIGHTHOUSE
Body of Water: Portsmouth Harbor
Near: New Castle, NH
Lat & Long: 43.0708, -70.7083
First Lit: 1877
Height & Type: 48 ft tower
Focal Plane: 52 ft fp
Current Lens Information: fourth order Fresnel
Miscellaneous Information:
  • Original fourth order Fresnel lens transmits continuous green light
Volunteer & Contribution Information:
  www.portsmouthharborlighthouse.org

New Jersey

ABSECON LIGHTHOUSE
Body of Water: Atlantic Ocean
Near: Atlantic City, NJ
Lat & Long: 39.36647, -74.41413
National Park Service Inventory
First Lit: 1857
Height & Type: 169 ft tower
Focal Plane: 168 ft fp
Current Lens Information: first order Fresnel
Miscellaneous Information:
  • Most of restoration completed (1998)
  • Keepers house lost in fire
Volunteer & Contribution Information:
  www.abseconlighthouse.org

BARNEGAT "OLD BARNEY" LIGHTHOUSE
Body of Water: Atlantic Ocean
Near: Barnegat, NJ
Lat & Long: 39.7643, -74.106
National Park Service Inventory
First Lit: 1857

Height & Type: 172 ft tower
Focal Plane: 165 ft fp
Miscellaneous Information:
- Tallest NJ lighthouse

BARNEGAT LIGHTSHIP
Body of Water: Delaware River
Near: Camden, NJ
Lat & Long: 39.9573, -75.1124
First Lit: 1904
Height & Type: lightship
Current Lens Information: 3 oil lens lanterns at each masthead
Miscellaneous Information:
- DDL LV-79 WAL-506
- Privately owned

BRANDYWINE SHOAL LIGHTHOUSE
Body of Water: Delaware Bay
Near: Cape May, NJ
Lat & Long: 38.98636, -75.11353
National Park Service Inventory
First Lit: 1914
Height & Type: 45 ft caisson
Focal Plane: 60 ft fp
Miscellaneous Information:
- First US screwpile lighthouse (1850)

CAPE MAY LIGHTHOUSE
Body of Water: Delaware Bay
Near: Cape May, NJ
Lat & Long: 38.933332, -74.95997
National Park Service Inventory
First Lit: 1859
Height & Type: 157 ft tower
Focal Plane: 175 ft fp
Current Lens Information: DCB-36
Miscellaneous Information:
- Two previous lighthouses built (1823 and 1847)
Volunteer & Contribution Information:
www.capemaymac.org

CHAPEL HILL RANGE REAR LIGHTHOUSE
Body of Water: New York Bay
Near: Leonardo, NJ

Lat & Long: 40.3983, -74.0588
National Park Service Inventory
First Lit: 1941
Height & Type: 31 ft tower with house
Current Lens Information: none
Miscellaneous Information:
- Privately owned
- Lens displayed at Navesink Lighthouse Museum

CONOVER BEACON (CHAPEL HILL RANGE FRONT) LIGHTHOUSE
Body of Water: New York Bay
Near: Leonardo, NJ
Lat & Long: 40.421395, -74.05562
First Lit: 1941
Height & Type: 40 ft skeleton – white/red
Focal Plane: 45 ft fp
Current Lens Information: 375 MM
Miscellaneous Information:
- Owned by Monmouth County

CROSS LEDGE LIGHTHOUSE
Body of Water: Delaware Bay
Near: Cape May, NJ
Lat & Long: 39.20396, -75.23074
Height & Type: ruins
Miscellaneous Information:
- Only the granite foundation remains

EAST POINT LIGHTHOUSE
Body of Water: Delaware Bay / Maurice River
Near: Maurice River, NJ
Lat & Long: 39.1957, -75.02709
National Park Service Inventory
First Lit: 1849
Height & Type: 40 ft tower with house
Focal Plane: 43 ft fp
Current Lens Information: 250 MM
Miscellaneous Information:
- Maintained by Maurice River Historical Society

ELBOW OF CROSS LEDGE LIGHTHOUSE
Body of Water: Delaware Bay
Near: Cape May, NJ

Lat & Long: 39.18162, -75.26828
Height & Type: caisson
Miscellaneous Information:
- Best viewed from boat

FINNS POINT (FORT MOTT) LIGHTHOUSE
Body of Water: Delaware River
Near: Pennsville, NJ
Lat & Long: 39.617175, -75.53389
National Park Service Inventory
First Lit: 1877
Height & Type: 115 ft skeleton – black
Focal Plane: 105 ft fp
Current Lens Information: none
Miscellaneous Information:
- Part of Supawna Meadows Wildlife Refuge

GREAT BEDS LIGHTHOUSE
Body of Water: Raritan River
Near: South Amboy, NJ
Lat & Long: 40.4867, -74.2532
National Park Service Inventory
First Lit: 1880
Height & Type: 47 ft caisson
Focal Plane: 61 ft fp
Current Lens Information: 300 MM (red)
Miscellaneous Information:
- Emits flashing red light

HEREFORD INLET LIGHTHOUSE
Body of Water: Hereford Inlet
Near: North Wildwood, NJ
Lat & Long: 39.0067, -74.79166
National Park Service Inventory
First Lit: 1874
Height & Type: 57 ft tower with house
Focal Plane: 53 ft fp
Current Lens Information: fourth order Fresnel
Miscellaneous Information:
- Museum
Volunteer & Contribution Information:
www.herefordlighthouse.org

LIBERTY (WINTER QUARTER) LIGHTSHIP
Body of Water: New York Harbor
Near: Jersey City, NJ

Lat & Long: 40.7097, -74.0403
First Lit: 1923
Height & Type: lightship
Current Lens Information: 375 MM electric lens lanterns at each masthead
Miscellaneous Information:
- LV-107 WAL-529
- Used as floating office building in Liberty State Park

LUDLUM BEACH LIGHTHOUSE
Body of Water: Atlantic Ocean
Near: Sea Isle City, NJ
Lat & Long: 39.1597, -74.668
Height & Type: only residence remains
Current Lens Information: none
Miscellaneous Information:
- Plan to relocate and renovate
Volunteer & Contribution Information:
www.ludlamsbeachlight.org

MIAH MAULL SHOAL LIGHTHOUSE
Body of Water: Delaware Bay
Near: Cape May, NJ
Lat & Long: 39.12643, -75.20966
National Park Service Inventory
First Lit: 1913
Height & Type: 45 ft caisson – red
Focal Plane: 59 ft fp
Current Lens Information: 500 MM
Miscellaneous Information:
- Best viewed from boat

NAVESINK ("TWIN LIGHT") LIGHTHOUSE
Body of Water: New York Bay
Near: Highlands, NJ
Lat & Long: 40.39587, -73.98562
National Park Service Inventory
First Lit: 1862
Height & Type: 73 ft twin towers
Focal Plane: 246 ft fp
Current Lens Information: North tower: sixth order Fresnel
Miscellaneous Information:
- First Fresnel lens sent to US (1841)

Volunteer & Contribution Information:
www.twin-lights.org

ROBBINS REEF (KATES) LIGHTHOUSE
Body of Water: New York Harbor
Near: Staten Island, NY, NJ
Lat & Long: 40.6574, -74.0656
National Park Service Inventory
First Lit: 1883
Height & Type: 46 ft caisson – brown/white
Focal Plane: 56 ft fp
Current Lens Information: 300 MM (green)
Miscellaneous Information:
- Kate Walker – lightkeeper (1846-1931)

ROMER SHOAL LIGHTHOUSE
Body of Water: New York Harbor
Near: Staten Island, NY, NJ
Lat & Long: 40.5126, -74.0135
National Park Service Inventory
First Lit: 1898
Height & Type: 54 ft caisson – white/red
Focal Plane: 54 ft fp
Current Lens Information: 190MM
Miscellaneous Information:
- Best viewed from boat

SANDY HOOK LIGHTHOUSE
Body of Water: New York Harbor
Near: Highlands, NJ
Lat & Long: 40.4617, -74.00167
National Park Service Inventory
First Lit: 1764
Height & Type: 85 ft tower
Focal Plane: 88 ft fp
Current Lens Information: third order Fresnel
Miscellaneous Information:
- Oldest standing U.S. Lighthouse
- 1990 USPS stamp
Volunteer & Contribution Information:
www.njlhs.org

SEA GIRT LIGHTHOUSE
Body of Water: Atlantic Ocean
Near: Sea Girt, NJ
Lat & Long: 40.13666, -74.02746
National Park Service Inventory
First Lit: 1896
Height & Type: 44 ft tower
Focal Plane: 60 ft fp
Miscellaneous Information:
- One of three locations with first radio beacon navigation system
Volunteer & Contribution Information:
www.seagirtboro.com

Sea Girt Lighthouse,
New Jersey

SHIP JOHN SHOAL LIGHTHOUSE
Body of Water: Delaware Bay
Near: Bridgeton, NJ
Lat & Long: 39.30496, -75.37651
National Park Service Inventory
First Lit: 1877
Height & Type: 45 ft caisson – brown
Focal Plane: 50 ft fp
Current Lens Information: VRB-25 SP
Miscellaneous Information:
  • Best viewed from boat

TINICUM ISLAND REAR (BILLINGSPORT ISLAND) LIGHTHOUSE
Body of Water: Delaware River
Near: Paulsboro, NJ
Lat & Long: 39.847443, -75.23956
National Park Service Inventory
First Lit: 1880
Height & Type: 86 ft skeleton
Focal Plane: 112 ft fp
Current Lens Information: DCB-24
Miscellaneous Information:
  • Tours once each month (April – October)

TUCKER'S BEACH LIGHTHOUSE
Body of Water: Barnegat Bay
Near: Tuckerton, NJ
Lat & Long: 39.6018, -74.3424
Height & Type: 45 ft square tower with house – replica
Miscellaneous Information:
  • Brandywine Lighthouse's third order Fresnel is displayed here
Volunteer & Contribution Information:
  www.tuckertonseaport.org (general info)

New York

AMBROSE LIGHTSHIP
Body of Water: New York Harbor
Near: Manhattan, NY
Lat & Long: 40.7056, -74.0029
First Lit: 1907
Height & Type: lightship
Current Lens Information: 3 oil lens lanterns at each masthead
Miscellaneous Information:
- LV-87 WAL-512
- Museum

BARBER'S POINT LIGHTHOUSE
Body of Water: Lake Champlain
Near: Westport, NY
Lat & Long: 44.1526, -73.4052
National Park Service Inventory
First Lit: 1873
Height & Type: 36 ft tower with house
Focal Plane: 83 ft fp
Current Lens Information: none
Miscellaneous Information:
- Privately owned

BARCELONA (PORTLAND HARBOR) LIGHTHOUSE
Body of Water: Lake Erie
Near: Westfield, NY
Lat & Long: 42.3411, -79.5948
National Park Service Inventory
First Lit: 1829
Height & Type: 40 ft stone tower
Miscellaneous Information:
- Privately owned
- First US light to use natural gas (1831)

BLACKWELL ISLAND LIGHTHOUSE
Body of Water: Harlem River
Near: Manhattan, NY
Lat & Long: 40.7718, -73.9408
Height & Type: 50 ft stone tower
Miscellaneous Information:
- **National Park Service Inventory** "significant unmanned aid"

BLUFF POINT (VALCOUR ISLAND) LIGHTHOUSE
Body of Water: Lake Champlain
Near: Plattsburgh, NY
Lat & Long: 44.6231, -73.4304
National Park Service Inventory
First Lit: 1874
Height & Type: 35 ft tower with house
Focal Plane: 95 ft fp
Current Lens Information: 300 MM
Miscellaneous Information:
- Deactivated (1930); relit (2003)
Volunteer & Contribution Information: www.clintoncountyhistorical.org

BRADDOCK POINT LIGHTHOUSE
Body of Water: Lake Ontario
Near: Rochester, NY
Lat & Long: 43.34, -77.762
National Park Service Inventory
First Lit: 1896
Height & Type: 110 ft octagonal tower – red brick
Miscellaneous Information:
- Privately owned

BUFFALO MAIN LIGHTHOUSE
Body of Water: Lake Erie
Near: Buffalo, NY
Lat & Long: 42.8774, -78.89
National Park Service Inventory
First Lit: 1833
Height & Type: 61 ft octogonal tower
Focal Plane: 76 ft fp
Miscellaneous Information:
- Oldest building in Buffalo
Volunteer & Contribution Information: www.buffalohistoryworks.com

BUFFALO HARBOR BREAKWATER LIGHTHOUSE
Body of Water: Lake Erie
Near: Buffalo, NY
Lat & Long: 42.87067, -78.90238
Height & Type: 20 ft tower

Miscellaneous Information:
- Best viewed from boat
- Can be seen from Buffalo Main Lighthouse

BUFFALO INTAKE CRIB LIGHTHOUSE
Body of Water: Lake Erie
Near: Buffalo, NY
Lat & Long: 42.8818, -78.9107
Height & Type: crib
Miscellaneous Information:
- Best viewed from boat
- Owned by the City of Buffalo

BUFFALO NORTH BREAKWATER (SOUTH END) LIGHTHOUSE
Body of Water: Lake Erie
Near: Buffalo, NY
Lat & Long: 42.8774, -78.89
First Lit: 1903
Height & Type: 29 ft "bottle"
Current Lens Information: 300 MM
Miscellaneous Information:
- Unique shape
- **National Park Service Inventory** "significant unmanned aid"

Buffalo North Breakwater (South End) Lighthouse, New York

BUFFALO SOUTH BREAKWATER LIGHTHOUSE
Body of Water: Lake Erie
Near: Dunkirk, NY
Lat & Long: 42.4936, -79.3537
Height & Type: 29 ft "bottle"
Miscellaneous Information:
- Relocated to Dunkirk Lighthouse

BREWERTON RANGE REAR LIGHTHOUSE
Body of Water: Oneida Lake
Near: Brewerton, NY
Lat & Long: 43.24117, -76.14464
First Lit: 1917
Height & Type: 85 ft tower
Miscellaneous Information:
- Town of Hastings to restore lighthouse, create Oneida River Lighthouse Park (2004)

CAPE VINCENT BREAKWATER LIGHTHOUSE
Body of Water: Lake Ontario
Near: Cape Vincent, NY
Lat & Long: 44.1191, -76.3317
National Park Service Inventory
Height & Type: 15 ft tower
Miscellaneous Information:
- Located from breakwater to Route 12 E (entrance to town)

CEDAR ISLAND LIGHTHOUSE
Body of Water: Gardiners Bay
Near: Sag Harbor, NY
Lat & Long: 41.0408, -72.261
National Park Service Inventory
First Lit: 1868
Height & Type: 40 ft stone tower with house
Focal Plane: 44 ft fp
Current Lens Information: none
Miscellaneous Information:
- DDL Cedar Island Preservation Committee
Volunteer & Contribution Information:
www.cedarislandlighthouse.org

CHARLOTTE-GENESEE (PORT GENESEE) LIGHTHOUSE
Body of Water: Lake Ontario / Genesee River
Near: Rochester, NY

Lat & Long: 43.253, -77.6108
National Park Service Inventory
First Lit: 1822
Height & Type: 40 ft tower
Focal Plane: 45 ft fp
Current Lens Information: fourth order Fresnel
Miscellaneous Information:
- Renovation by Charlotte Genesee Lighthouse Historical Society
Volunteer & Contribution Information:
www.geneseelighthouse.org

COLD SPRING HARBOR LIGHTHOUSE
Body of Water: Long Island Sound
Near: Cold Spring Harbor, NY
Lat & Long: 40.9143, -73.4931
National Park Service Inventory
First Lit: 1890
Height & Type: caisson
Focal Plane: 37 ft fp
Current Lens Information: 300 MM
Miscellaneous Information:
- Moved to privately owned residence

CONEY ISLAND (NORTON/ NORTONS POINT) LIGHTHOUSE
Body of Water: New York Harbor
Near: Brooklyn, NY
Lat & Long: 40.5765, -74.01185
National Park Service Inventory
First Lit: 1920
Height & Type: 70 ft tower
Focal Plane: 75 ft fp
Current Lens Information: 190 MM
Miscellaneous Information:
- Located in a private community
- Best viewed from boat

CROSSOVER ISLAND LIGHTHOUSE
Body of Water: St Lawrence River
Near: Alexandria Bay, NY
Lat & Long: 44.4974, -75.7821
National Park Service Inventory
First Lit: 1882
Height & Type: 30 ft tower
Focal Plane: 30 ft fp

Miscellaneous Information:
- Distant views from land
- Privately owned

CROWN POINT (CHAMPLAIN MEMORIAL) LIGHTHOUSE

Body of Water: Lake Champlain
Near: Crown Point, NY
Lat & Long: 44.0299, -73.4214
First Lit: 1912
Height & Type: 55 ft former lighthouse
Miscellaneous Information:
- Located across from Crown Point State Historic Point

CUMBERLAND HEAD LIGHTHOUSE

Body of Water: Lake Champlain
Near: Plattsburgh, NY
Lat & Long: 44.6908, -73.3862
National Park Service Inventory
First Lit: 1868
Height & Type: 50 ft conical stone tower
Miscellaneous Information:
- Privately owned
- Can be viewed from ferry

DUNKIRK (POINT GRATIOT) LIGHTHOUSE

Body of Water: Lake Erie
Near: Dunkirk, NY
Lat & Long: 42.4936, -79.3537
National Park Service Inventory
First Lit: 1875
Height & Type: 61 ft tower with house
Focal Plane: 82 ft fp
Current Lens Information: third order Fresnel
Miscellaneous Information:
- Current lighthouse is fifth one at this location
Volunteer & Contribution Information:
  www.dunkirklighthouse.com

EAST CHARITY SHOAL(S) LIGHTHOUSE

Body of Water: Lake Ontario
Near: Cape Vincent, NY
Lat & Long: 43.9912, -76.5422
National Park Service Inventory
First Lit: 1877

Height & Type: 16 ft tower
Focal Plane: 52 ft fp
Miscellaneous Information:
- Distant view from Tibbetts Point lighthouse

EATONS NECK LIGHTHOUSE

Body of Water: Long Island Sound
Near: Northport, NY
Lat & Long: 40.9533, -73.3949
National Park Service Inventory
First Lit: 1799
Height & Type: 73 ft tower
Focal Plane: 144 ft fp
Current Lens Information: third order Fresnel
Miscellaneous Information:
- Only active Fresnel lens in Long Island lighthouse

ELM TREE (SWASH CHANNEL RANGE FRONT) LIGHTHOUSE

Body of Water: Atlantic Ocean
Near: Staten Island, NY
Lat & Long: 40.5634, -74.095
First Lit: 1912
Height & Type: 59 ft tower
Miscellaneous Information:
- Part of Gateway National Recreation Area
- **National Park Service Inventory** "significant unmanned aid"

ESOPUS MEADOWS (MIDDLE HUDSON RIVER) LIGHTHOUSE

Body of Water: Hudson River
Near: Esopus, NY
Lat & Long: 41.8851, -73.9484
National Park Service Inventory
First Lit: 1872
Height & Type: 25 ft tower with house
Focal Plane: 52 ft fp
Current Lens Information: fifth order Fresnel
Miscellaneous Information:
- DDL
- Owned and restored by Esopus Meadows Lighthouse Commission
Volunteer & Contribution Information:
  www.esopuslighthouse.org

EXECUTION ROCK(S) LIGHTHOUSE

Body of Water: Long Island Sound
Near: Sands Point, NY
Lat & Long: 40.87804, -73.7373
National Park Service Inventory
First Lit: 1850
Height & Type: 60 ft tower – red/white
Focal Plane: 62 ft fp
Current Lens Information: APRB-251 SP
Miscellaneous Information:
- Tower open twice a month in summer
- See website for dates
Volunteer & Contribution Information:
  www.lighthouserestorations.org

FIRE ISLAND LIGHTHOUSE

Body of Water: Atlantic Ocean
Near: West Islip, NY
Lat & Long: 40.63167, -73.21789
National Park Service Inventory
First Lit: 1858
Height & Type: 168 ft tower – black/white
Focal Plane: 180 ft fp
Current Lens Information: DCB-224
Miscellaneous Information:
- Relit and reinstated as an official aid to navigation (1986)
Volunteer & Contribution Information:
  www.fireislandlighthouse.com

FIRE ISLAND LIGHTHOUSE (1826 RUINS)

Body of Water: Atlantic Ocean
Near: West Islip, NY
Lat & Long: 40.63167, -73.21789
Height & Type: ruins
Current Lens Information: none
Miscellaneous Information:
- Stone used to build the terrace for the present lighthouse

Fire Island Lighthouse,
New York

FORT NIAGARA LIGHTHOUSE

Body of Water: Lake Ontario / Niagara River
Near: Youngstown, NY
Lat & Long: 43.2617, -79.0633
National Park Service Inventory
First Lit: 1872
Height & Type: 61 ft tower
Focal Plane: 91 ft fp
Current Lens Information: fourth order Fresnel
Miscellaneous Information:
- Museum
- Managed by Old Fort Niagara Association

Fort Niagara Lighthouse,
New York

FORT WADSWORTH LIGHTHOUSE
Body of Water: New York Harbor
Near: Staten Island, NY
Lat & Long: 40.6041, -74.0539
National Park Service Inventory
First Lit: 1903
Height & Type: 15 ft tower
Focal Plane: 75 ft fp
Current Lens Information: none
Miscellaneous Information:
  • Under Verrazano Narrows Bridge

FRYING PAN LIGHTSHIP
Body of Water: Hudson River
Near: Manhattan, NY
Lat & Long: 40.7501, -74.01
First Lit: 1930
Height & Type: lightship
Current Lens Information: 375 MM electric lens lantern at masthead
Miscellaneous Information:
  • LV-115 WAL-537
  • Sunk for three years
  • Museum
Volunteer & Contribution Information:
  www.fryingpan.com (general info)

GALLOO ISLAND LIGHTHOUSE
Body of Water: Lake Ontario
Near: Watertown, NY
Lat & Long: 43.9912, -76.5422
National Park Service Inventory
First Lit: 1867
Height & Type: 55 ft tower
Focal Plane: 58 ft fp
Current Lens Information: 190 MM
Miscellaneous Information:
  • Best viewed from boat
  • First tower built (1820)
  • Privately owned

GRAND ISLAND RANGE FRONT LIGHTHOUSE
Body of Water: Lake Ontario
Near: Buffalo, NY
Lat & Long: 42.9761, -78.9474
First Lit: 1917

Height & Type: 36 ft tower
Focal Plane: 23 ft fp
Miscellaneous Information:
  • Located at Buffalo Launch Club

HORSE ISLAND (SACKETS/ SACKETTS HARBOR) LIGHTHOUSE
Body of Water: Lake Ontario
Near: Sackets Harbor, NY
Lat & Long: 43.9429, -76.1427
National Park Service Inventory
First Lit: 1870
Height & Type: 70 ft square tower with house
Miscellaneous Information:
  • WLTL
  • Privately owned
  • Foliage makes it difficult to view

HORSESHOE REEF LIGHTHOUSE
Body of Water: Lake Erie
Near: Buffalo, NY
Lat & Long: 42.8866, -78.9125
Height & Type: 50 ft tower
Miscellaneous Information:
  • Best viewed from boat
  • Distant view from Buffalo Main Lighthouse

HORTON POINT LIGHTHOUSE
Body of Water: Long Island Sound
Near: Southold, NY
Lat & Long: 41.085, -72.44668
National Park Service Inventory
First Lit: 1857
Height & Type: 58 ft tower
Focal Plane: 103 ft fp
Current Lens Information: VRB-25
Miscellaneous Information:
  • Museum
Volunteer & Contribution Information:
  www.southoldhistoricalsociety.org

HUDSON (HUDSON-ATHENS) LIGHTHOUSE
Body of Water: Hudson River
Near: Hudson, NY
Lat & Long: 42.2517, -73.81
National Park Service Inventory
First Lit: 1874

Height & Type: 30 ft square tower with house
Focal Plane: 46 ft fp
Current Lens Information: 300 MM
Miscellaneous Information:
  • Built to warn ships about the middle ground flats
Volunteer & Contribution Information:
  www.hudsonathenslighthouse.org

HUNTINGTON (LLOYD) HARBOR LIGHTHOUSE
Body of Water: Huntington Harbor
Near: Huntington, NY
Lat & Long: 40.91078, -73.4311
National Park Service Inventory
First Lit: 1912
Height & Type: 42 ft tower
Focal Plane: 41 ft fp
Current Lens Information: 300 MM
Miscellaneous Information:
  • Tours once (or twice) each month (May–September)
Volunteer & Contribution Information:
  www.huntingtonlighthouse.org

JEFFREYS HOOK LIGHTHOUSE
Body of Water: Hudson River
Near: Manhattan, NY
Lat & Long: 40.85015, -73.94641
First Lit: 1895
Height & Type: 40 ft tower – red
Focal Plane: 61 ft fp
Current Lens Information: 300 MM
Miscellaneous Information:
  • Book: The Little Red Lighthouse and the Great Gray Bridge
Volunteer & Contribution Information:
  www.historichousetrust.org

LATIMER REEF LIGHTHOUSE
Body of Water: Fisher Island Sound
Near: Stonington, CT, NY
Lat & Long: 41.3045, -71.9335
National Park Service Inventory
First Lit: 1884
Height & Type: 49 ft caisson – brown/white
Focal Plane: 55 ft fp

Current Lens Information: 300 MM
Miscellaneous Information:
• Best viewed from boat

LITTLE GULL ISLAND LIGHTHOUSE
Body of Water: Block Island Sound
Near: Greenport, NY
Lat & Long: 41.20611, -72.1067
National Park Service Inventory
First Lit: 1869
Height & Type: 81 ft tower
Focal Plane: 91 ft fp
Miscellaneous Information:
• Original Fresnel lens on display at East End Seaport Maritime Museum

LONG BEACH BAR "BUG LIGHT" LIGHTHOUSE
Body of Water: Gardiners Bay
Near: Greenport, NY
Lat & Long: 41.11, -72.3066
Height & Type: 65 ft caisson
Current Lens Information: 250 MM
Miscellaneous Information:
• WLTL
• Restored (1990)
• Owned by East End Seaport
Volunteer & Contribution Information:
www.eastendseaport.org

MONTAUK POINT LIGHTHOUSE
Body of Water: Atlantic Ocean
Near: Montauk, NY
Lat & Long: 41.0717, -71.85677
National Park Service Inventory
First Lit: 1797
Height & Type: 110 ft tower – white/brown
Focal Plane: 168 ft fp
Current Lens Information: DCB-224
Miscellaneous Information:
• First NY lighthouse
• Museum
Volunteer & Contribution Information:
www.montauklighthouse.com

MONTAUK YACHT CLUB LIGHTHOUSE
Body of Water: Lake Montauk

Near: Montauk, NY
Lat & Long: 41.07, -71.9333
Height & Type: 60 ft tower w/building (faux)
Miscellaneous Information:
• Restaurant

NEW DORP (SWASH CHANNEL RANGE REAR) LIGHTHOUSE
Body of Water: New York Bay
Near: Staten Island, NY
Lat & Long: 40.58077, -74.1201
National Park Service Inventory
First Lit: 1856
Height & Type: 80 ft tower with house
Focal Plane: 190 ft fp
Current Lens Information: sixth order
Miscellaneous Information:
• Privately owned
• Restored by owner

NORTH BROTHER ISLAND LIGHTHOUSE
Body of Water: East River
Near: Manhattan, NY
Lat & Long: 40.7993, -73.8996
Height & Type: ruins – only oil house remains
Miscellaneous Information:
• Tower gone and keeper's house collapsed due to neglect

NORTH DUMPLING LIGHTHOUSE
Body of Water: Long Island Sound
Near: Groton, CT, NY
Lat & Long: 41.2881, -72.0195
National Park Service Inventory
First Lit: 1871
Height & Type: 31 ft tower with house
Focal Plane: 60 ft fp
Current Lens Information: 300 MM
Miscellaneous Information:
• Privately owned

OGDENSBURG HARBOR LIGHTHOUSE
Body of Water: St Lawrence River
Near: Ogdensburg, NY
Lat & Long: 44.6978, -75.5036
National Park Service Inventory
First Lit: 1900

Height & Type: 65 ft tower
Miscellaneous Information:
• Privately owned
Volunteer & Contribution Information:
www.ogdensburgharborlight.com (general info)

OLD FIELD POINT LIGHTHOUSE
Body of Water: Long Island Sound
Near: Old Field Village, NY
Lat & Long: 40.9767, -73.1183
National Park Service Inventory
First Lit: 1868
Height & Type: 35 ft tower with house
Focal Plane: 74 ft fp
Current Lens Information: FA-251
Miscellaneous Information:
• After Pearl Harbor bombing station seized for national defense (1941)
Volunteer & Contribution Information:
www.oldfieldny.org (general info)

OLD ORCHARD SHOAL LIGHTHOUSE
Body of Water: New York Harbor
Near: Staten Island, NY
Lat & Long: 40.5117, -74.1
National Park Service Inventory
First Lit: 1893
Height & Type: 35 ft caisson
Focal Plane: 51 ft fp
Current Lens Information: 250 MM
Miscellaneous Information:
• Best viewed from boat

ORIENT POINT "COFFEE POT" LIGHTHOUSE
Body of Water: Long Island Sound
Near: Greenport, NY
Lat & Long: 41.1634, -72.2234
National Park Service Inventory
First Lit: 1899
Height & Type: 45 ft caisson
Focal Plane: 64 ft fp
Current Lens Information: 190 MM
Miscellaneous Information:
• USCG added solar panels and batteries (2000)

OSWEGO (HARBOR) WEST PIERHEAD LIGHTHOUSE

Body of Water: Lake Ontario
Near: Oswego, NY
Lat & Long: 43.4736, -76.5169
National Park Service Inventory
First Lit: 1934
Height & Type: 57 ft tower with house
Focal Plane: 57 ft fp
Current Lens Information: VRB-25
Miscellaneous Information:
- Transferred to City of Oswego
- Fresnel lens displayed at H Lee White Marine Museum

PLUM ISLAND (PLUM GUT) LIGHTHOUSE

Body of Water: Long Island Sound
Near: Greenport, NY
Lat & Long: 41.1736, -72.2114
National Park Service Inventory
First Lit: 1870
Height & Type: 55 ft tower with house
Focal Plane: 69 ft fp
Current Lens Information: none
Miscellaneous Information:
- WLTL
- Owned by Homeland Security
Volunteer & Contribution Information:
www.eastendlighthouses.org

POINT AU ROCHE (AUX ROCHES) LIGHTHOUSE

Body of Water: Lake Champlain
Near: Plattsburgh, NY
Lat & Long: 44.7994, -73.3601
National Park Service Inventory
First Lit: 1858
Height & Type: 50 ft tower
Focal Plane: 59 ft fp
Current Lens Information: 250 MM
Miscellaneous Information:
- Property privately owned
- Tower owned by USCG

PRINCES (PRINCESS) BAY LIGHTHOUSE

Body of Water: New York Bay
Near: Staten Island, NY
Lat & Long: 40.5076, -74.2133
National Park Service Inventory
First Lit: 1864
Height & Type: 106 ft skeleton – black
Focal Plane: 106 ft fp
Miscellaneous Information:
- Located on Mt. Loretto Unique Area

RACE ROCK LIGHTHOUSE

Body of Water: Long Island Sound
Near: Groton, CT
Lat & Long: 41.2434, -72.0466
National Park Service Inventory
First Lit: 1879
Height & Type: 45 ft tower with house
Focal Plane: 67 ft fp
Current Lens Information: DCB-24
Miscellaneous Information:
- Best viewed from boat

ROCK ISLAND LIGHTHOUSE

Body of Water: Lake Ontario / St Lawrence River
Near: Alexandria, NY
Lat & Long: 44.2802, -76.0166
National Park Service Inventory
First Lit: 1882
Height & Type: 40 ft tower
Focal Plane: 40 ft fp
Current Lens Information: none
Miscellaneous Information:
- Owned by NY Office of Parks and Historic Preservation
Volunteer & Contribution Information:
www.rockislandlighthouse.org

RONDOUT CREEK (KINGSTON) LIGHTHOUSE

Body of Water: Hudson River
Near: Kingston, NY
Lat & Long: 41.9217, -73.9633
National Park Service Inventory
First Lit: 1915
Height & Type: 48 ft tower
Focal Plane: 52 ft fp

Current Lens Information: 250 MM
Miscellaneous Information:
- Tours available (June–August)
Volunteer & Contribution Information:
www.hrmm.org (tour info)

SANDS POINT LIGHTHOUSE

Body of Water: Long Island Sound
Near: North Hempstead, NY
Lat & Long: 40.8659, -73.7294
National Park Service Inventory
First Lit: 1809
Height & Type: 65 ft tower brownstone
Focal Plane: 68 ft fp
Current Lens Information: fourth order Fresnel
Miscellaneous Information:
- Privately owned
- Third oldest lighthouse in NY

SAUGERTIES LIGHTHOUSE

Body of Water: Hudson River
Near: Saugerties, NY
Lat & Long: 42.0716, -73.93
National Park Service Inventory
First Lit: 1869
Height & Type: 46 ft tower
Focal Plane: 42 ft fp
Miscellaneous Information:
- Bed & breakfast
Volunteer & Contribution Information:
www.saugertieslighthouse.com (general info)

SELKIRK (SALMON RIVER) LIGHTHOUSE

Body of Water: Lake Ontario / Salmon River
Near: Pulaski, NY
Lat & Long: 43.5742, -76.2019
National Park Service Inventory
First Lit: 1838
Height & Type: 32 ft tower with house
Focal Plane: 49 ft fp
Current Lens Information: 190 MM
Miscellaneous Information:
- Can be rented for overnight stays
- "Birdcage" lantern room

SHINNECOCK (GREAT WEST BAY) (PONQUOGUE POINT) LIGHTHOUSE

Body of Water: Atlantic Ocean
Near: Hampton Bays, NY
Lat & Long: 40.8505, -72.5041
First Lit: 1858
Height & Type: ruins (160 ft tower) oil house remains
Miscellaneous Information:
• Demolished by USCG (1948)

SISTERS ISLAND (THREE SISTERS ISLAND) LIGHTHOUSE

Body of Water: St Lawrence River
Near: Alexandria Bay, NY
Lat & Long: 44.414, -75.8446
National Park Service Inventory
First Lit: 1870
Height & Type: 60 ft tower with house
Miscellaneous Information:
• Privately owned
• Can be viewed from boat

SODUS OUTER (SODUS BAY WEST PIER) LIGHTHOUSE

Body of Water: Lake Ontario / Sodus Bay
Near: Sodus Point, NY
Lat & Long: 43.2772, -76.9741
National Park Service Inventory
First Lit: 1938
Height & Type: 50 ft tower
Focal Plane: 51 ft fp
Miscellaneous Information:
• Current cast iron tower replaced original wooden one (built 1858)

SODUS POINT (SODUS BAY) LIGHTHOUSE

Body of Water: Lake Ontario / Sodus Bay
Near: Sodus Point, NY
Lat & Long: 43.27259, -76.98608
National Park Service Inventory
First Lit: 1871
Height & Type: 45 ft tower
Focal Plane: 70 ft fp
Current Lens Information: third & half order Fresnel

Miscellaneous Information:
• Museum
Volunteer & Contribution Information:
www.soduspointlighthouse.org

Sodus Point (Sodus Bay) Lighthouse, New York

SOUTH BUFFALO (HARBOR SOUTH ENTRANCE) LIGHTHOUSE
Body of Water: Lake Erie
Near: Buffalo, NY
Lat & Long: 42.8337, -78.8673
National Park Service Inventory
First Lit: 1903
Height & Type: 43.5 ft tower
Current Lens Information: none
Miscellaneous Information:
• Relocated from Buffalo Harbor South Entrance

SPLIT ROCK LIGHTHOUSE
Body of Water: Lake Champlain
Near: Plattsburgh, NY
Lat & Long: 44.2676, -73.3226
National Park Service Inventory
First Lit: 1867
Height & Type: 39 ft tower
Focal Plane: 100 ft fp
Miscellaneous Information:
• Privately owned
• Deactivated (1934) relit (2003)

STATEN ISLAND RANGE (REAR) LIGHTHOUSE
Body of Water: New York Harbor
Near: Staten Island, NY
Lat & Long: 40.5762, -74.1409
National Park Service Inventory
First Lit: 1912
Height & Type: 90 ft tower
Focal Plane: 231 ft fp
Current Lens Information: second order
Miscellaneous Information:
• Privately owned

STATUE OF LIBERTY LIGHTHOUSE
Body of Water: New York Harbor
Near: Manhattan, NY
Lat & Long: 40.6897, -74.0446
National Park Service Inventory
First Lit: 1886
Height & Type: 305 ft tower – former lighthouse

Miscellaneous Information:
• First use of electricity in lighthouse (1886)

STEPPING STONES LIGHTHOUSE
Body of Water: Long Island Sound
Near: Kings Point, NY
Lat & Long: 40.8247, -73.7748
National Park Service Inventory
First Lit: 1877
Height & Type: 38 ft tower with house
Focal Plane: 46 ft fp
Current Lens Information: 300 MM
Miscellaneous Information:
• Can be seen from Throgs Neck Bridge but best viewed from boat

STONY POINT (HENDERSON) LIGHTHOUSE
Body of Water: Lake Ontario
Near: Henderson, NY
Lat & Long: 43.8391, -76.2985
National Park Service Inventory
First Lit: 1869
Height & Type: 73 ft square tower with house
Current Lens Information: none
Miscellaneous Information:
• Privately owned

STONY POINT (HUDSON RIVER) LIGHTHOUSE
Body of Water: Hudson River
Near: Kingston, NY
Lat & Long: 41.2416, -73.97
National Park Service Inventory
First Lit: 1826
Height & Type: 30 ft tower
Focal Plane: 22 ft fp
Current Lens Information: fourth order Fresnel SP
Miscellaneous Information:
• Restored and relit (1995)
Volunteer & Contribution Information:
www2.lhric.org/spbattle/spbattle.htm

SUNKEN ROCK LIGHTHOUSE
Body of Water: St Lawrence River
Near: Alexandria Bay, NY
Lat & Long: 44.337444, -75.918428
National Park Service Inventory
First Lit: 1884
Height & Type: 30 ft conical tower -white/green
Current Lens Information: sixth order Fresnel
Miscellaneous Information:
• Can be viewed from Alexandria Bay's downtown waterfront

TARRYTOWN (KINGSLAND POINT) LIGHTHOUSE
Body of Water: Hudson River
Near: Sleepy Hollow, NY
Lat & Long: 41.08468, -73.87481
National Park Service Inventory
First Lit: 1883
Height & Type: 60 ft caisson – white/red/black
Focal Plane: 56 ft fp
Miscellaneous Information:
• Open for group tours (by appointment)
Volunteer & Contribution Information:
www.hudsonlights.com (general info)

THIRTY MILE POINT LIGHTHOUSE
Body of Water: Lake Ontario - Niagara River
Near: Somerset, NY
Lat & Long: 43.3747, -78.4861
National Park Service Inventory
First Lit: 1876
Height & Type: 61 ft tower with house
Focal Plane: 71 ft fp
Miscellaneous Information:
• 1994 USPS stamp
• Located in Golden Hill State Park

THROGS NECK LIGHTHOUSE
Body of Water: Long Island Sound
Near: Bronx, NY
Lat & Long: 40.805, -73.7916
First Lit: 1906
Height & Type: 56 ft navigation aid

Miscellaneous Information:
- Only keeper's house remains
- Owned by SUNY Maritime College

TIBBETTS POINT LIGHTHOUSE
Body of Water: Lake Ontario - St Lawrence River
Near: Cape Vincent, NY
Lat & Long: 44.1005, -76.37
National Park Service Inventory
First Lit: 1854
Height & Type: 58 ft tower
Focal Plane: 69 ft fp
Current Lens Information: fourth order Fresnel
Miscellaneous Information:
- Hostel accommodations available on lighthouse property
Volunteer & Contribution Information:
www.capevincent.org

TITANTIC MEMORIAL LIGHTHOUSE
Body of Water: New York Harbor
Near: Manhattan, NY
Lat & Long: 40.7074, -74.0042
Height & Type: 60 ft tower
Miscellaneous Information:
- Donated to and relocated at South Street Seaport Museum (1965)

VERONA BEACH LIGHTHOUSE
Body of Water: Oneida Lake
Near: Verona, NY
Lat & Long: 43.1894, -75.7317
Height & Type: 85 ft tower
Miscellaneous Information:
- Being renovated by Verona Beach Lighthouse Association
Volunteer & Contribution Information:
www.townverona.org

WEST BANK (STATEN ISLAND RANGE FRONT) LIGHTHOUSE
Body of Water: New York Harbor
Near: Staten Island, NY
Lat & Long: 40.5384, -74.0433
National Park Service Inventory
First Lit: 1901
Height & Type: 55 ft caisson – brown

Focal Plane: 69 ft fp
Current Lens Information: 300 MM
Miscellaneous Information:
- Privately owned
- Best viewed from boat

North Carolina

BALD HEAD ISLAND "OLD BALDY" LIGHTHOUSE
Body of Water: Cape Fear River
Near: Southport, NC
Lat & Long: 33.8736, -78.0004
National Park Service Inventory
First Lit: 1817
Height & Type: 100 ft tower
Focal Plane: 110 ft fp
Miscellaneous Information:
- Accessible by ferry
Volunteer & Contribution Information:
www.oldbaldy.org

Bald Head Island "Old Baldy"
Lighthouse, North Carolina

BODIE ISLAND LIGHTHOUSE
Body of Water: Atlantic Ocean
Near: Nags Head, NC
Lat & Long: 35.8185, -75.5633
National Park Service Inventory
First Lit: 1872
Height & Type: 170 ft tower – black/white
Focal Plane: 156 ft fp
Current Lens Information: first order Fresnel
Miscellaneous Information:
  • DDL
  • Pronounced: "body"
Volunteer & Contribution Information:
  www.outerbankslighthousesociety.org

CAPE FEAR LIGHTHOUSE
Body of Water: Atlantic Ocean
Near: Southport, NC
Lat & Long: 33.8459, -77.9677
Height & Type: ruins
Miscellaneous Information:
  • Located on Bald Head Island
Volunteer & Contribution Information:
  www.outerbankslighthousesociety.org

CAPE HATTERAS LIGHTHOUSE
Body of Water: Atlantic Ocean
Near: Buxton, NC
Lat & Long: 35.2501, -75.5295
National Park Service Inventory
First Lit: 1870
Height & Type: 197 ft tower – black/white
Focal Plane: 192 ft fp
Current Lens Information: DCB-224 rotating
Miscellaneous Information:
  • Tallest U.S. lighthouse (268 steps)
  • 1990 USPS stamp
  • Spiral-striped day mark
Volunteer & Contribution Information:
  www.outerbankslighthousesociety.org

CAPE LOOKOUT LIGHTHOUSE
Body of Water: Atlantic Ocean
Near: Beaufort, NC
Lat & Long: 34.6226, -76.5247

National Park Service Inventory
First Lit: 1859
Height & Type: 169 ft tower – black/white
Focal Plane: 156 ft fp
Miscellaneous Information:
  • 2002 USPS stamp
  • Diamond-patterned day mark
Volunteer & Contribution Information:
  www.outerbankslighthousesociety.org

CURRITUCK BEACH LIGHTHOUSE
Body of Water: Atlantic Ocean
Near: Corolla, NC
Lat & Long: 36.3767, -75.83
National Park Service Inventory
First Lit: 1875
Height & Type: 162 ft tower – brick
Focal Plane: 158 ft fp
Current Lens Information: first order Fresnel
Miscellaneous Information:
  • Northernmost Outer Banks lighthouse
Volunteer & Contribution Information:
  www.outerbankslighthousesociety.org

DIAMOND SHOAL LIGHTHOUSE
Body of Water: Atlantic Ocean
Near: Buxton, NC
Lat & Long: 35.333333, -75.5
National Park Service Inventory
First Lit: 1966
Height & Type: 175 ft tower
Miscellaneous Information:
  • Light failed (2001)
  • Tower unsafe for repairs
  • Replaced with buoy

FRYING PAN SHOALS LIGHTHOUSE
Body of Water: Atlantic Ocean
Near: Southport, NC
Lat & Long: 33.80083, -77.94722
Height & Type: 125 ft "Texas" tower
Miscellaneous Information:
  • Accessible only by boat
  • Replaced by floating buoy (2003)

OAK ISLAND LIGHTHOUSE
Body of Water: Atlantic Ocean
Near: Caswell Beach, NC
Lat & Long: 33.8929, -78.0351
National Park Service Inventory
First Lit: 1958
Height & Type: 169 ft tower black/white/gray
Miscellaneous Information:
  • Newest (1958) and most powerful US lighthouse
Volunteer & Contribution Information:
  www.outerbankslighthousesociety.org

OCRACOKE LIGHTHOUSE
Body of Water: Atlantic Ocean
Near: Ocracoke, NC
Lat & Long: 35.109, -75.986
National Park Service Inventory
First Lit: 1823
Height & Type: 65 ft tower
Focal Plane: 75 ft fp
Current Lens Information: fourth order Fresnel
Miscellaneous Information:
  • Accessible by ferry
  • Repainted and repaired (2009)
Volunteer & Contribution Information:
  www.outerbankslighthousesociety.org

PRICES CREEK LIGHTHOUSE
Body of Water: Cape Fear River
Near: Southport, NC
Lat & Long: 33.936, -77.9896
First Lit: 1849
Height & Type: base only – no lantern room
Miscellaneous Information:
  • DDL
  • Inactive since 1861
  • Located on private property
Volunteer & Contribution Information:
  www.outerbankslighthousesociety.org

ROANOKE MARSHES LIGHTHOUSE
Body of Water: Roanoke Sound
Near: Manteo, NC
Lat & Long: 35.90813, -75.66819

Height & Type: tower with house - 1877 replica
Current Lens Information: fifth order Fresnel
Miscellaneous Information:
- Collapsed attempting to move it on shore (1995)

Volunteer & Contribution Information:
www.manteo.govoffice.com (general info)

ROANOKE RIVER LIGHTHOUSE

Body of Water: Albemarle Sound
Near: Edenton, NC
Lat & Long: 36.05956, -76.61669
National Park Service Inventory
First Lit: 1903
Height & Type: 75 ft tower with house
Focal Plane: 35 ft fp
Current Lens Information: fourth order Fresnel
Miscellaneous Information:
- WLTL original screwpile - relocated to Colonial Park (2007)

Volunteer & Contribution Information:
www.edentonhistoricalcommission.org

ROANOKE RIVER LIGHTHOUSE (REPLICA)

Body of Water: Albemarle Sound
Near: Plymouth, NC
Lat & Long: 35.8666, -76.7523
Height & Type: replica
Miscellaneous Information:
- Museum
- Owned by Town of Plymouth

Volunteer & Contribution Information:
www.roanokeriverlighthouse.org (general info)

Ohio

ASHTABULA LIGHTHOUSE

Body of Water: Lake Erie
Near: Ashtabula, OH
Lat & Long: 41.9183, -80.7966
National Park Service Inventory
First Lit: 1905
Height & Type: 40 ft tower

Focal Plane: 51 ft fp
Miscellaneous Information:
- Difficult (uneven) breakwater

Volunteer & Contribution Information:
www.ashtabulalighthouse.com

CEDAR POINT LIGHTHOUSE

Body of Water: Lake Erie
Near: Sandusky, OH
Lat & Long: 41.4882, -82.69378
First Lit: 1867
Height & Type: square wood tower with house
Miscellaneous Information:
- Restored (2000-2001)
- Owned by Cedar Point Amusement Park

CELINA LIGHTHOUSE

Body of Water: Grand Lake
Near: Celina, OH
Lat & Long: 40.5441, -84.5706
First Lit: 1986
Height & Type: 40 ft tower
Focal Plane: 50 ft fp
Miscellaneous Information:
- Owned by City of Celina

CLEVELAND EAST ENTRANCE LIGHTHOUSE

Body of Water: Lake Erie
Near: Cleveland, OH
Lat & Long: 41.54316, -81.6516
Height & Type: 31 ft tower – white & red
Miscellaneous Information:
- "D9"

CLEVELAND HARBOR EAST PIERHEAD LIGHTHOUSE

Body of Water: Lake Erie
Near: Cleveland, OH
Lat & Long: 41.5102, -81.7155
National Park Service Inventory
First Lit: 1911
Height & Type: 25 ft tower
Focal Plane: 31 ft fp
Current Lens Information: 300 MM SP
Miscellaneous Information:
- Sold privately (2008)

CLEVELAND HARBOR (WEST PIERHEAD) MAIN ENTRANCE LIGHTHOUSE

Body of Water: Lake Erie
Near: Cleveland, OH
Lat & Long: 41.5089, -81.7176
National Park Service Inventory
First Lit: 1911
Height & Type: 67 ft tower with house
Focal Plane: 63 ft fp
Current Lens Information: 300 MM
Miscellaneous Information:
- Fresnel lens displayed at Great Lakes Science Center

CONNEAUT (RIVER) WEST BREAKWATER LIGHTHOUSE

Body of Water: Lake Erie
Near: Conneaut, OH
Lat & Long: 41.9794, -80.5584
First Lit: 1906
Height & Type: 60 ft square tower – white & black
Focal Plane: 80 ft fp
Current Lens Information: 375 MM
Miscellaneous Information:
- Sold privately (2008)

FAIRPORT HARBOR (GRAND RIVER) LIGHTHOUSE

Body of Water: Lake Erie
Near: Fairport, OH
Lat & Long: 41.757, -81.2773
National Park Service Inventory
First Lit: 1871
Height & Type: 69 ft tower
Focal Plane: 102 ft fp
Current Lens Information: third order Fresnel
Miscellaneous Information:
- Museum

Volunteer & Contribution Information:
www.ncweb.com/org/fhlh

FAIRPORT HARBOR WEST BREAKWATER LIGHTHOUSE

Body of Water: Lake Erie
Near: Fairport, OH
Lat & Long: 41.7679, -81.2811
National Park Service Inventory
First Lit: 1925
Height & Type: 42 ft square tower
Focal Plane: 56 ft fp
Current Lens Information: 300 MM
Miscellaneous Information:
• Sold privately (2009)

Fairport Harbor West
Breakwater Lighthouse, Ohio

GREEN ISLAND LIGHTHOUSE
Body of Water: Lake Erie
Near: Port Clinton, OH
Lat & Long: 41.645, -82.8683
First Lit: 1865
Height & Type: ruins – skeleton only
Focal Plane: 57 ft fp
Miscellaneous Information:
  • DDL
  • Bird sanctuary managed by Ohio Division
  of Wildlife

HURON HARBOR LIGHTHOUSE
Body of Water: Lake Erie
Near: Huron, OH
Lat & Long: 41.399, -82.5465
National Park Service Inventory
First Lit: 1936
Height & Type: 72 ft tower
Focal Plane: 80 ft fp
Current Lens Information: 375 MM
Miscellaneous Information:
  • Ohio's tallest lighthouse

LORAIN HARBOR (EAST BREAKWATER) LIGHTHOUSE
Body of Water: Lake Erie
Near: Lorain, OH
Lat & Long: 41.4766, -82.19
First Lit: 1965
Height & Type: 55 ft tower
Focal Plane: 60 ft fp
Miscellaneous Information:
  • Can be viewed from behind water
  treatment plant on Oberlin Street

LORAIN HARBOR (WEST HARBOR BREAKWATER) LIGHTHOUSE
Body of Water: Lake Erie
Near: Lorain, OH
Lat & Long: 41.4766, -82.19
National Park Service Inventory
First Lit: 1917
Height & Type: 51 ft tower with house
Focal Plane: 60 ft fp

Miscellaneous Information:
  • Best viewed from boat
  • Owned by Port of Lorain Foundation
Volunteer & Contribution Information:
  www.lorainlighthouse.com

MANHATTAN RANGE REAR LIGHTHOUSE
Body of Water: Lake Erie
Near: Northriver, OH
Lat & Long: 41.677, -83.4982
First Lit: 1918
Height & Type: 20 ft tower on stilts
Focal Plane: 105 ft fp
Miscellaneous Information:
  • Two lights unceremoniously removed
  (1980s)
  • Both relocated

MARBLEHEAD (SANDUSKY BAY) LIGHTHOUSE
Body of Water: Lake Erie
Near: Marblehead, OH
Lat & Long: 41.5364, -82.7115
National Park Service Inventory
First Lit: 1821
Height & Type: 65 ft tower
Focal Plane: 67 ft fp
Miscellaneous Information:
  • 1994 USPS stamp
  • Oldest continuously operating Great Lakes
  lighthouse
Volunteer & Contribution Information:
  www.marbleheadlighthouseohio.org

NORTHWOOD (EDDYSTONE) LIGHTHOUSE
Body of Water: Grand Lake
Near: Northmoor, OH
Lat & Long: 40.5437, -84.4815
Height & Type: 50 ft tower
Miscellaneous Information:
  • Privately owned & on private property
  • Best viewed from boat

PERRY MEMORIAL LIGHTHOUSE
Body of Water: Lake Erie
Near: Port Clinton, OH

Lat & Long: 41.6542, -82.81151
First Lit: 1915
Height & Type: 352 ft tower
Focal Plane: 335 ft fp
Miscellaneous Information:
  • Accessible by ferry
  • Tallest US aid to navigation

PORT CLINTON LIGHTHOUSE
Body of Water: Lake Erie
Near: Port Clinton, OH
Lat & Long: 41.5162, -82.9477
First Lit: 1896
Height & Type: 20 ft tower
Focal Plane: 70 ft fp
Miscellaneous Information:
  • Owned by Brands' Marina

SOUTH BASS ISLAND LIGHTHOUSE
Body of Water: Lake Erie
Near: Port Clinton, OH
Lat & Long: 41.6286, -82.8417
National Park Service Inventory
First Lit: 1897
Height & Type: 60 ft square tower with house
Focal Plane: 74 ft fp
Current Lens Information: none
Miscellaneous Information:
  • Owned by Ohio State University
  • Best views from boat or ferry

TOLEDO HARBOR LIGHTHOUSE
Body of Water: Lake Erie
Near: Toledo, OH
Lat & Long: 41.7618, -83.3286
National Park Service Inventory
First Lit: 1904
Height & Type: 69 ft tower with house
Focal Plane: 72 ft fp
Miscellaneous Information:
  • Fresnel lens displayed at Maumee Bay
  State Park Lodge
Volunteer & Contribution Information:
  www.toledoharborlighthouse.org

Turtle Island Lighthouse
Body of Water: Lake Erie
Near: Point Place, OH
Lat & Long: 41.7525, -83.391
Height & Type: tower without lantern room
Miscellaneous Information:
- DDL
- Privately owned
- Best viewed from boat

Vermilion Lighthouse
Body of Water: Lake Erie
Near: Vermillion, OH
Lat & Long: 41.4245, -82.3666
First Lit: 1992
Height & Type: 16 ft tower (replica) – white & red
Focal Plane: 35 ft fp
Current Lens Information: fifth order Fresnel
Miscellaneous Information:
- Replica of 1877 light
- Maintained by Inland Seas Maritime Museum

Volunteer & Contribution Information:
www.inlandseas.org

West Sister Island Lighthouse
Body of Water: Lake Erie
Near: Toledo, OH
Lat & Long: 41.7364, -83.1102
First Lit: 1848
Height & Type: 55 ft tower
Focal Plane: 57 ft fp
Current Lens Information: 300 MM
Miscellaneous Information:
- WLTL
- Part of West Sister Island National Wildlife Refuge

Oregon

Cape Arago (Cape Gregory) Lighthouse
Body of Water: Coos Bay
Near: Coos Bay, OR
Lat & Long: 43.3415, -124.3754
National Park Service Inventory
First Lit: 1934
Height & Type: 44 ft tower with house
Focal Plane: 100 ft fp
Current Lens Information: VRB-25 SP
Miscellaneous Information:
- Owned by Confederated tribes of Coos, Lower Umpqua and Siuslaw Indians since 2008

Cape Blanco Lighthouse
Body of Water: Pacific Ocean
Near: Port Orford, OR
Lat & Long: 42.8373, -124.5628
National Park Service Inventory
First Lit: 1870
Height & Type: 59 ft tower with house
Focal Plane: 245 ft fp
Current Lens Information: second order Fresnel
Miscellaneous Information:
- Oldest continuously operating Oregon lighthouse

Volunteer & Contribution Information:
www.portorfordoregon.com/Friends

Cape Meares Lighthouse
Body of Water: Tillamook Bay
Near: Tillamook, OR
Lat & Long: 45.4864, -123.9781
National Park Service Inventory
First Lit: 1890
Height & Type: 38 ft tower
Focal Plane: 217 ft fp
Current Lens Information: first order Fresnel
Miscellaneous Information:
- All four bulls eyes were stolen from Fresnel lens
- Three have been recovered

Volunteer & Contribution Information:
www.capemeareslighthouse.org

Cleft of the Rock (Cape Perpetua) Lighthouse
Body of Water: Pacific Ocean
Near: Yachats, OR
Lat & Long: 44.2816, -124.1119
First Lit: 1976
Height & Type: 35 ft square tower with house
Focal Plane: 110 ft fp
Miscellaneous Information:
- Privately owned
- Can be seen from Highway 101

Coquille River (Bandon) Lighthouse
Body of Water: Coquille River
Near: Bandon, OR
Lat & Long: 43.1222, -124.4234
National Park Service Inventory
First Lit: 1896
Height & Type: 40 ft tower with house
Focal Plane: 47 ft fp
Current Lens Information: second and half order Fresnel
Miscellaneous Information:
- Owned by Oregon State Parks
- Located in Bullards Beach State Park

Heceta Head Lighthouse
Body of Water: Pacific Ocean
Near: Yachats, OR
Lat & Long: 44.1373, -124.1284
National Park Service Inventory
First Lit: 1894
Height & Type: 56 ft tower
Focal Plane: 205 ft fp
Current Lens Information: first order Fresnel
Miscellaneous Information:
- Bed & breakfast

Volunteer & Contribution Information:
www.hecetalighthouse.com (general info)

Columbia Lightship
Body of Water: Columbia River
Near: Astoria, OR

Lat & Long: 46.1904, -123.8242
First Lit: 1950
Height & Type: lightship
Current Lens Information: duplex 550 MM electric
Miscellaneous Information:
- WAL-604
- Museum
- Owned by Columbia River Maritime Museum

PELICAN BAY (PORT OF BROOKINGS) LIGHTHOUSE
Body of Water: Pacific Ocean
Near: Brookings, OR
Lat & Long: 42.46583, -122.08139
First Lit: 1999
Height & Type: 35 ft tower with house (faux)
Focal Plane: 141 ft fp
Miscellaneous Information:
- Privately owned
- Newest US lighthouse

TILLAMOOK ROCK LIGHTHOUSE
Body of Water: Pacific Ocean
Near: Cannon Beach, OR
Lat & Long: 45.9375, -124.019
National Park Service Inventory
First Lit: 1881
Height & Type: 62 ft tower
Focal Plane: 133 ft fp
Current Lens Information: first order Fresnel
Miscellaneous Information:
- Can be seen from Ecola State Park
- Owned by Eternity at Sea Columbarium

UMPQUA RIVER LIGHTHOUSE
Body of Water: Pacific Ocean
Near: Reedsport, OR
Lat & Long: 43.6615, -124.1984
National Park Service Inventory
First Lit: 1894
Height & Type: 61 ft tower
Focal Plane: 165 ft fp
Current Lens Information: first order Fresnel

Miscellaneous Information:
- Beautiful red/white lens
- 2006 USPS stamp

WARRIOR ROCK LIGHTHOUSE
Body of Water: Columbia River
Near: St Helens, OR
Lat & Long: 45.8484, -122.7884
Height & Type: 40 ft tower
Focal Plane: 28 ft fp
Miscellaneous Information:
- Accessible by boat or a six-mile round-trip hike

YAQUINA BAY LIGHTHOUSE
Body of Water: Yaquina Bay
Near: Newport, OR
Lat & Long: 44.624, -124.063
National Park Service Inventory
First Lit: 1871
Height & Type: 51 ft tower with house
Focal Plane: 161 ft fp
Current Lens Information: 250 MM
Miscellaneous Information:
- Museum
- Yaquina Bay State Park
Volunteer & Contribution Information:
www.yaquinalights.org

YAQUINA HEAD (FOULWEATHER) LIGHTHOUSE
Body of Water: Pacific Ocean
Near: Newport, OR
Lat & Long: 44.6767, -124.08
National Park Service Inventory
First Lit: 1873
Height & Type: 93 ft tower
Focal Plane: 162 ft fp
Current Lens Information: first order Fresnel
Miscellaneous Information:
- Oregon's tallest lighthouse
Volunteer & Contribution Information:
www.yaquinalights.org

Yaquina Bay Lighthouse, Oregon

Pennsylvania

Erie Land (Old Presque Isle) Lighthouse
Body of Water: Erie Harbor
Near: Erie, PA
Lat & Long: 42.1442, -80.0621
National Park Service Inventory
First Lit: 1867
Height & Type: 49 ft tower
Focal Plane: 128 ft fp
Current Lens Information: none
Miscellaneous Information:
- Lens and lantern room removed and transferred to Ohio's Marblehead Lighthouse (1901)

Presque Isle Lighthouse
Body of Water: Lake Erie
Near: Erie, PA
Lat & Long: 42.1659, -80.1153
National Park Service Inventory
First Lit: 1873
Height & Type: 68 ft tower with house
Focal Plane: 73 ft fp
Current Lens Information: 300 MM
Miscellaneous Information:
- Located in Presque Isle State Park

Presque Isle (Erie Harbor) North Pierhead Lighthouse
Body of Water: Lake Erie
Near: Erie, PA
Lat & Long: 42.1567, -80.0716
First Lit: 1858
Height & Type: 34 ft square tower – black/white bands
Focal Plane: 42 ft fp
Miscellaneous Information:
- Located at Presque Isle Peninsula's eastern point

Turtle Rock Lighthouse
Body of Water: Schuylkill River
Near: Philadelphia, PA
Lat & Long: 39.97, -75.1898
First Lit: 1887
Height & Type: 30 ft tower
Miscellaneous Information:
- Owned by The Sedgeley Club
- Can be rented for private functions

Rhode Island

Beavertail Lighthouse
Body of Water: Narragansett Bay
Near: Jamestown, RI
Lat & Long: 41.44944, -71.39894
National Park Service Inventory
First Lit: 1856
Height & Type: 45 ft square tower
Focal Plane: 64 ft fp
Current Lens Information: DCB-24
Miscellaneous Information:
- Fourth-order Fresnel lens displayed in Beavertail Lighthouse Museum (in assistant keeper's dwelling)
Volunteer & Contribution Information: www.beavertaillight.org

Block Island North Lighthouse
Body of Water: Atlantic Ocean
Near: New Shoreham, RI
Lat & Long: 41.22751, -71.57606
National Park Service Inventory
First Lit: 1867
Height & Type: 55 ft tower with house
Focal Plane: 61 ft fp
Current Lens Information: DCB-24
Miscellaneous Information:
- Accessible by ferry

Block Island Southeast Lighthouse
Body of Water: Atlantic Ocean
Near: New Shoreham, RI
Lat & Long: 41.16247, -71.55198
National Park Service Inventory
First Lit: 1875
Height & Type: 52 ft tower with house
Focal Plane: 261 ft fp
Current Lens Information: first order Fresnel
Miscellaneous Information:
- Museum
- Accessible by ferry
- Moved and relit (1993-94)

Bristol Ferry Lighthouse
Body of Water: Mount Hope River
Near: Bristol, RI
Lat & Long: 41.64287, -71.2603
National Park Service Inventory
First Lit: 1855
Height & Type: 34 ft square tower
Focal Plane: 35 ft fp
Current Lens Information: none
Miscellaneous Information:
- Privately owned
- Tower raised six feet (1916)

Castle Hill Lighthouse
Body of Water: Narragansett Bay
Near: Newport, RI
Lat & Long: 41.46211, -71.36294
National Park Service Inventory
First Lit: 1890
Height & Type: 34 ft conical tower
Focal Plane: 40 ft fp
Current Lens Information: 300 MM
Miscellaneous Information:
- Emits an alternating red light

CONANICUT ISLAND LIGHTHOUSE
Body of Water: Narragansett Bay
Near: Jamestown, RI
Lat & Long: 41.5733, -71.73144
National Park Service Inventory
First Lit: 1886
Height & Type: 42 ft square tower without lantern room -red
Focal Plane: 47 ft fp
Current Lens Information: none
Miscellaneous Information:
• Privately owned
• Best viewed from boat

CONIMICUT SHOAL LIGHTHOUSE
Body of Water: Narragansett Bay
Near: Warwick, RI
Lat & Long: 41.71646, -71.34521
National Park Service Inventory
First Lit: 1883
Height & Type: 58 ft caisson
Focal Plane: 55 ft fp
Current Lens Information: 250 MM
Miscellaneous Information:
• Can be distantly viewed from Conimicut Point Park

DUTCH ISLAND LIGHTHOUSE
Body of Water: Narragansett Bay
Near: Jamestown, RI
Lat & Long: 41.49722, -71.40433
National Park Service Inventory
First Lit: 1857
Height & Type: 42 ft square tower
Focal Plane: 56 ft fp
Current Lens Information: none
Miscellaneous Information:
• DDL
• Land owned by Rhode Island Department of Environmental Management
Volunteer & Contribution Information:
www.dutchislandlighthouse.org

HOG ISLAND SHOAL LIGHTHOUSE
Body of Water: Narragansett Bay
Near: Portsmouth, RI
Lat & Long: 41.63166, -71.27329
National Park Service Inventory
First Lit: 1901
Height & Type: 60 ft caisson
Focal Plane: 54 ft fp
Current Lens Information: 250 MM
Miscellaneous Information:
• Best viewed from boat
• Sold privately (2006)

IDA LEWIS (LIME) ROCK LIGHTHOUSE
Body of Water: Narragansett Bay
Near: Newport, RI
Lat & Long: 41.47777, -71.32582
National Park Service Inventory
First Lit: 1854
Height & Type: 13 ft tower
Focal Plane: 30 ft fp
Current Lens Information: none
Miscellaneous Information:
• Privately owned Yacht Club
• Original sixth order Fresnel inside

NAYATT POINT LIGHTHOUSE
Body of Water: Providence River
Near: Barrington, RI
Lat & Long: 41.72535, -71.33869
National Park Service Inventory
First Lit: 1856
Height & Type: 25 ft square tower
Focal Plane: 31 ft fp
Current Lens Information: none
Miscellaneous Information:
• Privately owned

NEWPORT HARBOR (GOAT ISLAND) LIGHTHOUSE
Body of Water: Narragansett Bay
Near: Newport, RI
Lat & Long: 41.49307, -71.32719
National Park Service Inventory
First Lit: 1865
Height & Type: 35 ft tower
Focal Plane: 33 ft fp
Current Lens Information: 250 MM
Miscellaneous Information:
• Can be viewed near the Hyatt Regency Hotel
Volunteer & Contribution Information:
www.lighthousefoundation.org

PLUM BEACH LIGHTHOUSE
Body of Water: Narragansett Bay
Near: North Kingstown, RI
Lat & Long: 41.53035, -71.40529
National Park Service Inventory
First Lit: 1899
Height & Type: 53 ft caisson – red/white/black
Focal Plane: 54 ft fp
Current Lens Information: fourth order Fresnel
Miscellaneous Information:
• Best viewed from boat
Volunteer & Contribution Information:
www.plumbeachlighthouse.org

POINT JUDITH LIGHTHOUSE
Body of Water: Narragansett Bay
Near: Narragansett, RI
Lat & Long: 41.36095, -71.481476
National Park Service Inventory
First Lit: 1857
Height & Type: 51 ft tower – white/brown
Focal Plane: 65 ft fp
Current Lens Information: fourth order Fresnel
Miscellaneous Information:
   • Original rotating fourth order Fresnel lens
   was replaced with another (fixed) one (1907)

Point Judith Lighthouse,
Rhode Island

POMHAM ROCKS LIGHTHOUSE

Body of Water: Providence River
Near: East Providence, RI
Lat & Long: 41.7773, -71.3673
National Park Service Inventory
First Lit: 1871
Height & Type: 40 ft tower with house
Focal Plane: 54 ft fp
Current Lens Information: 250 MM
Miscellaneous Information:
- Original sixth order Fresnel lens emitted red light

Volunteer & Contribution Information:
www.lighthousefoundation.org

POPLAR POINT LIGHTHOUSE

Body of Water: Narragansett Bay
Near: North Kingstown, RI
Lat & Long: 41.5711, -71.4393
National Park Service Inventory
First Lit: 1831
Height & Type: square tower with house
Focal Plane: 48 ft fp
Current Lens Information: none
Miscellaneous Information:
- Privately owned
- One of few surviving American wooden towers

PRUDENCE ISLAND (SANDY POINT) LIGHTHOUSE

Body of Water: Narragansett Bay
Near: Prudence, RI
Lat & Long: 41.6059, -71.3037
National Park Service Inventory
First Lit: 1823
Height & Type: 30 ft tower
Focal Plane: 28 ft fp
Current Lens Information: 250 MM
Miscellaneous Information:
- Oldest Rhode Island lighthouse
- Moved from Goat Island

Volunteer & Contribution Information:
www.prudenceconservancy.org

Point Judith Lighthouse,
Rhode Island

Rose Island Lighthouse
Body of Water: Narragansett Bay
Near: Newport, RI
Lat & Long: 41.49585, -71.34213
National Park Service Inventory
First Lit: 1870
Height & Type: 35 ft square tower with house
Focal Plane: 48 ft fp
Miscellaneous Information:
- Museum
- Overnight stays are available

Volunteer & Contribution Information:
www.roseislandlighthouse.org

Sakonnet Lighthouse
Body of Water: Atlantic Ocean
Near: Little Compton, RI
Lat & Long: 41.45323, -71.2026
National Park Service Inventory
First Lit: 1884
Height & Type: 66 ft caisson
Focal Plane: 70 ft fp
Miscellaneous Information:
- Deactivated (1955) relit (1997)

Volunteer & Contribution Information:
www.sakonnetlighthouse.org

Warwick Lighthouse
Body of Water: Narragansett Bay
Near: Warwick, RI
Lat & Long: 41.6672, -71.3784
National Park Service Inventory
First Lit: 1932
Height & Type: 51 ft tower
Focal Plane: 66 ft fp
Current Lens Information: 250 MM – green
Miscellaneous Information:
- Moved (1939) when hurricane caused it to be at the water's edge

Watch Hill Lighthouse
Body of Water: Fishers Island Sound
Near: Watch Hill, RI
Lat & Long: 41.3034, -71.8583
National Park Service Inventory
First Lit: 1857

Height & Type: 45 ft tower
Focal Plane: 61 ft fp
Current Lens Information: VRB-25
Miscellaneous Information:
- Museum – emits red and white signal

South Carolina

Bloody Point Range Front Lighthouse
Body of Water: Atlantic Ocean
Near: Daufuskie Island, SC
Lat & Long: 32.0968, -80.8723
National Park Service Inventory
First Lit: 1883
Height & Type: house – dormer window
Miscellaneous Information:
- Privately owned
- Accessible by boat or ferry

Cape Romain Lighthouse
Body of Water: Atlantic Ocean
Near: McClellanville, SC
Lat & Long: 33.01872, -79.3739
National Park Service Inventory
First Lit: 1958
Height & Type: 150 ft tower – black/white
Focal Plane: 161 ft fp
Current Lens Information: none
Miscellaneous Information:
- Tower leans
- First order Fresnel lens installed
- WLTL

Cape Romain Lighthouse
Body of Water: Atlantic Ocean
Near: McClellanville, SC
Lat & Long: 33.01872, -79.3739
First Lit: n/a
Height & Type: ruins (65 ft tower without lantern room)
Current Lens Information: none
Miscellaneous Information:
- Can only be viewed from boat
- Part of Cape Romain National Wildlife Refuge
- WLTL

Cape Romain Lighthouse,
South Carolina, with ruins behind it

CHARLESTON (SULLIVANS ISLAND) LIGHTHOUSE
Body of Water: Charleston Harbor
Near: Sullivans Island, SC
Lat & Long: 32.7578, -79.8429
National Park Service Inventory
First Lit: 1962
Height & Type: 140 ft tower
Focal Plane: 163 ft fp
Current Lens Information: DCB-24
Miscellaneous Information:
- Last U.S. lighthouse built by government
- Unique triangle shape

GEORGETOWN (NORTH ISLAND) LIGHTHOUSE
Body of Water: Atlantic Ocean
Near: Georgetown, SC
Lat & Long: 33.2233, -79.185
National Park Service Inventory
First Lit: 1867
Height & Type: 87 ft tower
Focal Plane: 85 ft fp
Current Lens Information: VRB-25 SP
Miscellaneous Information:
- Original tower lit (1812)
- Best viewed from boat

GOVERNORS LIGHTHOUSE
Body of Water: Little River
Near: North Myrtle Beach, SC
Lat & Long: 33.860, -78.637
First Lit: 1985
Height & Type: 50 ft tower – black/white (faux)
Miscellaneous Information:
- Privately owned
- Located in Lightkeepers Village and Marina

HAIG POINT (DAUFUSKIE ISLAND) LIGHTHOUSE
Body of Water: Caliboque Sound
Near: Daufuskie Island, SC
Lat & Long: 32.145, -80.8366
National Park Service Inventory
First Lit: 1873
Height & Type: square tower with house
Focal Plane: 70 ft fp

Miscellaneous Information:
- Privately owned – located in private community

HARBOUR TOWN LIGHTHOUSE
Body of Water: Atlantic Ocean
Near: Hilton Head, SC
Lat & Long: 32.13898, -80.81238
First Lit: 1970
Height & Type: 90 ft tower – red/white
Focal Plane: 90 ft fp
Miscellaneous Information:
- Privately financed building
- **National Park Service Inventory** "significant unmanned aid"
Volunteer & Contribution Information:
www.seapines.com (general info)

HILTON HEAD RANGE REAR (LEAMINGTON) LIGHTHOUSE
Body of Water: Atlantic Ocean
Near: Hilton Head, SC
Lat & Long: 32.1644, -80.7398
First Lit: 1880
Height & Type: 94 ft skeleton
Focal Plane: 136 ft fp
Miscellaneous Information:
- Located on Arthur Hills Golf Course at Palmetto Dunes Resort

HUNTING ISLAND LIGHTHOUSE
Body of Water: Atlantic Ocean
Near: Beaufort, SC
Lat & Long: 32.37499, -80.43829
National Park Service Inventory
First Lit: 1875
Height & Type: 136 ft tower – black/white
Focal Plane: 140 ft fp
Miscellaneous Information:
- WLTL
- Tower located only 400 feet from shore
- Reactivated (1995)
Volunteer & Contribution Information:
www.huntingisland.com (general info)

MORRIS ISLAND (OLD CHARLESTON) LIGHTHOUSE
Body of Water: Atlantic Ocean
Near: Folly Beach, SC
Lat & Long: 32.6895, -79.883
National Park Service Inventory
First Lit: 1876
Height & Type: 161 ft tower – black/white stripes
Focal Plane: 158 ft fp
Miscellaneous Information:
- DDL
- 2002 USPS stamp
- Being renovated by Save The Light
Volunteer & Contribution Information:
www.savethelight.org

PARRIS ISLAND LIGHTHOUSE
Body of Water: Atlantic Ocean
Near: Port Royal, SC
Lat & Long: 32.3129, -80.6774
First Lit: n/a
Height & Type: ruins (131 ft skeleton)
Current Lens Information: none
Miscellaneous Information:
- Oil house only
- Located at Marine Corps Recruit Depot

Texas

ARANSAS PASS (LYDIA ANN) LIGHTHOUSE
Body of Water: Gulf of Mexico
Near: Aransas Pass, TX
Lat & Long: 27.8635, -97.0564
National Park Service Inventory
First Lit: 1857
Height & Type: 68 ft octagon tower – brick
Miscellaneous Information:
- Best viewed from boat
- Privately owned

BOLIVAR POINT LIGHTHOUSE
Body of Water: Gulf of Mexico
Near: Port Bolivar, TX
Lat & Long: 29.36661, -94.76718
National Park Service Inventory
First Lit: 1872
Height & Type: 116 ft tower – black
Current Lens Information: none
Miscellaneous Information:
- WLTL
- Privately owned
- Original third order Fresnel at the Smithsonian Museum

GALVESTON (SOUTH) JETTY LIGHTHOUSE
Body of Water: Gulf of Mexico
Near: Galveston, TX
Lat & Long: 29.3297, -94.7074
National Park Service Inventory
First Lit: 1918
Height & Type: ruins - (84 ft tower)
Current Lens Information: none
Miscellaneous Information:
- Tower toppled in 2000 storm
- Fresnel lens displayed at Galveston County Historical Museum

HALF MOON REEF LIGHTHOUSE
Body of Water: Matagorda Bay
Near: Port Lavaca, TX
Lat & Long: 28.6349, -96.6187
National Park Service Inventory
First Lit: 1858
Height & Type: 45 ft screwpile
Current Lens Information: none
Miscellaneous Information:
- Located next to Port Lavaca's Bauer Community Center

MATAGORDA ISLAND LIGHTHOUSE
Body of Water: Matagorda Bay
Near: Port Lavaca, TX
Lat & Long: 28.3417, -96.431

National Park Service Inventory
First Lit: 1852
Height & Type: 79 ft tower – black
Focal Plane: 90 ft fp
Current Lens Information: 250 MM
Miscellaneous Information:
- Original Fresnel lens displayed at Calhoun County Museum

POINT ISABEL (PORT ISABEL) LIGHTHOUSE
Body of Water: Gulf of Mexico
Near: Port Isabel, TX
Lat & Long: 26.0777, -97.2075
National Park Service Inventory
First Lit: 1853
Height & Type: 57 ft tower
Focal Plane: 82 ft fp
Current Lens Information: none
Miscellaneous Information:
- Owned by Texas Parks and Wildlife

SABINE BANK LIGHTHOUSE
Body of Water: Sabine River
Near: Port Arthur, TX
Lat & Long: 29.7345, -93.8934
National Park Service Inventory
First Lit: 1906
Height & Type: 72 ft caisson
Focal Plane: 72 ft fp
Current Lens Information: 190 MM
Miscellaneous Information:
- Refurbished top at Lions Park in Sabine Pass

Vermont

BURLINGTON BREAKWATER NORTH LIGHTHOUSE
Body of Water: Lake Champlain
Near: Burlington, VT
Lat & Long: 44.4802, -73.2298
First Lit: 2003

Height & Type: 35 ft tower
Focal Plane: 35 ft fp
Miscellaneous Information:
- Replica built and lit (2003)
- **National Park Service Inventory** "significant unmanned aid"
Volunteer & Contribution Information:
www.cedoburlington.org/waterfront/lighthouse

BURLINGTON BREAKWATER SOUTH LIGHTHOUSE
Body of Water: Lake Champlain
Near: Burlington, VT
Lat & Long: 44.4694, -73.2258
First Lit: 2003
Height & Type: 26 ft tower
Focal Plane: 12 ft fp
Miscellaneous Information:
- Replica built and lit (2003)
Volunteer & Contribution Information:
www.cedoburlington.org/waterfront/lighthouse

COLCHESTER REEF LIGHTHOUSE
Body of Water: Lake Champlain
Near: Shelburne, VT
Lat & Long: 44.3733, -73.2306
National Park Service Inventory
First Lit: 1871
Height & Type: 35 ft tower with house
Current Lens Information: sixth order Fresnel (inactive)
Miscellaneous Information:
- Renovated in 2009
- Museum
- Relocated from Lake Champlain
Volunteer & Contribution Information:
www.shelburnemuseum.org

ISLE LA MOTTE LIGHTHOUSE
Body of Water: Lake Champlain
Near: Isle La Motte, VT
Lat & Long: 44.90657, -73.34328
National Park Service Inventory
First Lit: 1881

Height & Type: 25 ft tower – pink
Focal Plane: 46 ft fp
Current Lens Information: 300 MM
Miscellaneous Information:
• Privately owned
• Best viewed from boat

JUNIPER ISLAND LIGHTHOUSE
Body of Water: Lake Champlain
Near: Burlington, VT
Lat & Long: 44.4502, -73.2762
National Park Service Inventory
First Lit: 1846
Height & Type: 25 ft tower
Focal Plane: 93 ft fp
Current Lens Information: none
Miscellaneous Information:
• Privately owned
• Best viewed from boat

WINDMILL POINT LIGHTHOUSE
Body of Water: Lake Champlain
Near: Alburg, VT
Lat & Long: 44.98361, -73.4058
National Park Service Inventory
First Lit: 1858
Height & Type: 40 ft stone tower
Focal Plane: 52 ft fp
Current Lens Information: 300 MM
Miscellaneous Information:
• Privately owned
• Relit (2002)

Virginia

ASSATEAGUE ISLAND LIGHTHOUSE
Body of Water: Atlantic Ocean
Near: Chincoteague, VA
Lat & Long: 37.9117, -75.3567
National Park Service Inventory
First Lit: 1867
Height & Type: 142 ft tower – red/white
Focal Plane: 154 ft fp

Current Lens Information: DCB-224
Miscellaneous Information:
• Open every Friday and Saturday (from Easter to Thanksgiving)

CAPE CHARLES LIGHTHOUSE
Body of Water: Atlantic Ocean
Near: Cape Charles, VA
Lat & Long: 37.1233, -75.9067
National Park Service Inventory
First Lit: 1895
Height & Type: 191 ft skeleton – white
Focal Plane: 180 ft fp
Current Lens Information: 190 MM SP
Miscellaneous Information:
• Tallest Virginia lighthouse

CHESAPEAKE LIGHTHOUSE
Body of Water: Chesapeake Bay
Near: Virginia Beach, VA
Lat & Long: 37.06941, -75.79073
National Park Service Inventory
First Lit: 1965
Height & Type: 120 ft "Texas" tower
Miscellaneous Information:
• Used by University of Maryland, Baltimore County for research projects (2002-2003)

JONES POINT LIGHTHOUSE
Body of Water: Chesapeake Bay
Near: Alexandria, VA
Lat & Long: 38.7904, -77.0408
National Park Service Inventory
First Lit: 1856
Height & Type: 20 ft tower with house
Current Lens Information: 155 MM
Miscellaneous Information:
• Northernmost lighthouse in VA

JORDAN POINT REAR RANGE LIGHTHOUSE
Body of Water: James River
Near: Hopewell, VA
Lat & Long: 37.3132, -77.2234
First Lit: 1941
Height & Type: 35 ft skeleton tower

Miscellaneous Information:
• Two previous wooden towers were built on this site

NEW CAPE HENRY LIGHTHOUSE
Body of Water: Chesapeake Bay
Near: Virginia Beach, VA
Lat & Long: 36.9265, -76.0074
National Park Service Inventory
First Lit: 1881
Height & Type: 163 ft tower – black/white alternating stripes
Focal Plane: 164 ft fp
Current Lens Information: first order Fresnel
Miscellaneous Information:
• Southernmost Virginia lighthouse

NEW POINT COMFORT LIGHTHOUSE
Body of Water: Mobjack Bay
Near: Yorktown, VA
Lat & Long: 37.3054, -76.2782
National Park Service Inventory
First Lit: 1806
Height & Type: 58 ft tower
Focal Plane: 56 ft fp
Current Lens Information: none
Miscellaneous Information:
• DDL
• Best viewed from water
• Owned by Matthews County

NEWPORT NEWS MIDDLE GROUND LIGHTHOUSE
Body of Water: Chesapeake Bay
Near: Newport News, VA
Lat & Long: 36.9452, -76.3919
National Park Service Inventory
First Lit: 1891
Height & Type: 35 ft caisson – red
Focal Plane: 52 ft fp
Current Lens Information: 375 MM
Miscellaneous Information:
• Sold privately (2005)
• Best viewed from boat

OLD CAPE HENRY LIGHTHOUSE
Body of Water: Chesapeake Bay
Near: Virginia Beach, VA
Lat & Long: 36.9258, -76.0083
National Park Service Inventory
First Lit: 1792
Height & Type: 90 ft tower
Focal Plane: 72 ft fp
Current Lens Information: none
Miscellaneous Information:
• First US lighthouse built by federal government
• 2002 USPS stamp
Volunteer & Contribution Information:
www.apva.org

Old Cape Henry Lighthouse,
Virginia

OLD PLANTATION FLATS LIGHTHOUSE
Body of Water: Chesapeake Bay
Near: Cape Charles, VA
Lat & Long:
First Lit: 2005
Height & Type: screw pile (replica) original lighthouse demolished in 1962
Miscellaneous Information:
  • Privately owned by Bay Creek Resort and Club

OLD POINT COMFORT LIGHTHOUSE
Body of Water: Chesapeake Bay
Near: Hampton, VA
Lat & Long: 37.0017, -76.3064
National Park Service Inventory
First Lit: 1802
Height & Type: 54 ft tower
Focal Plane: 54 ft fp
Current Lens Information: fourth order Fresnel
Miscellaneous Information:
  • Remained undisturbed during the Civil War

PORTSMOUTH LIGHTSHIP
Body of Water: Chesapeake Bay
Near: Portsmouth, VA
Lat & Long: 36.837, -76.2967
First Lit: 1916
Height & Type: lightship
Current Lens Information: 500 MM
Miscellaneous Information:
  • LV-101 WAL-524
  • Museum
Volunteer & Contribution Information:
  www.portsnavalmuseums.com (general info)

RAPPAHANNOCK SHOAL CHANNEL SOUTH RANGE REAR LIGHTHOUSE
Body of Water: Chesapeake Bay
Near: Cape Charles, VA
Lat & Long: 37.534167, -76.0025
First Lit: 1991
Height & Type: 224 ft skeleton (built on caisson)
Current Lens Information: Fresnel lens built in 2004

Miscellaneous Information:
  • Second tallest US aid to navigation

SMITH POINT LIGHTHOUSE
Body of Water: Potomac River
Near: Reedville, VA
Lat & Long: 37.8802, -76.1833
National Park Service Inventory
First Lit: 1897
Height & Type: 35 ft caisson
Focal Plane: 52 ft fp
Current Lens Information: DCB-24
Miscellaneous Information:
  • Best viewed from boat

STINGRAY POINT LIGHTHOUSE
Body of Water: Chesapeake Bay
Near: Deltaville, VA
Lat & Long: 37.560833, -76.306667
First Lit: 2003
Height & Type: screw pile (replica)
Miscellaneous Information:
  • Museum
  • Owned by Stingray Harbor Marina
Volunteer & Contribution Information:
  www.stingrayharbor.com (general info)

THIMBLE SHOAL LIGHTHOUSE
Body of Water: Chesapeake Bay
Near: Hampton, VA
Lat & Long: 37.0145, -76.2404
National Park Service Inventory
First Lit: 1914
Height & Type: 40 ft caisson – red
Focal Plane: 55 ft fp
Current Lens Information: RB-355 SP
Miscellaneous Information:
  • Sold privately (2005)
  • Best viewed from boat

WOLF TRAP LIGHTHOUSE
Body of Water: Chesapeake Bay
Near: Cape Charles, VA
Lat & Long: 37.3904, -76.1897

National Park Service Inventory
First Lit: 1894
Height & Type: 52 ft caisson – red
Focal Plane: 52 ft fp
Current Lens Information: VRB-25 SP
Miscellaneous Information:
  • Privately owned since (2005)
  • Restoration began (2007)

Washington

ADMIRALTY HEAD LIGHTHOUSE
Body of Water: Puget Sound
Near: Coupeville, WA
Lat & Long: 48.15702, -122.67943
National Park Service Inventory
First Lit: 1903
Height & Type: 30 ft tower
Focal Plane: 127 ft fp
Current Lens Information: none
Miscellaneous Information:
  • Museum
  • 1990 USPS stamp
Volunteer & Contribution Information:
  www.admiraltyhead.wsu.edu

ALKI POINT LIGHTHOUSE
Body of Water: Puget Sound
Near: Seattle, WA
Lat & Long: 47.5762, -122.4206
National Park Service Inventory
First Lit: 1913
Height & Type: 37 ft tower
Focal Plane: 39 ft fp
Current Lens Information: VRB-25
Miscellaneous Information:
  • Open on weekends (June - August)
  • "Alki" is the Washington State motto; a Chinook word meaning "by and by"

BROWNS POINT LIGHTHOUSE
Body of Water: Puget Sound
Near: Tacoma, WA
Lat & Long: 47.3059, -122.444

National Park Service Inventory
First Lit: 1933
Height & Type: 34 ft tower
Focal Plane: 38 ft fp
Current Lens Information: VRB-25
Miscellaneous Information:
• Keeper's dwelling available for weekly rentals
Volunteer & Contribution Information:
www.pnehs.dreamhosters.com/lighthouse (general info)

BURROWS ISLAND LIGHTHOUSE
Body of Water: Bellingham Bay
Near: Oak Harbor, WA
Lat & Long: 48.4781, -122.7134
National Park Service Inventory
First Lit: 1906
Height & Type: 34 ft tower with house
Focal Plane: 57 ft fp
Current Lens Information: 300 MM
Miscellaneous Information:
• Best viewed from boat

BUSH POINT LIGHTHOUSE
Body of Water: Puget Sound
Near: Freeland, WA
Lat & Long: 48.0309, -122.6071
First Lit: 1933
Height & Type: 20 ft tower without lantern room
Focal Plane: 25 ft fp
Miscellaneous Information:
• Owned by USCG – grounds and tower closed to public

CAPE DISAPPOINTMENT LIGHTHOUSE
Body of Water: Columbia River
Near: Ilwaco, WA
Lat & Long: 46.2756, -124.0518
National Park Service Inventory
First Lit: 1856
Height & Type: 53 ft tower – black/white
Focal Plane: 220 ft fp
Current Lens Information: fourth order Fresnel

Miscellaneous Information:
• Original first order Fresnel lens displayed at Lewis and Clark Interpretive Center
Volunteer & Contribution Information:
www.funbeach.com/attractions/lighthouse.html (general info)

CAPE FLATTERY LIGHTHOUSE
Body of Water: Pacific Ocean
Near: Port Angeles, WA
Lat & Long: 48.3917, -124.7366
National Park Service Inventory
First Lit: 1857
Height & Type: 65 ft tower with house
Focal Plane: 165 ft fp
Current Lens Information: VRB-25
Miscellaneous Information:
• Ownership transferred to Makah tribe who own the island (2009)

CATTLE POINT LIGHTHOUSE
Body of Water: Friday Harbor
Near: Friday Harbor, WA
Lat & Long: 48.5404, -122.9634
First Lit: 1935
Height & Type: 34 ft tower without lantern room
Focal Plane: 94 ft fp
Miscellaneous Information:
• **National Park Service Inventory** "significant unmanned aid"
• Accessible by ferry

DESTRUCTION ISLAND LIGHTHOUSE
Body of Water: Pacific Ocean
Near: Forks, WA
Lat & Long: 47.6752, -124.4868
National Park Service Inventory
First Lit: 1891
Height & Type: 94 ft tower
Focal Plane: 147 ft fp
Current Lens Information: VRB-25
Miscellaneous Information:
• USCG switched off the light for good (2008)

DIMICK LIGHTHOUSE
Body of Water: Puget Sound
Near: Port Townsend, WA
Lat & Long: 48.11057, -122.7676
First Lit: 1990
Height & Type: 50 ft tower with house – faux
Miscellaneous Information:
• Privately built and owned replica of the 1906 Mukilteo

DOFFLEMYER (DOFFLEMEYER) POINT LIGHTHOUSE
Body of Water: Puget Sound
Near: Olympia, WA
Lat & Long: 47.1404, -122.907
First Lit: 1934
Height & Type: 30 ft tower
Miscellaneous Information:
• **National Park Service Inventory** "significant unmanned aid"

EDIZ HOOK LIGHTHOUSE
Body of Water: Puget Sound
Near: Port Angeles, WA
Lat & Long: 48.11274, -123.42693
First Lit: 1908
Height & Type: house without tower
Miscellaneous Information:
• Original lighthouse relocated to 4th & Albert Streets
• Privately owned

GIG HARBOR LIGHTHOUSE
Body of Water: Puget Sound
Near: Gig Harbor, WA
Lat & Long: 47.3266, -122.5748
First Lit: 1989
Height & Type: 15 ft square tower
Focal Plane: 13 ft fp
Miscellaneous Information:
• Emits a red flashing light
• To raise funds, public purchased time capsules placed in the lighthouse

GRAYS HARBOR LIGHTHOUSE
Body of Water: Pacific Ocean
Near: Westport, WA
Lat & Long: 46.888216 -124.116914
National Park Service Inventory
First Lit: 1898
Height & Type: 107 ft tower
Focal Plane: 123 ft fp
Current Lens Information: FA-251
Miscellaneous Information:
- 2006 USPS stamp
- Tallest Washington lighthouse

Volunteer & Contribution Information:
www.westportwa.com/museum

Lightship name: Swiftsure LIGHTHOUSE
Body of Water: Puget Sound
Near: Seattle, WA
Lat & Long: 47.6275, -122.3383
First Lit: 1904
Height & Type: lightship
Miscellaneous Information:
- LV-83 WAL-508
- Museum
- Oldest remaining lightship

Volunteer & Contribution Information:
www.nwseaport.org

LIME KILN LIGHTHOUSE
Body of Water: Puget Sound
Near: Friday Harbor, WA
Lat & Long: 48.5159, -123.1524
National Park Service Inventory
First Lit: 1919
Height & Type: 38 ft tower with house
Focal Plane: 55 ft fp
Current Lens Information: VRB-25
Miscellaneous Information:
- Accessible by Washington state ferry

MARROWSTONE POINT LIGHTHOUSE
Body of Water: Puget Sound
Near: Port Townsend, WA
Lat & Long: 48.1018, -122.6879
National Park Service Inventory
First Lit: 1912

Height & Type: 28 ft tower
Focal Plane: 28 ft fp
Current Lens Information: 250 MM
Miscellaneous Information:
- Located in Fort Flagler State Park

MUKILTEO LIGHTHOUSE
Body of Water: Puget Sound
Near: Mukilteo, WA
Lat & Long: 47.9487, -122.306
National Park Service Inventory
First Lit: 1906
Height & Type: 30 ft tower
Focal Plane: 33 ft fp
Current Lens Information: fourth order Fresnel
Miscellaneous Information:
- Two Fresnel lenses are here (one from Desdemona Sands Light)

Volunteer & Contribution Information:
www.mukilteohistorical.org

NEW DUNGENESS LIGHTHOUSE
Body of Water: Puget Sound
Near: Sequim, WA
Lat & Long: 48.18174, -123.10962
National Park Service Inventory
First Lit: 1857
Height & Type: 63 ft tower
Focal Plane: 67 ft fp
Current Lens Information: VRB-25
Miscellaneous Information:
- Keepers Program provides weekly accommodations for work

Volunteer & Contribution Information:
www.newdungenesslighthouse.com

NORTH HEAD LIGHTHOUSE
Body of Water: Pacific Ocean
Near: Ilwaco, WA
Lat & Long: 46.299, -124.0785
National Park Service Inventory
First Lit: 1898
Height & Type: 65 ft tower
Focal Plane: 194 ft fp
Current Lens Information: VRB-25

Miscellaneous Information:
- Keepers house (just inland from the lighthouse) offers vacation rentals

Volunteer & Contribution Information:
www.funbeach.com/attractions/lighthouse-northhead.html (general info)

PATOS ISLAND LIGHTHOUSE
Body of Water: Puget Sound
Near: Eastsound, WA
Lat & Long: 48.789, -122.9715
National Park Service Inventory
First Lit: 1908
Height & Type: 35 ft tower with house
Focal Plane: 52 ft fp
Current Lens Information: 300 MM SP
Miscellaneous Information:
- Best viewed from boat

POINT NO POINT LIGHTHOUSE
Body of Water: Puget Sound
Near: Hansville, WA
Lat & Long: 47.9123, -122.5267
National Park Service Inventory
First Lit: 1879
Height & Type: 30 ft tower with house
Focal Plane: 27 ft fp
Current Lens Information: fourth order Fresnel
Miscellaneous Information:
- Headquarters of US Lighthouse Society
- Keeper's house available as vacation rental

Volunteer & Contribution Information:
www.uslhs.org

POINT ROBINSON LIGHTHOUSE
Body of Water: Puget Sound
Near: Vashon Island, WA
Lat & Long: 47.3881, -122.3746
National Park Service Inventory
First Lit: 1915
Height & Type: 40 ft tower
Focal Plane: 40 ft fp
Current Lens Information: fifth order Fresnel
Miscellaneous Information:
- Accessible by Vashon Island ferry

Point Robinson
Lighthouse,
Washington

POINT WILSON LIGHTHOUSE
Body of Water: Puget Sound
Near: Port Townsend, WA
Lat & Long: 48.1442, -122.7551
National Park Service Inventory
First Lit: 1914
Height & Type: 46 ft tower/house
Focal Plane: 51 ft fp
Current Lens Information: fourth order Fresnel
Miscellaneous Information:
- Located in Fort Wilson State Park
- Is shown in the movie "An Officer and a Gentleman"

SKUNK BAY LIGHTHOUSE
Body of Water: Puget Sound
Near: Hansville, WA
Lat & Long: 47.92, -122.5696
First Lit: 1964
Height & Type: 30 ft octagon tower
Focal Plane: 210 ft fp
Miscellaneous Information:
- Privately owned
- Lantern room salvaged from Smith Island Lighthouse

SLIP POINT LIGHTHOUSE
Body of Water: Puget Sound
Near: Port Angeles, WA
Lat & Long: 48.2645, -124.251
First Lit: 1916
Height & Type: keeper's dwelling only
Miscellaneous Information:
- House and land owned by Clallam County who make erect a replica

TURN POINT LIGHTHOUSE
Body of Water: Puget Sound
Near: Sidney Canada, WA
Lat & Long: 48.68877, -123.23725
National Park Service Inventory
First Lit: 1936
Height & Type: 44 ft tower
Focal Plane: 44 ft fp
Current Lens Information: 300 MM

Miscellaneous Information:
- From public dock there's a two-mile hike to the lighthouse
Volunteer & Contribution Information:
www.tplps.org

WEST POINT LIGHTHOUSE
Body of Water: Puget Sound
Near: Seattle, WA
Lat & Long: 47.6619, -122.4355
National Park Service Inventory
First Lit: 1881
Height & Type: 23 ft tower with house
Focal Plane: 27 ft fp
Current Lens Information: fourth order
Miscellaneous Information:
- Located in Discovery Park

Wisconsin

ALGOMA PIERHEAD LIGHTHOUSE
Body of Water: Lake Michigan
Near: Algoma, WI
Lat & Long: 44.6074, -87.4292
National Park Service Inventory
First Lit: 1932
Height & Type: 48 ft tower – red
Focal Plane: 42 ft fp
Current Lens Information: fifth order Fresnel
Miscellaneous Information:
- Located on a detached breakwater good views possible from land

ASHLAND HARBOR BREAKWATER LIGHTHOUSE
Body of Water: Lake Superior
Near: Ashland, WI
Lat & Long: 46.6285, -90.8697
National Park Service Inventory
First Lit: 1915
Height & Type: 58 ft tower
Focal Plane: 60 ft fp
Current Lens Information: 250 MM SP

Miscellaneous Information:
- Can be viewed from Bayview Park

ASYLUM POINT LIGHTHOUSE
Body of Water: Lake Winnebago
Near: Oshkosh, WI
Lat & Long: 44.0626, -88.5159
First Lit: 1937
Height & Type: 30 ft stone tower
Miscellaneous Information:
- Owned by Winnebago County

BAILEYS HARBOR LIGHTHOUSE
Body of Water: Lake Michigan
Near: Baileys Harbor, WI
Lat & Long: 45.0513, -87.0955
National Park Service Inventory
First Lit: 1853
Height & Type: 21 ft tower
Focal Plane: 21 ft fp
Current Lens Information: none
Miscellaneous Information:
- DDL
- Privately owned

BAILEYS HARBOR RANGE LIGHTHOUSE
Body of Water: Lake Michigan
Near: Baileys Harbor, WI
Lat & Long: 45.07, -87.12
First Lit: 1870
Height & Type: 35 ft tower with house
Focal Plane: 39 ft fp
Miscellaneous Information:
- Tower was equipped with window that directed beam to the lake
Volunteer & Contribution Information:
www.ridgessanctuary.org/rangelights

BOYER BLUFF LIGHTHOUSE
Body of Water: Lake Michigan
Near: Marinette, WI
Lat & Long: 45.42, -86.9364
Height & Type: 80 ft skeleton
Focal Plane: 220 ft fp

Miscellaneous Information:
- Accessible by ferry
- Highest Great Lakes focal plane

BRAYS POINT (ROCKWELL) LIGHTHOUSE
Body of Water: Lake Winnebago
Near: Oshkosh, WI
Lat & Long: 44.0075, -88.52
First Lit: 1909
Height & Type: 42 ft octagon tower (faux)
Miscellaneous Information:
- Privately owned
- Located at Lake St & Bay Shore Drive

CALUMET HARBOR (COLUMBIA HARBOR) LIGHTHOUSE
Body of Water: Lake Winnebago
Near: Pipe, WI
Lat & Long: 43.9147, -88.3322
First Lit: 1936
Height & Type: 70 ft skeleton
Miscellaneous Information:
- Tower restored and re-opened for climbing (1992)

CANA ISLAND LIGHTHOUSE
Body of Water: Lake Michigan
Near: Baileys Harbor, WI
Lat & Long: 45.0883, -87.0466
National Park Service Inventory
First Lit: 1869
Height & Type: 81 ft tower
Focal Plane: 89 ft fp
Current Lens Information: third order
Miscellaneous Information:
- Damaged exterior was encased in steel (1902)
- Museum
Volunteer & Contribution Information:
www.dcmm.org

Cana Island Lighthouse, Wisconsin

CHAMBERS ISLAND LIGHTHOUSE
Body of Water: Lake Michigan
Near: Menominee, WI
Lat & Long: 45.2025, -87.3647
National Park Service Inventory
First Lit: 1868
Height & Type: 67 ft tower without lantern room – yellow
Focal Plane: 68 ft fp
Current Lens Information: none
Miscellaneous Information:
 • Located in Gibraltar Township Park

CHEQUAMEGON POINT LIGHTHOUSE
Body of Water: Lake Superior
Near: Washburn, WI
Lat & Long: 46.7283, -90.8093
First Lit: 1896
Height & Type: 35 ft tower
Focal Plane: 42 ft fp
Current Lens Information: none
Miscellaneous Information:
 • Best viewed from boat
 • Moved 150 feet from shoreline & replaced by D9 cylindrical tower (1987)

DEVILS ISLAND LIGHTHOUSE
Body of Water: Lake Superior
Near: Washburn, WI
Lat & Long: 47.08, -90.7283
National Park Service Inventory
First Lit: 1898
Height & Type: 71 ft tower
Focal Plane: 100 ft fp
Current Lens Information: third order Fresnel
Miscellaneous Information:
 • Winds caused tower to shake violently so external braces were added (1914)

DUNLAP REEF RANGE REAR LIGHTHOUSE
Body of Water: Lake Michigan
Near: Sturgeon Bay, WI
Lat & Long: 44.8321, -87.3727
First Lit: 1881
Height & Type: square tower with house

Miscellaneous Information:
 • Privately owned
 • Relocated to 400 S 4th Ave (w/o square tower on roof)

EAGLE BLUFF LIGHTHOUSE
Body of Water: Lake Michigan
Near: Fish Creek, WI
Lat & Long: 45.1683, -87.2367
National Park Service Inventory
First Lit: 1868
Height & Type: 43 ft tower
Focal Plane: 75 ft fp
Current Lens Information: 300 MM SP
Miscellaneous Information:
 • Restored by Door County Historical Society
 • Museum
Volunteer & Contribution Information:
 www.eagleblufflighthouse.org

FISHERMANS ROAD LIGHTHOUSE
Body of Water: Lake Winnebago
Near: Fond du Lac, WI
Lat & Long: 43.8737, -88.3617
Height & Type: 25 ft hourglass tower
Miscellaneous Information:
 • Moved from its location next to Calumet Harbor (c. 2001)

FOND DU LAC (LAKESIDE PARK) LIGHTHOUSE
Body of Water: Lake Winnebago
Near: Fond du Lac, WI
Lat & Long: 43.7977, -88.4372
First Lit: 1933
Height & Type: 56 ft octagon tower (faux)
Miscellaneous Information:
 • Renovated (1966)

GRASSY ISLAND RANGE FRONT LIGHTHOUSE
Body of Water: Lake Michigan
Near: Green Bay, WI
Lat & Long: 44.5366, -88.0029
First Lit: 1872
Height & Type: 26 ft square tower – being renovated

Focal Plane: 27 ft fp
Current Lens Information: none
Miscellaneous Information:
 • Owned, moved and restored by Grassy Range Yacht Club

GRASSY ISLAND RANGE REAR LIGHTHOUSE
Body of Water: Lake Michigan
Near: Green Bay, WI
Lat & Long: 44.5366, -88.0029
First Lit: 1872
Height & Type: 36 ft square tower
Focal Plane: 35 ft fp
Current Lens Information: none
Miscellaneous Information:
 • Owned, moved and restored by Grassy Range Yacht Club

GREEN BAY HARBOR ENTRANCE LIGHTHOUSE
Body of Water: Lake Michigan
Near: Green Bay, WI
Lat & Long: 44.6533, -87.9016
First Lit: 1935
Height & Type: tower – crib
Focal Plane: 72 ft fp
Miscellaneous Information:
 • Best viewed from boat
 • **National Park Service Inventory** "significant unmanned aid"

GREEN ISLAND LIGHTHOUSE
Body of Water: Lake Michigan
Near: Marinette, WI
Lat & Long: 45.057, -87.4937
First Lit: 1956
Height & Type: 65 ft skeleton – black
Focal Plane: 80 ft fp
Miscellaneous Information:
 • Privately owned island
 • Best viewed by boat

GULL ISLAND LIGHTHOUSE
Body of Water: Lake Superior
Near: Bayfield, WI
Lat & Long: 46.9066, -90.4433

First Lit: 1928
Height & Type: ruins – skeleton only
Current Lens Information: none
Miscellaneous Information:
- Best viewed by boat

KENOSHA (SOUTHPORT) LIGHTHOUSE
Body of Water: Lake Michigan
Near: Kenosha, WI
Lat & Long: 42.5893, -87.8152
National Park Service Inventory
First Lit: 1866
Height & Type: 55 ft tower
Focal Plane: 74 ft fp
Current Lens Information: 300 MM
Miscellaneous Information:
- Owned by City of Kenosha
Volunteer & Contribution Information:
www.kenoshahistorycenter.org

KENOSHA PIERHEAD LIGHTHOUSE
Body of Water: Lake Michigan
Near: Kenosha, WI
Lat & Long: 42.5888, -87.8086
First Lit: 1931
Height & Type: 50 ft tower – red
Focal Plane: 50 ft fp
Current Lens Information: 250 MM
Miscellaneous Information:
- **National Park Service Inventory** "significant unmanned aid"

KEVICH LIGHTHOUSE
Body of Water: Lake Michigan
Near: Grafton, WI
Lat & Long: 43.3233, -87.8883
First Lit: 1981
Height & Type: 50 ft tower
Focal Plane: 163 ft fp
Miscellaneous Information:
- Privately owned

KEWAUNEE PIERHEAD LIGHTHOUSE
Body of Water: Lake Michigan
Near: Kewaunee, WI
Lat & Long: 44.4581, -87.4906

National Park Service Inventory
First Lit: 1931
Height & Type: 43 ft tower with house
Focal Plane: 45 ft fp
Current Lens Information: fifth order Fresnel
Miscellaneous Information:
- Declared excess
- PETA expressed interest in ownership

LA POINTE (LONG ISLAND) LIGHTHOUSE
Body of Water: Lake Superior
Near: Bayfield, WI
Lat & Long: 46.7289, -90.7851
National Park Service Inventory
First Lit: 1896
Height & Type: 65 ft skeleton – white
Focal Plane: 70 ft fp
Current Lens Information: 300 MM
Miscellaneous Information:
- Accessible only by boat

LONG TAIL POINT LIGHTHOUSE
Body of Water: Lake Michigan
Near: Green Bay, WI
Lat & Long: 44.59699, -87.9828
First Lit: 1849
Height & Type: 67 ft tower without lantern room
Focal Plane: 38 ft fp
Miscellaneous Information:
- DDL
- Located in Long Tail Point National Wildlife Refuge

MANITOWOC BREAKWATER LIGHTHOUSE
Body of Water: Lake Michigan
Near: Manitowoc, WI
Lat & Long: 44.0942, -87.6435
National Park Service Inventory
First Lit: 1918
Height & Type: 40 ft tower with house
Focal Plane: 52 ft fp
Miscellaneous Information:
- Deemed excess by the USCG and offered through NHLPA (2009)

MANITOWOC SOUTH BREAKWATER LIGHTHOUSE
Body of Water: Lake Michigan
Near: Manitowoc, WI
Lat & Long: 44.0942, -87.6435
Height & Type: hourglass tower – white/green
Focal Plane: 63 ft fp
Miscellaneous Information:
- End of pier – opposite Manitowoc

MICHIGAN ISLAND (NEW) LIGHTHOUSE
Body of Water: Lake Superior
Near: Washburn, WI
Lat & Long: 46.8714, -90.497
National Park Service Inventory
First Lit: 1880
Height & Type: 118 ft skeleton – white
Focal Plane: 170 ft fp
Current Lens Information: DCB-24
Miscellaneous Information:
- Accessible by boat

MICHIGAN ISLAND (OLD) LIGHTHOUSE
Body of Water: Lake Superior
Near: Washburn, WI
Lat & Long: 46.8714, -90.497
National Park Service Inventory
First Lit: 1869
Height & Type: 64 ft tower
Focal Plane: 129 ft fp
Current Lens Information: none
Miscellaneous Information:
- Accessible by boat

MILWAUKEE BREAKWATER LIGHTHOUSE
Body of Water: Lake Michigan
Near: Milwaukee, WI
Lat & Long: 43.0267, -87.8816
National Park Service Inventory
First Lit: 1926
Height & Type: 53 ft tower with house
Focal Plane: 61 ft fp
Miscellaneous Information:
- Original fourth order Fresnel lens displayed at WI Maritime Museum

MILWAUKEE PIERHEAD LIGHTHOUSE
Body of Water: Lake Michigan
Near: Milwaukee, WI
Lat & Long: 43.02583, -87.89424
National Park Service Inventory
First Lit: 1906
Height & Type: 41 ft tower – red
Focal Plane: 45 ft fp
Miscellaneous Information:
- Original fourth order Fresnel lens moved to Milwaukee Breakwater Lighthouse

NEENAH (KIMBERLY POINT) LIGHTHOUSE
Body of Water: Lake Winnebago
Near: Neenah, WI
Lat & Long: 44.1853, -88.4425
First Lit: 1945
Height & Type: 40 ft hexagon tower
Focal Plane: 40 ft fp
Miscellaneous Information:
- Located in Kimberly Point Park

NORTH POINT (MILWAUKEE) LIGHTHOUSE
Body of Water: Lake Michigan
Near: Milwaukee, WI
Lat & Long: 43.0649, -87.87223
National Park Service Inventory
First Lit: 1888
Height & Type: 74 ft tower
Focal Plane: 154 ft fp
Miscellaneous Information:
- Managed by North Point Lighthouse Friends
Volunteer & Contribution Information:
www.northpointlighthouse.org

OUTER ISLAND LIGHTHOUSE
Body of Water: Lake Superior
Near: Ashland, WI
Lat & Long: 47.0764, -90.4168
National Park Service Inventory
First Lit: 1874

Height & Type: 80 ft tower
Focal Plane: 129 ft fp
Current Lens Information: 190 MM SP
Miscellaneous Information:
- DDL
- Accessible only by boat

PILOT ISLAND (PORT DES MORTS) LIGHTHOUSE
Body of Water: Lake Michigan
Near: Washington Island, WI
Lat & Long: 45.2841, -86.9178
National Park Service Inventory
First Lit: 1873
Height & Type: 41 ft tower with house
Focal Plane: 48 ft fp
Current Lens Information: 300 MM SP
Miscellaneous Information:
- DDL
- Accessible only by boat
Volunteer & Contribution Information:
www.plumandpilot.org

PESHTIGO REEF LIGHTHOUSE
Body of Water: Lake Michigan
Near: Peshtigo, WI
Lat & Long: 44.9538, -87.579
National Park Service Inventory
First Lit: 1936
Height & Type: 72 ft tower
Focal Plane: 72 ft fp
Miscellaneous Information:
- Accessible only by boat
- **National Park Service Inventory** "significant unmanned aid"

PLUM ISLAND RANGE REAR LIGHTHOUSE
Body of Water: Lake Michigan
Near: Washington Island, WI
Lat & Long: 45.3078, -86.9577

National Park Service Inventory
First Lit: 1897
Height & Type: 65 ft skeleton – white
Focal Plane: 80 ft fp
Current Lens Information: fourth order Fresnel
Miscellaneous Information:
- DDL
- Accessible only by boat
Volunteer & Contribution Information:
www.plumandpilot.org

PORT WASHINGTON LIGHTHOUSE
Body of Water: Lake Michigan
Near: Port Washington, WI
Lat & Long: 43.39102, -87.8671
National Park Service Inventory
First Lit: 1860
Height & Type: house without tower
Current Lens Information: none
Miscellaneous Information:
- Museum
Volunteer & Contribution Information:
www.portwashingtonhistoricalsociety.org

PORT WASHINGTON BREAKWATER LIGHTHOUSE
Body of Water: Lake Michigan
Near: Port Washington, WI
Lat & Long: 43.3884, -87.8633
First Lit: 1935
Height & Type: 58 ft tower without lantern
Focal Plane: 78 ft fp
Current Lens Information: none
Miscellaneous Information:
- **National Park Service Inventory** "significant unmanned aid"

POTTAWATOMIE (ROCK ISLAND) LIGHTHOUSE
Body of Water: Lake Michigan
Near: Washington Island, WI
Lat & Long: 45.4278, -86.8286

National Park Service Inventory
First Lit: 1858
Height & Type: 41 ft tower with house
Focal Plane: 137 ft fp
Current Lens Information: none
Miscellaneous Information:
- Oldest Wisconsin lighthouse
- Accessible by ferry
- Museum

RACINE (NORTH) BREAKWATER LIGHTHOUSE
Body of Water: Lake Michigan
Near: Racine, WI
Lat & Long: 42.7341, -87.7717
First Lit: 1901
Height & Type: 46 ft square tower – red
Focal Plane: 48 ft fp
Miscellaneous Information:
- No longer in service

RACINE HARBOR (ROOT RIVER) LIGHTHOUSE
Body of Water: Lake Michigan
Near: Racine, WI
Lat & Long: 42.7342, -87.7789
National Park Service Inventory
First Lit: 1866
Height & Type: square tower
Miscellaneous Information:
- Owned by Pugh Marina

RASPBERRY ISLAND LIGHTHOUSE
Body of Water: Lake Superior
Near: Washburn, WI
Lat & Long: 46.9717, -90.805
National Park Service Inventory
First Lit: 1863
Height & Type: 35- ft tower with house
Focal Plane: 80 ft fp
Current Lens Information: none
Miscellaneous Information:
- DDL
- Accessible only by boat

RAWLEY POINT (TWIN RIVER POINT) LIGHTHOUSE
Body of Water: Lake Michigan
Near: Two Rivers, WI
Lat & Long: 44.2116, -87.5083
National Park Service Inventory
First Lit: 1894
Height & Type: 111 ft skeleton
Focal Plane: 113 ft fp
Current Lens Information: DCB-36
Miscellaneous Information:
- Located in Point Beach State Forest

SAND ISLAND LIGHTHOUSE
Body of Water: Lake Superior
Near: Washburn, WI
Lat & Long: 47.0024, -90.9374
National Park Service Inventory
First Lit: 1881
Height & Type: 40 ft stone tower with house
Focal Plane: 52 ft fp
Current Lens Information: DCB-24
Miscellaneous Information:
- Accessible only by boat

SHEBOYGAN BREAKWATER LIGHTHOUSE
Body of Water: Lake Michigan
Near: Sheboygan, WI
Lat & Long: 43.75, -87.6917
First Lit: 1905
Height & Type: 50 ft tower without lantern – red
Focal Plane: 55 ft fp
Miscellaneous Information:
- Relocated (1915)
- **National Park Service Inventory** "significant unmanned aid"

SHERWOOD POINT LIGHTHOUSE
Body of Water: Lake Michigan
Near: Sturgeon Bay, WI
Lat & Long: 44.8922, -87.4334
National Park Service Inventory
First Lit: 1883
Height & Type: 37 ft tower with house and bell tower
Focal Plane: 61 ft fp
Miscellaneous Information:
- Open during the Door County Lighthouse Walk in May

STURGEON BAY SHIP CANAL (CANAL STATION) LIGHTHOUSE
Body of Water: Lake Michigan
Near: Sturgeon Bay, WI
Lat & Long: 44.795, -87.3133
National Park Service Inventory
First Lit: 1899
Height & Type: 98 ft skeleton
Focal Plane: 107 ft fp
Current Lens Information: third order Fresnel
Miscellaneous Information:
- Last US lighthouse to be automated (1983)

STURGEON BAY SHIP CANAL NORTH PIERHEAD LIGHTHOUSE
Body of Water: Lake Michigan
Near: Sturgeon Bay, WI
Lat & Long: 44.792, -87.3089
National Park Service Inventory
First Lit: 1903
Height & Type: 39 ft tower with house – red
Focal Plane: 40 ft fp
Current Lens Information: 300 MM
Miscellaneous Information:
- Still staffed by USCG
- Lighthouse remains in excellent condition

TWO RIVERS LIGHTHOUSE
Body of Water: Lake Michigan
Near: Two Rivers, WI
Lat & Long: 44.1529, -87.5621
First Lit: 1928
Height & Type: 36 ft square tower – red
Focal Plane: 35 ft fp
Miscellaneous Information:
- Relocated (1975)
- Owned by Rogers Street Fishing Village

Volunteer & Contribution Information:
www.lhinn.com (general info)

WIND POINT LIGHTHOUSE
Body of Water: Lake Michigan
Near: Wind Point, WI
Lat & Long: 42.78176, -87.75983
National Park Service Inventory
First Lit: 1880
Height & Type: 108 ft tower
Focal Plane: 111 ft fp
Current Lens Information: DCB-24R
Miscellaneous Information:
- Owned and managed by Village of Wind Point

Volunteer & Contribution Information:
www.windpoint-lighthouse.com

WISCONSIN POINT (SUPERIOR HARBOR ENTRY SOUTH BREAKWATER) LIGHTHOUSE
Body of Water: Lake Superior
Near: Duluth, WI
Lat & Long: 46.71, -92.0066
National Park Service Inventory
First Lit: 1913
Height & Type: 56 ft tower
Focal Plane: 70 ft fp
Current Lens Information: DCB-224
Miscellaneous Information:
- Displays green light every 15 seconds

Wisconsin Point (Superior Harbor Entry South Breakwater) Lighthouse, Wisconsin

10

Experiences of a Lifetime

General

Almost everything in Chapters 1 through 9 pertains to lighthouses and lighthouse keepers. This chapter describes some of my personal experiences while traveling around America's coasts visiting lighthouse after lighthouse after lighthouse.

Prior to this road trip, I had a "desk job" for almost 34 years. When I retired, I knew that I wanted to see America's wonderful lighthouses along with local people, wildlife, and varying landscapes. I drove alone in my car. During my 18 months of travel, I felt liberated, focused, and exhilarated. I woke up every morning wondering what I would see and experience for the first time. I imagined myself as a pioneer although I was clearly on the road more traveled. I sensed a feeling of urgency but did not fully understand it. Mostly I was excited about the adventure that lay ahead.

From August to November, 2006, I drove up the east coast from New York to Maine and just into Canada. In addition to seeing lighthouses, I saw the peak colors of New England's fall foliage. My plan was to drive from New England across the Great Lakes in late fall and winter. Despite all the warnings that I'd "freeze up north," I wanted to see and photograph frozen waves on the Great Lakes lighthouses (waves freeze because it's fresh, not salt, water). However, after reaching the east coast of Canada in November, I knew that I wouldn't be able to handle the northern winter's cold. As a result, I slowly traveled south, visiting lighthouses along the east coast until I arrived at Key West, Florida in March 2007. From there I began traveling north up the Gulf Coast, but I changed my itinerary again when I realized that I wouldn't be able to tolerate the southern, summer's heat. (A pioneer? I guess not!) I headed north, again, and finally arrived at the Great Lakes in July 2007.

After spending two months traveling around the southern Great Lakes coastline, I headed west. I consider this leg of my journey (through Minnesota, North Dakota, South Dakota, Iowa, Kansas, Idaho, and Washington), my non-lighthouse travel. It was the first time I had been to any of these states. Although I missed seeing lighthouses, the adventures were just as remarkable. In October after I arrived in northwest Washington, I spent one month traveling south as I visited lighthouses along the west coast.

Except for one time, it never mattered that I got lost so often...I'll explain later. In fact, I began to look forward to being lost; it was then that I'd experience landscapes and animals I would not have otherwise seen had I stayed on the main trail or road. I love nature and, because so many lighthouses are in secluded areas, it's amazing what I saw. My spirits were high and my mind welcomed everything. I've written about personally rewarding "firsts." It seems appropriate because I've never before taken off in my car and traveled around America. Most of the experiences were simple ones. I merely appreciated and enjoyed all of America around me.

Sea Life

Visiting lighthouses is reward enough. However, there are so many other benefits of being near the shore. I can spend hours looking for shells and sea glass, observing the wildlife (both fish and birds), enjoying the flowers, and waiting for the sunset. I loved being on the road, experiencing America's wonderful variety of wildlife.

Near the Bass Harbor Head Lighthouse in Acadia National Park, Maine, thousands of star fish floated near the shoreline. Near the Tybee Island Lighthouse in Georgia, hundreds of jelly fish were washed up on shore. I suspect it was simply the end of their life-cycles. I wasn't sad to think about life in these terms; their existence and departure from it had created food for other wildlife. It just seemed natural.

To reach the Rockland Breakwater Lighthouse in Maine, I had to walk on a long wall made of large, flat stones that formed a breakwater. Hundreds of gulls rested all along it. Also, along the breakwater were shells of sea urchins. I assume that the gulls caught the sea urchins, then dropped them while flying over the rocks to crack them open and eat the animal inside. I've never before seen sea urchins, although I've found evidence of gulls cracking open clam and oyster shells in the same fashion in other places.

I've never seen pelicans on the northern shores where I grew up. Now I enjoy watching them for hours on end. I began noticing pelicans when I reached Georgia. They are plentiful in Florida, where I observed them dive for food, bathe, and stretch out the skin on the underside of their beaks. It is incredible the way they twist and snap their necks causing the underside of their pouched bills to soar up through their mouths, reaching toward the sky. I assume this is how pelicans keep this body part pliable.

When you travel along the west coast you will, at some point, see entire herds of giant elephant seals playing and sleeping in the sand along the California beaches. Although there is little action on their part, they captivated me. While they slept in the hot sun, they used their flippers to throw sand on their backs, which I assume keeps them cool. Now and again two elephant seals became territorial and loudly "barked" at each other, butting heads until one of them finally retreated.

In Georgia I saw schools of dolphins swimming about 20 feet from the shoreline. Once, the dolphins swam closer to me and we seemed to share an equal curiosity. They never came close enough for me to touch but quite unexpectedly I felt giggly and childlike at being unexpectedly close to them.

In Minnesota I heard and saw loons. The loon's black and white markings are as unique as their red eyes are distinct. The sound they make is peaceful with an underlying sadness about it. I recognized the loon's unmistakable call again while I was traveling along the northern west coast.

In Alaska, whales swam very close to the lighthouse and stayed for hours. I saw whales "bubble hunting," breaching, waving, swimming in pairs (mother and child), and exhaling spray from their blow holes. They are huge creatures that are very graceful in their environment. While Alaskan tourist pay to go on whale cruises, many Alaska lighthouse volunteers have an almost non-stop whale show for free!

Artists

One of my first special moments occurred at the Ned's Point Lighthouse in Mattapoisett, Massachusetts. When I arrived, a grandfather and his 12-year grandson were sitting near the lighthouse. They both had chairs, easels, pencils, pads, charcoal, and other art gear. The grandfather was sketching the lighthouse, talking, and encouraging the boy. The grandson was listening, watching, sketching, and asking questions. These were the first of what I now refer to as "lighthouse artists." It was so wonderful to see two generations so beautifully working together. I now consider it a special and personal blessing if an artist is there painting or drawing a lighthouse when I happen to be photographing it. I visited the Port Boca Grande Lighthouse in Florida on the same day that senior citizens were there painting landscapes. Although most painted ocean scenes, my favorite artist was painting the lighthouse.

Port Boca Grande
Lighthouse, Florida

Flying

After visiting the Key West Lighthouse, I traveled back through the Florida Keys to reach the mainland. At Sugarloaf Key, I saw a large advertisement sign about Skydiving with Fantasy Dan. I found myself driving off the main road in search of Fantasy Dan. When I found him I explained that although I had no desire to jump out of a plane, I would love to fly over two lighthouses (the American Shoal Lighthouse and the Sand Key Lighthouse) that I couldn't see from land. We talked about the cost. Then we discussed the date and time; the conversation was simple: "How 'bout now?" I should have been scared to ride along in the little two-seater plane, but I was far too excited for anxiety. Dan opened my window so I could take better photos. The wind was a rush and the view of aquamarine water everywhere, with white sandbars peaking through, and lighthouses off in the distant growing larger as we neared them was a fantasy beyond my wildest dreams. After flying around the two lighthouses we discussed, Dan flew to and circled around the Key West Lighthouse. Throughout the flight and for two days after, I couldn't stop smiling.

Key West Lighthouse, Florida
(aerial view)

Michigan

Unless you live around the Great Lakes or have visited them, it is hard to imagine that America has a "north" coast. But it does and the lakes are gigantic. It is also hard to believe just how many lighthouses you'll see, especially in Michigan. Michigan has far more lighthouses than any other state. Lighthouses are simply everywhere on Michigan's coastline. If you like lighthouses, you must visit Michigan's coastline! Because pictures are worth a thousand words, I'll let them speak for themselves.

Point Betsie
Lighthouse, Michigan

Muskegon South Pier
Lighthouses, Michigan

Big Sable Point Lighthouse,
Michigan

Mackinac Point Lighthouse, Michigan

Tawas Point Lighthouse, Michigan

Point Iroquois Lighthouse, Michigan

Staying Overnight in a Lighthouse

Another memorable experience was the first time I stayed overnight at the Selkirk Lighthouse in New York. It's beautiful and old and no other guests were there the night I stayed. It was a great adventure to be there alone throughout the night.

For a unique lighthouse experience, stay overnight at a lighthouse. You can choose a lighthouse, a lighthouse inn, bed & breakfast lighthouse, or a lighthouse hostel across the country. Some are actual lighthouses, while others are replicas. If you stay in some of the actual lighthouses, you may be required to become a member and/or volunteer some of your time to help maintain the lighthouse or give tours. To find the right location, search The Listing of U.S. Lighthouses & Lightships in Chapter 9, which contains web links to most American lighthouses, or search the Internet using "lighthouse accommodation" or "lighthouse overnights."

Selkirk Lighthouse, New York

Lost in a Forest (Literally)

While searching for the Crisp Point Lighthouse near the Chippewa National Forest in Michigan, I became terribly lost. What should've been a 17-mile drive through narrow, winding, back roads turned into an all-day fright-fest with the sinking realization that I might never find my way out of the forest. Although I frequently saw deer and other "cute" forest animals, I became increasingly worried that I might encounter a bear, wolf, or other animal not as harmless as deer. My car was running low on gas, my cell phone wouldn't pick up a signal (and even if it did, I didn't know how to explain where I was in the middle of the wilderness), and I hadn't seen any kind of road sign or another human being or vehicle in the past five or six hours. Finally, I stumbled across a main road (two dirt lanes) and followed it until I saw a sign indicating that I was near the lighthouse. I realized that if I backtracked on this two-lane road, I'd be headed in the right direction to safety. With that in mind I decided once again to find the lighthouse, which I did. I spent two well-earned hours there, overlooking Lake Superior, before safely heading out of the forest.

After leaving the Crisp Point Lighthouse, I planned to visit two other lighthouses before calling it a day in Munising, Michigan, about 100 miles west. I spent time at the Grand Marais Light but when I arrived in the parking area of the Au Sable Point Lighthouse, I found out that it was a two- or three-hour hike into the woods and I just didn't have the energy. More than that, I was simply too scared to put myself back in harm's way, whether perceived or real. I left there and drove the remaining forty miles to Munising. The next morning I had to prove to myself that I could face my fears and get back into a forest. If I couldn't, it was time to call a halt to my travels. I drove east 40 miles and then hiked through the woods and the rocks of the Pictured Rocks National Lakeshore to see the Au Sable Point Lighthouse. I realized that, instead of panicking, I could overcome my fears by being stronger than they were and literally just taking one step at a time until I reached my destination. It was very rewarding.

Crisp Point Lighthouse, Michigan

Lost In a Forest (Figuratively)

At some point in my travels I began to realize that I might have a serious health issue. Over the years, I've had five or six benign lumps removed from my breasts so I was aware that things were not "normal" and expected a similar diagnosis. While spending a week in Minnesota, I faced a crossroad. I had to decide if I should continue or cancel the remainder of my lighthouse adventure. I thought I'd need surgery, but I didn't know that it would be for breast cancer (nor did I have any idea how severe the surgery would turn out to be).

I decided to travel on to the west coast rather than return home to the east coast. I reasoned that a few months would not have a dramatic impact on the outcome. I also envisioned cutting my adventure short, returning to the east coast, making doctor appointments, receiving a terrible prognosis, and regretting that I had not finished traveling. I knew that regardless of the outcome, I'd regret more what I didn't do and I continued heading west.

I had a wonderful time slowly traveling through "non-lighthouse states" to reach the west coast. I had never been in that part of the country before and I was in absolute awe of everything around me. It took a few weeks before I arrived on the west coast. My best experiences at this point of my journey occurred in Yellowstone National Forest. As I reached higher elevations, it began snowing. When I stepped out of my car into the snow, I realized that I should probably buy some boots the first opportunity to do so. Until then, I removed the sandals I was wearing and walked barefoot in the snow.

I spent almost a week in the Seattle area before I began to get a sense of urgency about my health. Along my trip, I had gone hundreds of miles out of the way to see friends and relatives. Now, I decided that I would not stop and see friends on the west coast, but I still planned to see two of my nieces, near San Diego. This was the time that the 2007 fires in southern California were blazing. I finally made it down the west coast and continued to visit lighthouses on my journey south. After spending a couple of days with my nieces I made one side trip to Taos, New Mexico, to visit my sister. Then I headed due east until I arrived in Savannah, Georgia.

I began to realize that my life would drastically change after I went to a doctor. So I postponed the inevitable one last time, and traveled to Long Island to spend Thanksgiving with family. I then moved to Tybee Island and began making medical appointments. I was quickly diagnosed and referred to the next doctors. Within days I had a barrage of tests and biopsies and I was officially diagnosed with breast cancer. Oddly, I hadn't really expected that. It took me about a week to be convinced that I could not take care of myself alone in Georgia. I made appointments at Memorial Slone-Kettering Hospital in New York City and moved back to Long Island where I would have the support of family. The doctors there confirmed the diagnosis and in short order, I had a mastectomy and 40 lymph nodes removed. My prognosis was good. After recovering from surgery, I began chemo treatments, which were followed by radiation treatments. Although I never questioned for a minute that I'd be a breast cancer survivor, sometimes it was difficult to imagine that I'd survive the treatments. At times the recovery was similar to being "lost in the woods." The silver lining was that I now had experience finding my way safely out of the woods and I knew I'd be able to do it again.

Throughout all of this I "kept my glow on." I diligently wrote this book and looked forward to the future. The book helped to keep me focused on helping to save lighthouses, rather than concentrating on the seemingly endless treatments. I'm beyond blessed with family and friends who cared about me and helped keep my spirits high. The following poem was written by my nephew, Ric Brewer. It was one of the many thoughtful distractions that were sent my way while I recovered.

The Pink Ribbon Lighthouse

A storm looms on the horizon
Let's hope it stays at sea
It's in our family so,
Our medical history

We've weathered it in the past
And we'll beat it once again
Like a lighthouse on the shore
We'll stay through thick and thin

The storm grows closer now
The sky is getting dim
The doctor says it's hopeful
Now the treatments will begin

The waves are crashing harder
The sea seems mighty strong
But the lighthouse never falters
Giving up would just be wrong

We endure nature's wrath
Life's challenges and so on
But like the lighthouse with pink ribbons
We always keep our glow on
We ALWAYS keep our glow on.

Cape May Lighthouse,
New Jersey

Acknowledgments & Resources

Family and Friends

Norma Ali, Point Reyes Lighthouse
Nancy Banks, Sapelo Island Lighthouse
Carol Barnett, Point Loma Lighthouse
Bruce & Jeanne Bernard, Chesapeake Bay lighthouses, Overfalls
    Lightship
Bob Bigler, perpetual Godspeed
Doug Bingham, Boston Harbor lighthouses
Carolyn Blanton, Tybee Island Lighthouse
Cassie Brewer, Point Loma & Tybee Island Lighthouses
Kevin Brewer, Tybee Island Lighthouse
Ric Brewer, Pink Ribbon Lighthouse concept
Sharon Burke, Jupiter Lighthouse
Miles Byington, Sentinel Island and Point Retreat Lighthouses
Darlene Campbell, Tybee Island, Cockspur, & Wisconsin
    lighthouses
Chatt & Dawn Chapman, New York Harbor lighthouses
Pam Conti, perpetual Godspeed
Mariann Elkowitz, Ponce de Leon Inlet and Tybee Island
    Lighthouses
Lisa Falsetti, Fire Island Lighthouse
Rich Gales, Tybee Island Lighthouse
Pam Guenther, Tybee Island Lighthouse
Jon & Belinda Hall, Sapelo Island Lighthouse
Don Hayes, North Carolina lighthouses
Jeanne Janis, Fond du Lac Lighthouse
Steve Kelly, Minnesota
Lori Posey Kibby, Five Finger Islands Lighthouse
Bronwyn Klein, Five Finger Islands Lighthouse
Jennifer Klein, Five Finger Islands, Sentinel Island & Point Retreat
    Lighthouses

Deborah Krulewitch, Jeffrey's Hook Lighthouse
Ronnie Lazarus, Cape Cod lighthouses
Diane Lightsey, Sapelo Island Lighthouse
Susan Lott, Five Finger Islands Lighthouse
Dharmaja Maldonado, editor
Steve Martinez, Five Finger Islands Lighthouse
Anna Marie (Senzamici) McGovern, Montauk Point Lighthouse
Kathylynn McGrath, Tybee Island and Harbour Town Lighthouses
Ed McIntosh, Five Finger Islands Lighthouse
Fred McIntosh, Five Finger Islands Lighthouse
Janet McIntosh, Five Finger Islands Lighthouse
Judy McIntosh-Vatne, Five Finger Islands Lighthouse
Michelle Metz, Tybee Island Lighthouse
Alan & JoAnn Michaels, New York Harbor lighthouses, Fire Island,
    Blackwell Island, Huntington Harbor, Jeffrey's Hook, Montauk
    Yacht Club Lighthouses, Nantucket Lightship
Diane & Danny Moore, New York Harbor lighthouses
Alan, Dave, and Nancy Pallozzi, Five Finger Islands Lighthouse
Justine Pechuzal, Five Finger Islands Lighthouse
Ken Poplasky, Five Finger Islands Lighthouse
Trina Rambo, Tybee Island Lighthouse
Gus & Dawn Rehnstrom, Sapelo Island Lighthouse
Trisha Rhodes, Tybee Island Lighthouse
Steven Samuelson, Sentinel Island and Point Retreat Lighthouses
Lynda Sheets, Tybee Island Lighthouse
Josh Thomas, Five Finger Islands Lighthouse
US Lighthouse/Lightship employees & volunteers
Dan & Harriet Weber, Tybee Island Lighthouse
Audrey Wolfe, Sapelo Island Lighthouse

Medical Personnel Who Helped Save My Life

Doctors at Memorial Sloan-Kettering Cancer Centers in New York
City and Commack, New York)
Tari King
Andrea Pusic
Melissa Remis
Steven Sugarman
Nursing and technical staffs

Doctors in Savannah, Georgia
Paula Denitto, Memorial Health's Anderson
Center for Breast Cancer
Karen Panzitta, Breast Imaging of Savannah
Carmela Pettigrew, OB-GYN Center
Nursing staff

Physical Therapists Who Helped
Improve the Quality of My Life

Todd Bornfriend
Caesar Cantone
Eric Loughman
Debbie Materra
Tiffany Rathbauer

Kristen Spann
& support staffs

Businesses

Boston Harbor Lighthouse Cruise, www.bostonharborcruises.com
/boston-harbor-cruises/new-england-lghthouse-tour.aspx

Brad Fowler – "Song of Myself" Photography,
www.songofmyself.com

Fantasy Dan – aerial tours Florida Keys,
www.floridaairplanetours.com

Capt. George Gallager, www.spottails.com

Long Island Sound Lighthouse Cruise,
www.longislandlighthouses.com
/sunbeam.htm

New York Harbor Lighthouse Cruise

Dharmaja Maldonado – editing and proofreading;
email: dharmajam@gmail.com

Microsoft Streets and Trips (2006)

Reference Sources

Absolute Astronomy, www.absoluteastronomy.com
Alabama Lighthouse Association, www.alabamalighthouses.com
American Lighthouse Foundation, www.lighthousefoundatin.org
Federal Communications Commission, www. fcc.gov/mb/audio/bickel/
    DDDMMSS-decimal.html
History Link, www.historylink.org
Lighthouse Friends, www.lighthousefriends.com
Michigan Lighthouse Conservancy, www.michiganlights.com
Michigan Lighthouse Fund,
    www.michiganlighthouse.org

National Park Services, www.nps.gov/history/maritime
Seeing The Light, www.terrypepper.com/lights
Smithsonian Institute, www.americanhistory.si.edu/collections/lighthouses
Stephen P. Morse, www.stevenmores.org/jcal/latlon.ph
U.S. Coast Guard, www.uscg.mil/history/h_lhindex.asp
The United States Coast Guard Lightship Sailors Site Menu, www.
    uscglightshipsailors.org/site_index
United States Lighthouse Society, www.uslhs.org
University of North Carolina, www.unc.edu/rowlett/lighthouse
Virginia Lighthouses, www.geocities.com/valights13